English Language Learners at School

A Guide for Administrators

English Language Learners at School

A Guide for Administrators

edited by

ELSE HAMAYAN

and

REBECCA FREEMAN

With 57 Contributors

Caslon Publishing
Philadelphia

Acknowledgments

The editors and the publisher would like to express their appreciation and gratitude for the timely generosity of all those whose contributions made this volume possible. The publisher wishes to thank the editors, Else Hamayan and Rebecca Freeman, for their tireless efforts and cheerful acceptance of short deadlines.

Copyright © Caslon, Inc. 2006

Caslon, Inc.
P.O. Box 3248
Philadelphia, Pennsylvania 19130
caslonpublishing.com

9 8 7 6 5 4 3

Library of Congress Cataloging-in-Publication Data

English language learners at school : a guide for administrators /
edited by Else Hamayan, Rebecca Freeman ; with 57 contributors.
   p. cm.
  Summary: "A practical handbook for administrators of schools serving ELLs; experts answer administrators' questions with 72 research-based responses on policy and accountibility, parents and community, learning in two languages, program development, implementation and evaluation, classroom instruction and assessment, professional development, and advocacy; includes self-surveys to guide program implementation" — Provided by publisher.
  Includes bibliographical references and index.
  ISBN 0-9727507-6-2 (pbk. : alk. paper) — ISBN 0-9727507-8-9 (case cover : alk. paper)
  1. English language—Study and teaching (Elementary)—Foreign speakers—Handbooks, manuals, etc. 2. Education, Bilingual—United States—Handbooks, manuals, etc. 3. School administrators—United States—Handbooks, manuals, etc. 4. School management and organization—United States—Handbooks, manuals, etc.
I. Hamayan, Else V. II. Freeman, Rebecca D. (Rebecca Diane), 1960– III. Title.

PE1128.A2E487 2005
428'.0071—dc22   2005030470

Contributing Experts

Diane August
Senior Research Scientist
Center for Applied Linguistics
Washington, DC

María Estela Brisk
Professor
Lynch School of Education
Boston College
Boston, Massachusetts

Donna Christian
President and Director
Center for Applied Linguistics (CAL)
Washington, DC

Nancy Cloud
Professor and Co-Director
Urban, Multicultural Special Education
Program
Feinstein School of Education and
Human Development
Rhode Island College
Providence, Rhode Island

Nancy L. Commins
Independent Consultant and
Curriculum Specialist
Bilingual ESL Network
School of Education
University of Colorado at Denver
Denver, Colorado

JoAnn (Jodi) Crandall
Professor
University of Maryland, Baltimore
County
Baltimore, Maryland

James Crawford
Executive Director
National Association for Bilingual
Education (NABE)
Washington, DC

Jim Cummins
Professor
Modern Language Centre
Ontario Institute for Studies
in Education (OISE)
University of Toronto
Toronto, Canada

Ester de Jong
Assistant Professor
Bilingual Education/ESOL
University of Florida
Gainesville, Florida

Lynne Díaz-Rico
Professor
College of Education
California State University, San
Bernardino
San Bernardino, California

Lynne Duffy
Bilingual and ESL Instructional Specialist
Community Consolidated School
District 21
Wheeling, Illinois

Jana Echevarria
Professor
California State University, Long Beach
Long Beach, California

Kelly Estrada
Assistant Professor of Education
Sonoma State University
Rohnert Park, California

Jack Fields
Director of Bilingual Education (retired)
U-46
Elgin, Illinois
Coordinator
Illinois Resource Center
Des Plaines, Illinois

Monica Maccera Filppu
Bilingual Programs
    Developer/Coordinator
Office of Bilingual Education
District of Columbia Public Schools
Washington, DC

David Freeman
Professor of Bilingual Education
The University of Texas at Brownsville
Brownsville, Texas

Rebecca Freeman
Adjunct Professor
Language Education Division
Graduate School of Education
University of Pennsylvania
Philadelphia, Pennsylvania

Yvonne S. Freeman
Professor of Bilingual Education
The University of Texas at Brownsville
Brownsville, Texas

Robert Fugate
ESL Teacher
Greenfield Elementary School
Chesterfield County, Virginia

Erminda García
Teacher and Instructional Coach
MK Udall K–8 School
Phoenix, Arizona

Eugene García
Vice-President for University School
    Partnerships
Dean of the College of Education
Arizona State University
Tempe, Arizona

Fred Genesee
Professor of Psychology
McGill University
Montreal, Quebec

María Paula Ghiso
Penn Literacy Network
Graduate School of Education
University of Pennsylvania
Philadelphia, Pennsylvania

Margo Gottlieb
WIDA Lead Developer
Worldclass Instructional Design and
    Assessment
Director of Assessment and Evaluation
Illinois Resource Center
Des Plaines, Illinois

Cindy Gross-Alvarez
Dual Language Program Coordinator
Eugenio María de Hostos Community
    Bilingual Charter School
Philadelphia, Pennsylvania

Else Hamayan
Director
Illinois Resource Center
Des Plaines, Illinois

Renea Hamilton
ESL Title III Coordinator
Delaware County Intermediate Unit
Morton, Pennyslvania

John Hilliard
Senior Educational Consultant
Illinois Resource Center
Des Plaines, Illinois

Marla Hori
Director of Curriculum and
  Instruction/Principal (retired)
Skokie District 73.5
Skokie, Illinois

Stephen Krashen
Professor Emeritus
University of Southern California
Los Angeles, California

Kathryn Lindholm-Leary
Professor
San Jose State University
San Jose, California

Joe Reeves Locke
ELL Program Teacher
Cohn Adult High School
Metropolitan Nashville Public Schools
Nashville, Tennessee

Barbara Marler
Senior Educational Consultant
Illinois Resource Center
Des Plaines, Ilinois

Kate Menken
Assistant Professor
Bilingual Education and TESOL
City College of New York (CUNY)
New York, New York

Maritza Meyers
ELL Program Coordinator
Long Beach Public Schools
Long Beach, New York

Lucía Morales
Dual Language Teacher
InterAmerican Magnet School
Chicago, Illinois

Cynthia Mosca
Director of ELL Programs
Cicero Public Schools
Cicero, Illinois

John Nelson
Co-director ESOL MA Program
University of Maryland Baltimore
  County (UMBC)
Baltimore, Maryland

Diep Nguyen
Bilingual and Multicultural Programs
  Director
Community Consolidated School
  District 54
Schaumburg, Illinois

Sharon M. O'Malley
Supervisor of ELL Programs
School District of the City of York
York, Pennsylvania

R.C. Rodriguez
Director of Bilingual and ESL Education
Northside Independent School District
San Antonio, Texas

David Rogers
Executive Director
Dual Language Education of New
  Mexico
Albuquerque, New Mexico

Nadeen Ruiz
Chair, Bilingual Multicultural Education
  Department
California State University Sacramento
Sacramento, California

Karen Sakash
Clinical Associate Professor
University of Illinois at Chicago
Chicago, Illinois

María Teresa Sánchez
Doctoral Candidate
Lynch School of Education
Boston College
Boston, Massachusetts

Cristina Sanchez-Lopez
Educational Consultant
Illinois Resource Center
Des Plaines, Illinois

Nancy Santiago Negrón
School District of Philadelphia
Philadelphia, Pennsylvania

Deborah J. Short
Director, Language Education and
  Academic Development
Center for Applied Linguistics
Washington, DC

Patrick H. Smith
Professor of Applied Linguistics
Programa de Lengua y Lingüística
  Aplicada
Universidad de las Américas, Puebla
Puebla, Mexico

Holly Stein
Adjunct Professor
University of Maryland, Baltimore
  County (UMBC) and College Park
  (UMCP)
Consultant, Center for Applied
  Linguistics
Former Supervisor of the ESOL/
  Language Minority Program
Prince George's County Public Schools,
  Maryland

Kimberly Thomasson
Dual Language Coordinator
Multicultural Education Department
The School District of Palm Beach
  County
West Palm Beach, Florida

María Torres-Guzman
Associate Professor and Program
  Coordinator
Program in Bilingual/Bicultural
  Education
Teachers College
Columbia University
New York, New York

Sue Wagner
Senior Educational Consultant
Illinois Resource Center
Des Plaines, Illinois

Adela Weinstein
Senior Educational Consultant
Illinois Resource Center
Des Plaines, Illinois

Wayne E. Wright
Assistant Professor
Division of Bicultural-Bilingual Studies
College of Education and Human
  Development
University of Texas, San Antonio
San Antonio, Texas

María Josefina (Josie) Yanguas
Coordinator
Illinois Resource Center
Des Plaines, Illinois

Judith Kwiat Yturriago
Director of Bilingual, ESL, Two-Way
  Immersion and State Pre-Kindergarten
  Programs
Evanston/Skokie School District 65
Evanston, Illinois

Preface

❦

Purpose of the Guide for Administrators

The education of English language learners (ELLs) is a pressing issue for schools across the United States today. The strict accountability requirements of the No Child Left Behind Act of 2001 have brought ELLs to the attention of the academic mainstream, in many cases for the first time. The whole school is held accountable for the performance of every student, which means that ELLs are everyone's responsibility. Administrators and mainstream teachers are asking questions, and most do not have time for intensive course work in TESOL (Teaching English to Speakers of Other Languages) or bilingual education. They want and need accessible information that they can use in their schools—now! This guide facilitates administrators' efforts to meet this challenge.

Although concern about the educational achievement of English language learners is not new to U.S. schools, there is a heightened sense of urgency in the popular media and education literature about the achievement gap between ELLs and native English speakers today. Genesee, Lindholm-Leary, Saunders, and Christian (2005) provide the following statistics to highlight the scope of this challenge:

> According to a compilation of reports from 41 state education agencies, only 18.7% of students classified as LEP (limited English proficient) met state norms for reading and English (Kindler, 2002). Students from language minority backgrounds also have higher drop-out rates and are more frequently placed in lower ability groups than English background students (Ruiz-de-Velasco & Fix, 2000). Across the nation, the number of students from non-English speaking backgrounds continues to rise. They represent the fastest growing segment of the student population by a wide margin. From 1991–1992 through 2001–2002, the number of identified ELLs in public schools (K–12) grew 95%, while total enrollment increased by only 12%. In 2002–2003, more than 5 million school

age children were identified as ELLs, 10.2% of the K–12 public school student population (Padolsky, 2004). These students speak more than 400 languages, but nearly 80% are native Spanish speakers. (Genesee et al., 2005, p. 354)

This challenge is not limited to urban schools or geographic areas; rather, ELLs are moving into rural, suburban, and urban schools all across the country, and the growth of the ELL population is the most dramatic (between 100 and 200 percent or more than 200 percent) in states that have not traditionally had the greatest numbers or density of this population (www.ncela.gwu.edu/policy/states/index.htm).

Meeting this challenge requires effective leadership. Administrators are probably the single most important factor in the effectiveness of a program for ELLs. This book highlights the critical role of administrators, emphasizes the need for collaboration among administrators and teachers at the local school district and school levels, and guides school-based efforts to address the language, literacy, and learning needs of ELLs in their classrooms. Without strong leadership and without a close link among staff, it is difficult if not impossible for schools to enable ELLs to access the educational opportunities to which they are legally entitled.

We draw on the notion of *professional learning communities* (DuFour & Baker, 1998) to describe how administrators and their staff might collaborate at the local level to address this challenge (see also Freeman, 1998). Researchers inside and outside of education maintain that professional learning communities can stimulate significant improvement in the ability of schools to reach their objectives. Schools that function as professional learning communities are "characterized by a shared mission, vision, and values; collective inquiry; collaborative teams; an orientation toward action and a willingness to experiment; commitment to continuous improvement; and a focus on results" (DuFour & Baker, 1998, p. 45). Strong leadership is critical, because the educational leader sets the tone and provides the structure for the professional learning community to articulate the mission, vision, and values statements that guide all educational decision making at the school. The professional learning community, supported and directed by the educational leader, ensures that the mission, vision, and values statements are oriented toward meaningful improvement in the performance of *all* students. The educational leader also sets the tone and provides the structure that enables the collaborative teams to conduct school-based inquiries into critical issues as they arise (Freeman, 1998). Closing the achievement gap for ELLs is a critical issue for students and schools today, and this book guides administrators' efforts to ensure that the professionals in their schools develop the expertise individually and in collaborative teams to take on this challenge.

This guide is intended to be accessible to administrators because we recognize the demands on their time. It is organized around the questions that administrators are actually asking about how they can meet the needs of ELLs in their schools. These questions are answered by experts in the field (over fifty total) in a clear and concise way. The range of questions, as well as the variety of responses given, clearly shows that there is no simple answer or one-size-fits-all solution for the education of ELLs. Instead, there are principled ways to approach the challenge of educating these students based on thirty years of research and practice in the field.

At a fundamental level, however, we do find a clear enrichment orientation toward the linguistic and cultural diversity that ELLs and their families bring to U.S. schools and communities. Administrators and teachers in effective programs for ELLs see linguistic and cultural diversity as resources to develop, not as problems to overcome. When administrators and teachers, working collaboratively in professional learning communities, approach their critical inquiry into the education of ELLs from this enrichment orientation, they are in a position to develop educationally sound programs and to implement those programs in ways that can deliver results. The experts in this guide also strongly encourage the use of data on ELL performance and development to inform instruction, guide program and professional development, and articulate sound policies that are based on empirical evidence of ELLs' English language development and academic achievement over time.

Content and Structure of the Guide

Since we wanted this guide to reflect the actual needs of administrators, we began by soliciting questions from administrators around the country who are looking for ways to educate their ELLs effectively. Based on our experiences working with administrators and teachers across the country, we also added some questions of our own. We organized the questions around common themes. We then invited experts (researchers and practitioners) to synthesize the research and offer their experiences in response to these questions in a brief, concise way.

By *experts*, we mean researchers and practitioners with extensive experience and expertise in the field. Collectively, the experts who contributed to this book brought expertise in second language acquisition, biliteracy development, and cross-cultural communication; educational policy for ELLs at the federal, state, district, and local school levels across the country; program development, implementation, monitoring, and evaluation in bilingual and English-only contexts; and effective instructional approaches and authentic assessments for ELLs. Some of the experts are university-based researchers; others are presidents of national organizations or directors of state resource centers, such as the Center for Applied Linguistics, the National Association of Bilingual Education, and the Illinois Resource Center. Some are administrators or teachers who work in different types of bilingual and English-only contexts in elementary and secondary schools in urban, suburban, and rural areas; and others are consultants who help schools mediate between theory, research, and practice in ways that make sense at the local school level. The responses these experts provide are based on solid research and grounded in experience. Some of the experts synthesize essential research regarding a question, while others describe how they have approached an issue and what has been successful for them. Many experts offer suggestions for action based on the research or on their own experience.

The guide begins with three foundation chapters: chapter 1 reviews policies and accountability requirements for ELLs, chapter 2 explores ways to link the school and the community, and chapter 3 provides a theoretical orientation about how children learn in two languages at school. The next two chapters cover programmatic issues: chapter 4 concerns program development, and chapter 5 addresses program implementation and evaluation. Chapter 6 concerns instruction and assessment in the classroom, and chapter 7 focuses on professional development. Chapter 8 addresses special challenges that may arise with ELLs who bring special characteristics to school, and chapter 9 addresses an issue that is crucial to administrators, namely, advocacy.

Each chapter begins with a set of guiding principles that emerged from our review of the experts' responses to the questions in the chapter. The guiding principles are followed by a brief introduction that synthesizes the major issues. The administrators' questions and the experts' responses make up the greater part of each chapter. The questions and answers are followed by a letter to an administrator from a constituent, for example a teacher, a parent, a consultant, or a student (in some cases the letter represents a composite of constituents, and in some cases the names of the addressees and authors are pseudonyms). The letter presents an actual challenge to the administrator from that constituent's perspective. Toward the end of each chapter, there is a survey for reflection and action that focuses administrators' attention on how the issues raised in the chapter are addressed at their school. Each chapter concludes with a list of references and additional resources that the experts have identified for those who want to explore the topic of the chapter in greater detail. The glossary at the end of the book clarifies the terms used in the book; this is intended to help administrators sort out some of the confusion in terminology that we find in the field.

How to Use this Guide

We hope that this guide will be useful in two major ways: for specific program development and improvement at school, and more broadly, for pre-service or in-service professional development. For specific program development and improvement, the guide can be used by school-based collaborative teams to guide them as they, for example, decide what kind of program is appropriate for their school, plan a schedule or a grouping method for their ELLs, decide on an instructional approach, or reflect on how well their current programs and practices address the needs of ELLs in their school. For professional development, the guide can be used by administrators and others responsible for in-service training to help school staff expand their expertise in ELL education. The guide can also be used in pre-service programs for administrators who need a grounded introduction to this critical aspect of their future work in schools; unfortunately, the needs of ELLs are addressed only cursorily in most educational leadership programs in the United States at this time.

In either specific program development or more general professional development, the guide can to be used in different ways, depending on the needs of the administrators or staff members, as well as on the time and structure that these professionals have available to them. Some examples follow.

- An administrator might consult the guide to help answer a particular question that has arisen at school (for example, how long does it take ELLs to acquire English?) and turn to an expert's response on that issue.

- A staff member who is responsible for professional development might use a letter from one of the constituents as the basis for a conversation about how administrators might address the challenge presented in the letter (for example, how to involve parents of ELLs).

- An administrator, group of administrators, or a school-based professional learning community might be concerned about a particular issue (such as program development) at their school. They might turn to the chapter on program development and begin with the guiding principles and surveys for reflection and action to assess their school's strengths and needs relative to the topic. After completing the school-based survey, these educators might look in the body of the chapter for answers to the specific questions that arose as they worked through the survey, and perhaps use the conversations around this focal area to develop school-based strategies for action. Ideally, administrators will incorporate these strategies for action into their school improvement plans.

- A study group of pre-service or in-service administrators might work through the guide, and develop an action plan that clearly articulates a problem or concern regarding ELLs at school. This action plan should be incorporated into the district strategic plan or into the school improvement plan.

- An administrator or staff member might draw on the recommended resources (such as the suggestions for further reading, Web sites of professional organizations, or lists of useful resources) at the end of the chapter to follow up on an area that they wanted to explore in greater detail.

We hope that the research and practical recommendations in this guide will prove helpful to administrators and staff in their efforts to help ELLs acquire English and achieve academically in all areas of the curriculum. At the same time, we hope that this guide enriches not only the education of ELLs but also the lives of all students and staff at the school.

References

DuFour, R., & Eaker, R. (1998). *Professional learning communities: Best practices for enhancing student achievement.* Bloomington, IN: National Education Service.

Freeman, D. (1998). *Doing teacher research: From inquiry to understanding.* Boston: Heinle & Heinle.

Genesee, F., Lindholm-Leary, K., Saunders, W., & Christian, D. (2005). English language learners in U.S. schools: An overview of research findings. *Journal of Education for Students Placed at Risk, 10*(4), 363–385.

Contents

Chapter 2

Linking the School and the Community

Chapter 3
How Children Learn in Two Languages

Chapter 4
Program Development

Chapter 5

Program Implementation and Evaluation

Chapter 6

Classroom Instruction and Assessment

Chapter 7

Professional Development

Chapter 8
When Challenges Arise

Chapter 9
Advocacy

English Language Learners at School

❦

A Guide for Administrators

Chapter 1

Policies and Accountability Requirements for English Language Learners

Guiding Principles

- We address all federal, state, and local mandates and accountability requirements regarding English language learners.
- We have developed an authentic accountability system for English language learners.
- We explicitly articulate local school district and school language education policies and procedures.
- We use valid and reliable data on the academic achievement and English language development of English language learners to inform our policies and accountability requirements for these students.

Introduction

The Civil Rights Act of 1964 mandates that U.S. public schools provide equal educational opportunities for all students. Educators are challenged to ensure that their English language learners (ELLs) have the language support that they need in order to access the educational opportunities to which they are legally entitled. More than thirty years of federal, state, and local legislation has led to the development of a wide range of policies, programs, and practices that are intended to support this effort. And more than thirty years of research on the educational experiences and outcomes of ELLs in a range of program types has contributed to our understanding of what is and is not effective for these students.

For the first time in the history of the United States, schools are being held accountable by the federal government for the English language development and academic achievement of ELLs in their classrooms. The good news is that the largely underserved ELL population is no longer invisible in our schools. ELLs have been moved from the margins to the mainstream of U.S. educational concerns by the accountability requirements of the No Child Left Behind Act of 2001. The national organization of Teachers of English to Speakers of Other Languages (TESOL) is developing new national TESOL standards that focus more attention on academic language used in the content areas of language arts, mathematics, science, and social studies. States are rapidly developing language policies, accountability requirements, language proficiency standards, and standardized language proficiency assessments, and they are mandating a wide range of professional development so that school districts and schools statewide can comply with the new federal mandates. These policies and mandates, however, often are issued without adequate funding and certainly without adequate time for effective implementation. Administrators and teachers are asking questions about how they should interpret and implement the new policies and requirements that are being handed down to them in ways that make sense for their schools and communities. The situation is made more difficult by the high degree of variation in expectations and accountability requirements for ELLs from one state, school, or school district to another—and the requirements are changing rapidly. This chapter aims to equip administrators with the background and resources they need to navigate the complexities of this dynamic policy context and make informed decisions at the local level, for programs, schools, and school districts.

This chapter answers questions about the policy mandates and accountability requirements for ELLs by first providing a brief historical overview of the federal policy context surrounding the education of ELLs today, and then by considering what an authentic accountability system for ELLs should include. Next, we look more closely at specific state policies on the education of ELLs that have received considerable media attention—those of Arizona, Massachusetts, and Colorado—to see how these policies are being interpreted by administrators at the level of the local school. We also explore how programs for ELLs are currently funded in specific states—Illinois, New York, and Pennsylvania. Our focus on specific states is intended to illustrate some of the variation that we find across the United States at this time and to stimulate administrators' thinking about policies, accountability requirements and funding in their own states. The questions in the last part of the chapter move to the local school district and school levels to explore how administrators can develop policies and accountability requirements that are appropriate for their school and community contexts, and how they can use the data they collect at the local level to drive their decision making.

The chapter concludes with a survey for reflection and action. School district and school administrators can use this survey to review the status of their current policies and accountability requirements for ELLs, and identify the strengths and needs of these policies and procedures. Equipped with this information, administrators can take the necessary action steps to ensure that their ELLs have equal access to the educational opportunities they offer all students at their schools.

Question

How have laws regarding English language learners evolved in the United States?

KATE MENKEN

Policies regarding the education of children who speak languages other than English are far from new in the United States. Historically, such policies have been decided by a combination of legislation, court mandates, and federal, state, and local educational policies that have shifted with the ebb and flow of immigration waves to this country. When the U.S. Constitution was written, linguistic diversity was the national norm, and instruction was multilingual in schools. Bilingual German-English schooling was authorized by law in several states in the nineteenth century and flourished unofficially elsewhere, and other European languages were taught in response to pressure from immigrant groups (Crawford, 1992). More than a dozen states passed legislation for schooling in languages other than English, either as a subject or as the medium of instruction.

With the arrival of the second great wave of immigrants to the United States in the early twentieth century, however, anti-immigrant sentiment increased, and the dominance of English grew. The "Americanization" campaign of this period corresponded to increased restrictions placed on the use on languages other than English. After the United States entered World War I in 1917, several states passed laws and decrees banning German from classrooms and other public arenas (Crawford, 1999). Similar attempts were made to prohibit the teaching of Japanese, Chinese, and Korean in California and Hawaii, and Spanish in New Mexico. In 1923, Congress considered a bill to make English the official American language. Although this bill did not pass, and anti-foreign language laws were eventually overturned, they had a great impact on public sentiment. From the period of mass immigration into the United States during the early twentieth century until the 1960s, few or no special services were offered to language-minority students in schools where English was the language of instruction.

It was after the Civil Rights Act of 1964 that the need to provide language support for non-native English speakers, and the recognition that language is tied to educational inequity, were first explicitly addressed in federal education legislation. This was enacted in the passage of Title VII of the Elementary and Secondary Education Act of 1965, entitled the Bilingual Education Act, passed by Congress in 1968. The Bilingual Education Act acknowledged the challenges posed by the linguistic diversity of U.S. public schools and authorized the funding of innovative programs for English language learners (ELLs), such as bilingual education and English as a second language (ESL).

Programs to meet the needs of ELLs, however, were only truly implemented in U.S. public schools after the *Lau v. Nichols* case of 1974. The suit was brought by Chinese parents in San Francisco who asserted that a child named Lau was unable to access the knowledge and skills needed to succeed in school owing to his limited English. The Supreme Court ruled in this case that "*identical* education does not constitute *equal* education under the Civil Rights Act." As a result, school districts were required to take "affirmative steps" to address the educational challenges for ELLs due to language in all schools (by, for example, implementing bilingual education or ESL programs). To this day, school districts across the country continue to cite "the Lau provisions" when making decisions about educational programming for ELLs.

In the wake of these mandates, a wide array of program models addressing the needs of ELLs have been implemented. These models are divided between those in which the students' native language is used in instruction (bilingual) and those in which the instruction is solely in English (ESL).

More immigrants arrived in the United States during the 1990s than in any other single decade, and there has been a backlash against the growing immigrant population and the languages they speak. With funding from Ron Unz, a millionaire software entrepreneur, anti-bilingual education ballot measures have recently passed at the state level in California, Arizona, and Massachusetts, prohibiting native language instruction in those states (despite research showing the effectiveness of bilingual education). In addition, the No Child Left Behind Act (NCLB) was passed into law by Congress in 2001, marking the end of the Bilingual Education Act. Title III of NCLB includes the English Language Acquisition, Language Enhancement, and Academic Achievement Act (Part A), which mandates that ELLs be included in state assessment systems for accountability purposes and requires that these students make "adequate yearly progress" toward mastering academic content and English proficiency—with only passing mention of bilingual education or native language use. As such, this law implicitly promotes an English-only policy, pressuring school districts to emphasize English acquisition and students to learn the language as quickly as possible. Taken together, these recent policies suggest a return to a period of language restrictionism like that seen during the Americanization campaign of a century ago (Menken, 2005).

On the other hand, states such as New York, New Jersey, and Illinois currently mandate bilingual education in schools where there are twenty or more students who speak the same language other than English. Other states that mandate bilingual education are Alaska, Connecticut, Indiana, Texas, Washington, and Wisconsin. California and Massachusetts had mandated bilingual education over English-only instruction for ELLs prior to the recent passage in these states of anti-bilingual education measures. Similarly, certain states, among them New Mexico and Michigan, effectively mandate bilingual education by funding only this type of program. And several states, including New Mexico, Oregon, Rhode Island, and Washington, have adopted what they call "English Plus" mandates. This is best described in New Mexico's legislation:

> NOW THEREFORE BE IT RESOLVED . . . Proficiency on the part of our citizens in more than one language is to the economic and cultural benefit of our state and the nation, whether that proficiency derives from second language study by English speakers or from home language maintenance plus English acquisition by speakers of other languages. Proficiency in English plus other languages should be encouraged throughout the State. (House Joint Memorial 16, New Mexico legislature, 1989)

Bilingual education is widely implemented in these states. Finally, programs using students' native languages in instruction in order to maintain those languages can also be found locally across the United States, even in states where native language instruction is not promoted.

Question

What does a valid and reliable accountability system for English language learners need to include?[1]

☙

JAMES CRAWFORD

Holding schools accountable for results is a goal with broad support among the American public, policymakers, and educators themselves. There is growing recognition that our children deserve no less, especially children whose academic needs have often been ignored, leading to achievement gaps that no just society should tolerate. The consensus falls apart, however, when it comes to means: How should accountability systems be designed to yield fair, accurate, and useful information on which to base decisions about school improvement? What kinds of oversight will ensure that students are achieving to their full potential while avoiding arbitrary, one-size-fits-all mandates that disrupt the educational process? In short, how can we ensure that the solution does not exacerbate the problem?

The No Child Left Behind (NCLB) Act is the latest attempt to resolve this question. The law's aims are worthy. Unfortunately, its approach to school accountability is overly rigid, punitive, unscientific, and likely to do more harm than good for the students who are now being left behind. Nowhere is this more true than in the case of English language learners (ELLs).

After just two years, it is clear that the goals of NCLB cannot be met. By setting arbitrary and unrealistic targets for student achievement, this accountability system cannot distinguish between schools that are neglecting ELLs and those that are making improvements. As achievement targets become increasingly stringent, virtually all schools serving ELLs are destined to be branded failures. The inevitable result will be to derail efforts toward genuine reform. Ultimately, a misguided accountability system means no accountability at all.

It is essential to develop high-quality assessments for ELLs—valid and reliable instruments to measure their academic achievement and their progress

---

1. This response was excerpted with permission from Crawford (2004), *No Child Left Behind: Misguided Approach to School Accountability for English Language Learners*. The complete text can be found at www.nabe.org.

in acquiring English. Such assessments are needed to serve numerous purposes. These purposes include:

- Identifying students with limited English proficiency, placing them in appropriate instructional programs, and determining when they are ready to be reassigned to mainstream classrooms.
- Evaluating alternative program models to gauge their effectiveness in serving ELLs.
- Diagnosing student strengths and weaknesses to assist educators in improving instruction.
- Tracking long-term trends of achievement in various groups and contexts.
- Holding schools accountable for student performance (Hakuta & Beatty, 2000).

Some progress is being made, especially in developing assessments of English language proficiency.

A broad consensus has emerged among testing experts that achievement tests of questionable validity and reliability—or, indeed, a single test of any kind—should not be used for high-stakes decision making (Gottlieb, 2003). The focus of concern has been primarily on decisions involving individual students, such as grade promotion and graduation. ELLs are at a huge disadvantage where test results are employed in this fashion. Given the widespread inequities in resources available to schools where minority students are concentrated, high-stakes testing has spawned civil rights litigation in several states.

What matters most in the final analysis is not the progress of the ELL subgroup but the progress of individual ELL students. A fair, reasonable, and useful accountability system would track cohorts of students to gauge their long-term academic achievement. It would use multiple measures, including grades; graduation, promotion, and dropout rates; and alternate forms of assessment. It would be accountable to local parents and communities, not just to top-down directives. Finally, it would consider a school's inputs in serving ELLs, such as program design and teacher qualifications, rather than merely outputs—test scores alone.

There is no question that schools' performance in educating ELLs requires close scrutiny. Services for these students remain inadequate in many districts, especially in parts of the country only recently affected by immigration. School officials have often been slow to respond to cultural and linguistic diversity, to recognize the unique needs of ELLs, and to adapt instructional practices accordingly. They should be held accountable for providing equal opportunities for these students. But judgments about school performance should be broad-based and well informed. Indicators of progress, or lack thereof, should be not only accurate but also sensitive enough to assist in the process of school improvement. NCLB's simplistic approach fails ELLs on all of these counts.

Fortunately, a more promising framework for accountability already exists. Known as the Castañeda standard, it provides a proven set of tools for determining whether schools are meeting their obligations toward students with limited proficiency in English. For two decades it has guided enforcement activities by the Office for Civil Rights of the U.S. Department of Education. The framework, first outlined by a federal appeals court in response to the 1981 *Castañeda v. Pickard* case, established a three-pronged test to gauge whether school districts are taking "affirmative steps to overcome language barriers," as required by the Equal Educational Opportunity Act of 1974. The court ruled that "good faith" efforts are insufficient. In serving ELLs, schools are obligated to meet three standards:

- Programs must be based on an educational theory recognized as sound by experts.
- Resources, personnel, and practices must be reasonably calculated to implement the program effectively.
- Programs must be evaluated and restructured, if necessary, to ensure that language barriers are being overcome.

Castañeda thus offers a comprehensive approach to school accountability, encompassing both inputs and outputs. Its broad focus includes instructional quality, teacher qualifications, language assessment and placement, classroom materials, and student outcomes. It emphasizes capacity building, requiring districts to address the specific needs of ELLs, while allowing them the flexibility to choose programs suited to local conditions and preferences. It stresses not merely the development of English language skills but also students' progress in reaching academic standards (Hakuta, 2001). And it emphasizes instructional reform—getting to the roots of underperformance—rather than imposing punitive sanctions for failing to reach arbitrary adequate yearly progress (AYP) targets.

Where the Castañeda standard has been applied by federal courts and the Office for Civil Rights, results have often been promising. Districts have been required to initiate serious capacity-building efforts for serving ELLs, sometimes with federal funding under Title VII of IASA (Improving America's Schools Act), also known as the Bilingual Education Act. The problem is that Castañeda has been applied on a very small scale, owing to political resistance and limited resources for enforcement. Moreover, the program evaluation component of Title VII was never adequately funded; nor were its provisions for professional development. NCLB exacerbated the situation by eliminating requirements for evaluating ELL programs altogether and capping funds for professional development at less than half the FY 2001 level.

As a result, the Castañeda framework has thus far played a relatively limited role in improving the education of ELLs. Yet there is no reason why this framework could not be successfully used in a comprehensive school accountability system. Under federal court orders, some states, including Illinois and Florida, are already providing this type of oversight to ensure that districts are adequately serving ELLs (*Gómez v. Illinois State Board of Education*, 1987; *LULAC v. Florida Board of Education*, 1990). The principles of Castañeda should be developed, refined, and extended for use in all state accountability plans.

Recommendations for Reforming NCLB

School accountability for ELLs should be authentic, comprehensive, and oriented toward reforming instruction to reflect what is known about best practices in the classroom. Toward that end, the National Association for Bilingual Education (NABE) recommends the following:

1. Until assessments for ELLs have been proven valid and reliable, they should never be used to make high-stakes decisions for students, educators, or schools. Meanwhile, the federal government should substantially increase funding for scientific research in ELL assessment.

2. Adequate yearly progress (AYP) should not be calculated for an ELL subgroup. Instead, the progress of ELLs toward English proficiency and high academic standards should be tracked on a longitudinal, cohort basis. Arbitrary achievement targets not based on scientific research should never be used.

3. ELLs' achievement should be measured using multiple indicators, including grades, graduation and dropout rates, and alternate forms of assessment. Local authorities should be responsible for deciding, on a case-by-case basis, when ELLs are ready to be assessed in English and what test accommodations may be used. ELLs should never be required to take standardized tests that have not been normed for children whose English is limited. The most important goal of assessment should be to help educators improve instruction and students achieve long-term academic success.

4. Accountability should concentrate on building schools' capacity to serve ELLs, not on stigmatizing labels or punitive sanctions. Sanc-

tions should only be used as a last resort, as a response to clear resistance to school improvement.

5. Schools should be accountable to all stakeholders, in particular local parents and communities, who should play an active role in accountability systems. Efforts should be required to facilitate the participation of limited English speakers.

6. Accountability for serving ELLs should consider both inputs and outputs, using the Castañeda framework to determine (a) whether schools are providing well-designed instructional programs based on sound theory; (b) whether programs are supported with sufficient funding, qualified teachers, appropriate assessment and placement, and adequate materials; (c) whether programs are evaluated comprehensively for effectiveness; and (d) whether programs are being restructured, when necessary, to ensure that students are acquiring high levels of English proficiency and academic achievement.

Question

What are the state mandates for educating English language learners?

WAYNE E. WRIGHT

As a consequence of Proposition 203 and the strict interpretation of this law by current state education leaders, Arizona is the most restrictive state in the country in terms of approaches schools may use to meet the needs of English language learners (ELLs) (Wright, in press). Although the law requires ELLs to be placed in "structured English immersion" (SEI), a clear description of this model has yet to be offered. Thus, local school administrators have the challenge of creating the most effective programs possible under the constraints of the new law. Programs for ELLs must still meet the requirements under federal law to help ELLs learn English and to provide ELLs with equal access to the core curriculum. This entails establishing programs that offer, at a minimum, daily instruction in English as a second language (ESL) and teaching content using "specially designed academic instruction in English" (SDAIE) or sheltered techniques. In addition, effective programs for ELLs provide ample primary language support.

Many school administrators have adopted commercial ESL curricular programs and require teachers to provide at least thirty minutes or more of daily ESL instruction. Others have adopted language arts programs specifically designed for ELLs. Although some confusion remains over whether the law allows pull-out ESL programs at the elementary level, many districts continue to offer them. In one large district, for example, ELLs are pulled from their mainstream classrooms during language arts instruction and receive this instruction from the ESL teacher. Such pull-out programs are unnecessary, however, in schools that offer self-contained SEI classrooms with trained teachers who are provided with the curricular materials necessary to provide daily ESL instruction in their own classrooms.

Key to effective ESL and content-area instruction using SDAIE (or sheltered) techniques is ensuring that teachers have proper and adequate training to work with ELLs. Administrators have been encouraging teachers to complete ESL endorsements through local colleges and universities. Incentives such as covering the costs of tuition and books, organizing cohorts of teachers within the school or district, pay bonuses, and salary increases have proved effective in increasing the number of endorsed teachers. Many districts also offer their own professional development programs. The Sheltered Instruction Observation Protocol (SIOP) model[2] has become a particularly popular training model (Echevarria, Vogt, & Short, 2004). Many administrators have found the SIOP model to be useful for evaluating effective teaching of ELL students.

Proposition 203 clearly states that teachers may "use a minimal amount of the child's language when necessary," but stresses that "no subject matter shall be taught in any language other than English." The fine line between these two is primary language support. Many school administrators have found that effective use of primary language support increases students' English language vocabulary and maximizes students' comprehension of lessons taught in English, thus leading to greater proficiency in English.

Bilingual education is still possible through the waiver provisions of Proposition 203. While current state-level interpretation of the waiver provisions makes it virtually impossible for an ELL student under the age of 10 to be in a bilingual program, some districts continue to offer transitional and dual-language programs in the upper elementary grades and secondary schools. A few dual-language programs exist at the K–2 level, but non-native English speakers must be designated as "fluent English proficient" to be enrolled. There are also a small number of immersion programs in Native American

2. © 2005 LessonLab, a division of Pearson Education. The SIOP Institute, trademark, and copyright are owned by LessonLab/Pearson Education.

languages that are attempting to prevent the death of these languages. These programs, however, are facing increasing opposition from current state education leaders.

In summary, administrators in Arizona are striving to provide the best possible programs for ELLs given the current restrictions in the state. It is likely that once the current state education leaders leave office, administrators will be afforded greater flexibility in meeting the needs of their ELLs.

❦

María Estela Brisk and María Teresa Sánchez

On November 5, 2002, Massachusetts voters passed a sister initiative to California's Proposition 227, known as Question 2, with 70 percent of voters approving. Similar to Arizona's Proposition 203, the text of Question 2 stated more restrictions for native language support, limited even more the waiver process, and included more severe measures for improper implementation than California's Proposition 227 (General Laws of Massachusetts, 2003). Question 2 modified the original Transitional Bilingual Education (TBE) Act of 1971 to practically eliminate bilingual education. Later, an amendment to the new legislation exempted two-way bilingual (immersion) programs.

Question 2 mandates went into effect at the beginning of the 2002–2003 school year. Most schools have restructured their programs serving bilingual students with limited English proficiency (BSLEPs) to accommodate the new mandates. Here we discuss ways in which several schools have restructured their programs to accommodate Question 2 mandates. We based our analysis on documentation from the Massachusetts Department of Education, on conversations with principals, teachers, and school administrators, and on school visits. A selection of these programs includes:

1. Two-way bilingual programs: These programs were not affected by the new legislation. There are twelve such programs in the state.

2. Waivers to maintain bilingual education programs: In a few schools parents have requested waivers to continue bilingual education programs. Under the law, it is easier to obtain waivers for students older than 10. In spite of waivers, these programs still need to place students below a certain level of English proficiency for the first thirty days of school in English-only classes.

3. Sheltered English immersion (SEI): Three forms of SEI have been implemented. The first form is *SEI classes for students from the same language group* with a former bilingual education teacher who does

all instruction in English but uses the students' language for clarification. The second group is *SEI classes for mixed language students.* All the instruction is in English. The legislation encourages this type of program because it lends itself to less use of the native language. The third group is *grade-level cohorts that include an SEI teacher.* In this version an SEI teacher has been added to each grade level. BSLEP students have been distributed among the SEI teacher and the mainstream teachers, reducing class size and mixing bilingual and English-speaking students. All teachers are in the process of receiving SEI training.

4. Mainstream classes: Many schools prior to Question 2 did not have particular programs for BSLEP students. A 2002 report notes that 15 percent of BSLEPs were not in TBE programs (*Boston Globe,* 2002). These schools have not been affected by the new mandates. However, the notion that BSLEP students were going to spend only one year in SEI concerned the principals that they would be receiving additional students with limited preparation in English. We know of at least one school that had a bilingual program but was slated to provide no SEI program. The teachers and many of the students decided to stay. Ostensibly a school without services for BSLEP students, the staff are using their skills as bilingual teachers to serve their mainly Spanish and Chinese background students.

5. Alternative school for older students: One high school has been opened for students who were in bilingual programs but who continue to have low-level English proficiency, and for newcomers to the United States. The instruction is in English but with as much native language support as possible.

Question 2, as well as the No Child Left Behind (NCLB) Act, requires districts annually to assess the English proficiency of BSLEPs regardless of their type of program. BSLEPs are now required to take a newly developed test, the MEPA (Massachusetts English Proficiency Assessment—Reading and Writing). In addition, *all* teachers are now required to be certified to administer the MELA-O (Massachusetts English Language Assessment—Oral), an observational instrument used by teachers to evaluate a student's English language listening and speaking skills.

Final Thoughts

We would like to address five issues in relation to the present legislation. First, as before the passage of Question 2, the level of support for teachers and principals varies, affecting the interpretation of the legislation and program quality. Second, principals are confused as to the promotion policy and the "one year in SEI" mandate. They are concerned that the inability to promote children out of SEI classes will result in a new form of segregation. Third, teachers from the ethnic group of the children who became the greatest asset to schools upon passage of the original TBE are being fired because they cannot pass the required English proficiency level. Fourth, this legislation seems to be more about eliminating languages other than English than about providing adequate education. The restrictions on materials, instruction, curricula, and qualification of personnel all point to this fact. And fifth, a positive aspect of this reform is that now there is more awareness of the specific needs of BSLEP students within the schools in general. In the past, teachers and administrators considered these students the responsibility of the TBE or ESL programs.

Ironically, those who proposed this new legislation have offered no support for its implementation. However, those of us who opposed it are working hard to make the best out of poor educational policy for the bilingual children in Massachusetts.

❧

NANCY L. COMMINS

Colorado, like all states in the Union, delivers services to English language learners (ELLs) guided by both federal and state policies. Colorado adheres to the guidelines of No Child Left Behind (NCLB), as well as the provisions of Title III as overseen by the Office of English Language Acquisition (OELA).

In 2002, Colorado voters soundly rejected a ballot measure that would have severely restricted the use of languages other than English in instruction. With the defeat of Amendment 31, bilingual education is still a viable option, and districts across the state are able to implement the full range of programs available for second language learners. This is a great victory for the children of Colorado.

Since 1981, the education of ELLs in Colorado has been governed by the state's English Language Proficiency Act (ELPA). This act provides a limited amount of per pupil funding to local school districts for students who have been identified as limited English proficient (LEP). ELPA requires districts to classify all students based on their English language proficiency levels. The categories are based on the LAU Guidelines, as follows: category A—Non English Proficient (NEP), B—Limited English Proficient (LEP), and C—Fluent English Proficient (FEP). Based on the specified eligibility criteria a student can be counted for funding for only two years. Because state funding is so limited, districts must rely on their general fund budgets and Title III funds to provide services for as long as students need additional support with English language and academic development. The nature of services to second language learners is determined at the local level by each school in the 176 school districts.

It is important to note that NCLB provides no restrictions on how long a language other than English can be used in instruction, only that testing must occur in English after three years. Denver Public Schools—the district with the largest number of second language learners in the state—operates under the guidelines of a court order that mandates a transitional bilingual program model for Spanish-speaking students whose parents choose primary language instruction for their children. Many districts offer two-way immersion programs. They are supported by the Dual Language Consortium, operated under the auspices of the Bilingual ESL Network at the University of Colorado at Denver.

Senate Bill 109, a Colorado law passed in 2002, outlines how Colorado will comply with federal guidelines. This bill calls for a single instrument by which to measure ELL student's English language proficiency. It also requires the state to establish levels of proficiency on the entire instrument and delineate guidelines for accommodations. Further, the law stipulates that assessment data must be disaggregated in order to be able to track academic progress of ELL learners. As a result, a major focus in Colorado has been the development of English language development (ELD) standards and participation in a consortium of several states to develop an assessment instrument based on these ELD Standards.

Question

How are programs for English language learners funded?

ADELA WEINSTEIN

Public schools in Illinois have access to two streams of supplemental funding for programs serving English language learners (ELLs), one stemming from a specific state appropriation and the second one derived from federal appropriation under Title III of the No Child Left Behind (NCLB) Act.

State of Illinois Funding

Illinois provides funding for the reimbursement of excess costs incurred by public school districts when providing bilingual/English as a second language (ESL) services to ELL students. There are two separate appropriations, one exclusively for the Chicago Public Schools and the other for all remaining school districts in the state.

Because school districts outside of the city of Chicago must share in a single appropriation amount, their applicable funding levels are determined through the use of a formula. Said formula takes into account several factors: (1) the number of students to be served, (2) grade levels (kindergarten, elementary, high school), (3) years in program, and (4) level of service (that is, five class periods versus ten or more class periods per week). Once the formula is applied, it sets a funding ceiling for each district that has applied for funding.

The approved level of funding, based on the ceiling, does not signify districts' full reimbursement of excess costs. This is because the legislature has never appropriated a sufficient amount to provide 100 percent reimbursement of excess costs. Therefore, the law provides for the application of a pro-ration to each year's claims. The pro-ration fluctuates annually and is dependent on the appropriation for that year and the amounts being claimed. Districts file quarterly reimbursement claims during the year, and an anticipated pro-ration is applied to each. The final quarterly claim used for adjustments in the reimbursement levels as that is when the final pro-ration is arrived at for that year.

The total state's appropriation for bilingual/ESL programs for the 2003–04 school year was $62,552,000. Of that amount, $27,655,400 had been earmarked for school districts outside of Chicago. Approximately 250 school districts outside of Chicago applied for reimbursement, with an estimated pro-ration of their reimbursement set at 60 percent. Pro-ration levels have fluctuated over the years, from a high of 89 percent in 1990 to a low of 35 percent in 1989.

Districts are not required to seek reimbursement from the state; however, most districts do so, particularly because state program approval allows ELLs to participate in IMAGE (Illinois Measure of Annual Growth in English) testing. The IMAGE is the state's test to determine whether ELLs meet state standards in language arts and mathematics. It is used, in conjunction with the other state tests to assess all students, for accountability purposes.

Federal Funding—Title III of NCLB

Districts have access to two types of programs funded under Title III of NCLB: Immigrant Education Programs and Language Instruction Educational Programs for Limited English Proficient Students. Illinois uses the acronyms of IEP for the first, and LIPLEPS for the second type of program. These are formula grants. The states' respective allotments are determined by the U.S. Department of Education on the basis of two separate sets of data. Twenty percent of the total allotment is based on the immigrant student enrollment count submitted to the Office of English Language Acquisition (OELA), U.S. Department of Education, for the preceding year. The U.S. Department of Education then determines the remaining 80 percent on the basis of data provided either by the Bureau of the Census or by the Department of Commerce's American Community Survey. These funds are to be used to supplement existing programs and services and cannot be used to take the place of services that the district and state are already required to support. Unexpended funds may be carried over into the second year.

1. Immigrant Education Programs (IEP)

Illinois sets aside 15 percent of its state grant allotment for Immigrant Education Programs, which is only for districts meeting the eligibility requirements under Section 3114(b) of Title III and further specified by the state. To be eligible, school districts need to meet all of the following criteria. They must have (a) submitted to the state, the preceding school year, a report of the number of eligible immigrant students, ages 3–21, by country of origin, who are enrolled in their public and nonpublic schools; (b) experienced an immigrant student enrollment increase of at least 3 percent or fifty students, whichever is less, as compared to the average of the preceding two years; (c) a minimum of ten eligible immigrant students; and (d) a state-approved bilingual/ESL program. The requirement of a minimum enrollment of ten students exists because a lower number would result in a sub-grant amount too small to make a significant impact; furthermore, the rationale for requiring a district to have a state-approved and funded bilingual/ESL program to qualify for the IEP grant rests on the need to ensure that these federal funds are used to supplement, not supplant, local and state funding.

Districts seeking funding must submit a grant application that includes detailed plans and required assurances, along with applicable budgets. Proposed activities are to be based on scientific research, and participating staff must meet program standards specified in NCLB. Final funding allocations to eligible districts that file an application with the state are based on the total amount available for these programs for that fiscal year and the state's total number of immigrant students reported by these districts the preceding school year. This generates the per capita allocation, and the funding level for the corresponding school district.

2. Language Instruction Programs for Limited English Proficient Students (LIPLEPS)

Eighty per cent of the state's grant is directed toward funding programs under this category. For districts to be eligible for a sub-grant under this program, they must meet all of the following requirements: (a) have a state-approved and state-funded bilingual/ESL program; (b) propose allowable activities based in scientific research; (c) have large enough ELL enrollments to generate a minimum grant of $10,000, or otherwise apply as part of a district cooperative; (d) operate a state-funded bilingual/ESL program that is in compliance with state regulations; (e) employ staff holding applicable qualifications; and (f) include all required documents, assurances, and budgets.

Final funding allocations are based on the available amount of funds for this program, the state's total number of ELL students receiving bilingual/ESL services in the public schools, and those ELL students in the participating nonpublic schools included in the sub-grant application. This generates the per capita allocation, which in turn is used to determine the funding level of the corresponding school district.

❦

MARITZA MEYERS

Programs for English language learners (ELLs) in New York State are funded through local tax-levy monies and state and federal grants.

State-funded Competitive Grants

- Two-Way Dual Language Grant—These competitive grants are used to plan and implement two-way bilingual education programs.

- Bilingual Excel Grant—This competitive grant is used to implement language arts programs in a school building with twenty-five or more ELLs. Programs must be implemented before or after school, during the summer, or on Saturdays.

State-funded Grants

- Limited English Proficient (LEP) Aid Grant—Funds are made available to assist school districts in implementing programs for ELLs that are consistent with the Regulations of the Commissioner of Education and with the department's initiatives in raising standards for all students.

Federally-funded Grants

- Title III, Part A—LEP and Immigrant Funds of the No Child Left Behind Act (NCLB): Language Instruction for ELLs and Immigrant Students is based on the number of students enrolled in a school. These funds are designated for language instruction programs to help ELLs attain English proficiency while meeting state academic achievement standards. Funds made available to eligible school districts under Title III, Part A of NCLB must be used to supplement the level of federal, State and local funds allocated for the education of LEP students.

- Title I, Part A Grant—This is a federal categorical program to ensure that all children have a fair, equal, and significant opportunity to obtain a high-quality education and reach minimum proficiency on the state content standards and assessments. The intent of the funding is to meet the educational needs of low-achieving students enrolled in the highest poverty schools.

Children who are economically disadvantaged, children with disabilities, migrant children, and ELLs are eligible for Part A services on the same basis as other children who are selected for services. Thus, schools are no longer required to demonstrate that the needs of ELLs stem from educational deprivation and not solely from their limited English proficiency. Similarly, schools are no longer required to demonstrate that the needs of children with disabilities stem from educational deprivation and not solely from their disabilities.

CINDY GROSS-ALVAREZ

In the School District of Philadelphia, programs for English language learners (ELLs) receive funding from several sources, including federal, state, and local revenues. Federal funding includes Titles I, III, and VII, until Title VII funding is phased out. In Pennsylvania, with the exception of a one-time allocation of funds for ELLs in the 2004 state budget procreated by a special governor's initiative, there is no state funding that exclusively targets ELLs. Pennsylvania is one of only a handful of states that have no ESL or bilingual education law or accompanying mandates and funding.[3] Since ELLs count as "regular" students, they are entitled to everything to which all students are

---

3. Guidelines for the development and implementation of ESL and bilingual-bicultural programs are provided by the Basic Education Circular, (BEC), which is prepared and disseminated by the Pennsylvania Department of Education.

entitled. However, since ELLs are also considered "at-risk" and "special needs" students, they receive additional entitlements that allow the district to supplement their instruction through the purchase of instructional materials or the offering of extended-day or enrichment activities, tutorials, and summer programs, which provide intensive instruction in language through content, particularly for pre-emergent or emergent level ELLs.

Though local operating funds are the primary source of funding used to finance the school district's instructional programs, including programs for ELLs, these monies are generated by a local real estate tax, which is insufficient to fully fund the district's schools. Therefore, the state must provide additional revenue to bring the district's level of funding up and provide a quality course of studies for its students.

In addition to local and state funding, the district ELL programs are supplemented with Title I and Title III programs, which fund everything from support personnel, including teachers, coaches, teacher assistants, and bilingual counselor assistants, to instructional materials and computer hardware and software. Family centers and professional development activities are also funded with these entitlements.

Grant Support/Development

The School District of Philadelphia is the fifth largest school district in the country. It has an Office of Grants Support and Development that provides support across the district to entities interested in responding to requests for proposals. Aside from sending out monthly grant alerts and opportunities for funding (both competitive and entitlements), the office coordinates across all district offices and facilitates meetings leading to joint applications and proposals. This accomplishes two major goals: it prevents duplication of efforts and it integrates the needs of ELLs into programs that would otherwise overlook serving this substantial population. For example, with the assistance of the office, the district was successful in receiving two Title VII Bilingual Systemwide Grants, and the district recently received funding for parents centers that include specific trainings and accommodations geared to the needs of the parents of ELLs. In addition, an Early Childhood grant has been submitted by that office that includes providing dual language instruction for ELL students in the program. Finally, a large grant given to the district by the National Science Foundation targeted schools with large language-minority populations, including Chinese, African, and Hispanic. Enough can't be said about the importance of cross-curricular collaboration on grant applications, since such collaborations ensure that services to ELLs and other at-risk groups are integrated into all of the district's initiatives, an important tenet of No Child Left Behind.

Question

How do you develop a language policy that is appropriate for your school and community context?

❦

REBECCA FREEMAN

Title III of the No Child Left Behind Act of 2001 holds school districts and schools accountable for the English language development and academic achievement in English of English language learners (ELLs). School district and school administrators are challenged to ensure that all of their constituents (teachers, support staff, parents, students, community partners) understand and support the ways that they organize their bilingual/English as a second language (ESL) programs and practices for ELLs at the local level. The effort to clearly articulate how ELLs are to reach the same high standards as all students in the school or district is complicated by the confusion, conflict, controversy, variation, and change that we find in the United States today about effective programs, practices, and assessments for ELLs. A school district or school language policy and implementation plan can help administrators navigate this complex challenge.

According to Corson (1999), a school language policy identifies areas in the school's scope of operations and programs in which language problems exist that need the commonly agreed approach offered by a policy. The language policy sets out what the school intends to do about areas of concern and includes provisions for follow-up, monitoring, and revision of the policy itself in light of changing circumstances. It is a dynamic action statement that changes along with the dynamic context of a school.

An effective school district or school language policy and implementation plan should (1) comply with all federal, state, and local policies, (2) respond to local community needs, interests, and concerns, (3) promote the development and implementation of educationally-sound programs for language learners (ELLs and/or English speakers) that deliver valid and reliable results, (4) be understood and supported by all constituents (administrators, teachers, students, parents, community members), and (5) drive decision making on the local level. The language policy should begin with a mission statement that clearly articulates the school district's or school's stance toward languages other than English. School districts and schools that are committed to maintaining and developing languages other than English, not only for ELLs but also for English speakers, must reflect this mission in all of their policies and procedures. This is critical, given the increasing English-only orientation that we find throughout the United States today.

Most schools and school districts today do not have one explicit, coherent language policy that is endorsed by the school board and supported by a written implementation plan that includes procedures guiding all aspects of program development, implementation, monitoring, and evaluation (in a readily accessible format). However, all schools with language learners do have language policies that guide practice at the local school level. In some cases the language policies are not explicitly written but are implicit in practices that we can observe within and across schools in the district. In other cases the policies are explicitly written but the practitioners working in classrooms throughout the school or the district are unaware of the existence or meaning of these policies, which leads to inconsistencies in implementation. In many cases we find gaps, confusion, or contradictions in policies and procedures that are to guide the education of language learners, including but not limited to ELLs.

Administrators can lead the effort to develop coherent language policies and implementation plans for their schools and school districts. For example, they can organize a retreat or an institute during which time educators can (1) review existing policies and procedures guiding all aspects of program development, implementation, monitoring, and evaluation, (2) identify gaps, inconsistencies, confusion, or contradiction in those policies and procedures, and (3) make recommendations for coherent policies and procedures to address these areas of concern. Administrators can provide models of language policies and implementation plans that have been developed by other school districts and schools to inform this process. Participants in the development of the language policy and implementation plan should represent the multiple levels of institutional authority in the school district (such as central, regional, and school-based administrators, teachers, counselors, and community liaisons) and the range of linguistic and cultural groups served by the schools. Including representation of participants with such a wide range of expertise and interests is essential because it increases the likelihood that the language policy and implementation plan that emerges will be understood and supported by all constituents throughout the school or district and community.

Since this is a relatively large task, it may be useful to divide into task forces with specific, clearly defined charges. Different groups may focus on, for example, programs for language learners, assessment and evaluation, students with special needs, professional development, or outreach and advocacy. Administrators can identify the task forces, charges, and participants prior to the retreat based on their assessment of district or school strengths and needs.

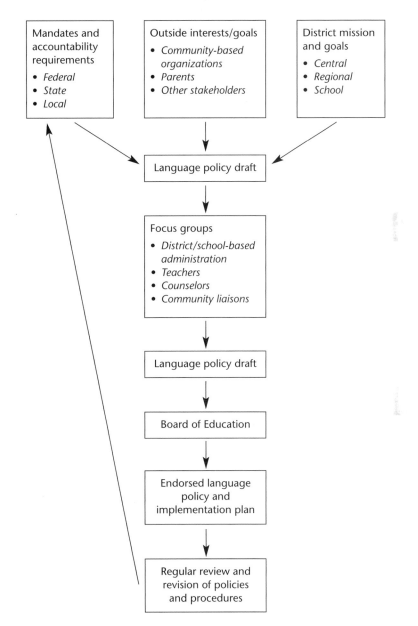

Figure 1-1. Dynamic processes of language policy development at local level.

Prior to submitting the language policy to the school board for approval, the language policy and implementation plan must be understood and supported by the various constituents. Administrators may choose to organize a series of focus groups, for example, with district administrators, school principals, teachers, and community representatives to review and respond to the proposed language policy draft. Feedback from these focus groups can be incorporated into the draft of the language policy and implementation plan. Administrators may choose to consult with external partners, for example from a university or resource center, to ensure that the policy and implementation plan is in fact aligned with all of the relevant federal and state policies and with research on effective programs, practices, and assessments for ELLs. Once this has been accomplished, the language policy is ready for board approval.

To ensure that the policy and implementation plan is actually implemented in practice, district and school administrators must regularly monitor its implementation and address program and professional development needs as they arise. To ensure that the policy and implementation plan changes with the dynamic context of the school—as federal, state, or local mandates are revised or developed, or as school or community demographics change, or as student performance or program effectiveness data yield important new insights— the policies and procedures included in the handbook must be regularly reviewed and revised. Administrators may choose to institutionalize an annual review of all data, policies, and procedures to ensure that the written policies and procedures actually drive decision making on the local level. Figure 1–1 represents the dynamic processes of language policy development at the local level.

Question

How do you use assessment data to drive decision making?

MARGO GOTTLIEB

Assessment involves a rational, logical progression of gathering, analyzing, and reporting information. Meaningful assessment data that are reliable, valid, fair, and useful should be the backbone of educational decision making. Increased numbers of measures with strong technical qualities and the involvement of stakeholders in the development process yield more useful and meaningful results.

The higher the level of decision making, the greater is the reliance on defensible assessment data. Table 1–1 shows the types of available assessment data and their links to specified purposes and uses at the classroom, program, and state levels. These are the chief kinds of assessment data that are used in making educational decisions regarding student academic performance.

Classroom data for English language learners (ELLs) are generally language dependent; that is, decisions rest on whether instruction is delivered

Table 1-1.   Data-driven decisions in programs for ELLs

Types of Assessment Data in L1 and L2	Purpose for Assessment	Decisions	Level of Decision Making
Standardized tests (Language proficiency and academic achievement in L2 [and L1])	• Meet accountability requirements • Identify ELLs • Reclassify ELLs	• Student and subgroup progress and attainment of standards • Eligibility and extent of support services	State
Intake data (Demographic data)	• Determine extent of support	• Initial placement of students	Program
Standard tasks (E.g., district writing prompts and rubric)	• Improve program services	• Reconfiguration of language allocation • Curriculum impact and adjustment	Program
Performance data (Student work samples)	• Monitor student progress • Inform instruction	• Differentiation of instruction • Effectiveness of unit or lesson • Diagnosis of student strengths and areas for improvement • Grading	Classroom
Student self-assessment	• Regulate and monitor learning	• Refinement of unit or lesson	Classroom
Observational/ anecdotal	• Document student behavior	• Grouping of students	Classroom

in the students' first (L1) or second (L2) language. At the classroom level, assessment *for* learning rather than assessment *of* learning is emphasized. For that reason, the students themselves should have opportunities to reflect on their work, and their voice should be part of everyday classroom decisions. Not only does self-assessment move students toward taking responsibility for their own learning, it also assists teachers in providing feedback on the effectiveness of instruction.

Formative assessment data, collected on an ongoing basis, are the foundation of classroom decision making. Teachers' reasons for classroom assessment are generally two-pronged: to monitor students' language proficiency and academic achievement in English, and in the L1 in dual language programs, while utilizing its constant feedback to improve the effectiveness of their lessons and delivery of instruction. The accumulation of formative assessment data forms a body of evidence that allows teachers to make fair judgments when it comes to grading their students. In addition, this continuous flow of information is useful in analyzing students' strengths and areas of improvement and for grouping students appropriately for different learning tasks.

At the program level, assessment data are used to make some important decisions regarding individual students and classrooms. First, intake data that extend beyond screening can provide a profile in regard to a student's language proficiency and academic achievement in L1 and L2. This baseline information is helpful in configuring classrooms and for planning instruction in ESL and dual language programs. Second, standard performance tasks, administered across classrooms within a specified time frame (such as quarterly) that are scored with a uniform rubric, provide insight into how the program as a whole is functioning. Further, these data serve to rate the performance of individual classrooms as well as contribute to program evaluation.

Finally, at the state level, assessment data need to be standardized in order to aggregate scores across programs and districts. Subsequently, data are disaggregated and results can be generalized for subgroups. For schools that implement dual language (two-way immersion) programs, it is critical that valid data be available for both groups of students participating in dual language education. Although it is required to carefully monitor ELL language and academic progress, as well as their attainment of English language proficiency, it is of equal importance that data related to proficient English speakers be maintained. In that way the viability and success of dual language education can be documented and disseminated.

Question

How do you use evidence on program effectiveness to inform policy?

JUDITH KWIAT YTURRIAGO

In the spring of 2004, Evanston School District 65 School Board took a vote that drastically changed the program for English language learners (ELLs) in the entire district. The board voted to eliminate the transitional bilingual education (TBE) program from kindergarten through fourth grade for the fall of 2004. What made this vote so unusual is that unlike many other districts that are eliminating TBE programs in favor of English-only programs, this board voted to establish dual language education programs for all Spanish-speaking students in the district. This decision did not come about overnight and was the result of many years of local data gathering and planned use of concrete evidence of the success of a program model, namely, two-way immersion (TWI), which was the type of dual language program offered in the district.

Prior to this significant decision, School District 65 had three program models to serve ELLs: (1) transitional bilingual education (TBE), (2) transitional program of instruction (TPI) which is a sheltered English instructional model, and (3) two-way immersion (TWI). When the TWI program was started, about 7 percent of the Spanish-speaking students were enrolled in it, with the rest in the TBE program. The TPI program had about 25 percent of ELLs in it from thirty countries who spoke twenty-seven languages. The TBE program was a half-day pull out program that had been in existence for more than twenty years. The academic performance of students who were in that program was consistently low year after year as measured by local curriculum-based assessments in reading and math, as well as by standardized tests. After the first year, the ELLs in the TWI program outperformed the Spanish-speaking TBE students on the three local kindergarten assessments in Spanish used to gauge readiness for first grade. Results were similar during the 2001–2002 school year for the same two groups on the district assessments for first graders going on to second grade. Other measures used to gauge teacher and parent opinions of the TWI program also demonstrated overwhelming satisfaction.

These data were presented to the school board with great fanfare, and the first significant vote that the board took was to expand the TWI program in the fall of 2002 to four kindergartens and two first grades in two schools. The TBE program continued to serve students in grades two through five. Local assessments in math and reading in the spring of 2003 again showed a significant difference in the scores of the Spanish-speaking TWI and TBE second-grade students. The TWI students consistently outperformed the TBE students on all measures. That spring, the school board again voted to expand and consolidate the TWI program in two schools.

The following spring, test results showed the same advantage for students in the TWI program. Spanish-speaking TWI students outperformed their peers in the TBE program, and, most impressive to the mostly English-speaking school board members, the TWI English-speaking students performed the same as or better than their English-speaking peers in the general education classrooms in the same school. This was despite the fact that the English-speaking student group in the TWI program was as racially and economically diverse as the general education students in this same school.

Spanish-speaking ELLs who had been in the TBE program in second and third grades were placed in the TWI program for third and fourth grade in fall 2004. This resulted in three TWI third grades and three TWI fourth grades with eight or nine English speakers in each class along with eleven to twelve Spanish speakers. In years past, the numbers of English speakers and Spanish speakers in each class had been more equal. The ratio of English speakers to Spanish speakers in the lower grades did remain equal. Spanish-speaking fifth- through eighth-grade ELLs are still served in a TBE program simply because TWI has not yet reached fifth grade.

The TWI program is now in four schools. There are now five TWI kindergartens, five TWI first grades, four TWI second grades, three TWI third grades, and three TWI fourth grades. The TWI Program nearly doubled, from eleven TWI classrooms during the 2003–2004 school year of about twenty-four students each to twenty TWI classrooms in the 2004–2005 school year. All TWI teachers are self-contained classroom teachers. The expansion of the program was a result of making data-driven decisions in the spring of each school year.

Letter to an Administrator:
From an English As a Second Language Teacher

To: Robert Magee, Principal
From: Lillian McConnell, Classroom Teacher
Re: Working with ELL Students

The State of Arizona has mandated that every teacher and administrator in our education system that does not already hold a bilingual or English as a Second Language endorsement get a provisional SEI endorsement by August 30, 2006 (15 clock hours) and a full endorsement by August 30, 2009 (an additional 45 hours). It will be impossible to get recertified to teach in Arizona without meeting the requirements for the SEI endorsement. I'd like you to consider the implications of this mandate so that we can be sure that all our teachers are well prepared. There are some specific restrictions given to educators by state legislation and federal court rulings that must be adhered to. Proposition 203 adopted sheltered English immersion as the model for all instruction, so it is important that teachers know the philosophy and strategies to implement this model.

Our district has been and will continue to offer the training necessary by providing our own in-house sessions or by bringing in workshops that meet our needs. We will be providing curriculum using the Arizona Academic Standards, so we will need to know how to use the ELL Proficiency Standards Correlation Guides provided by the State. Because English is the only language of instruction allowed, we will also have to know techniques that will work with students who are not native English speakers, including how we may use primary language support.

In addition to training, we also need support in the following areas:

Classroom Furniture. Our students will be actively involved in their learning. They will be working in various groups for specific purposes. They will be talking and moving around. Desks or tables and chairs that are easily movable and have flat surfaces that make group work easier, and as many bulletin boards as wall space will allow—our walls will be rich with written language!—would be very useful.

Supplies. Supplies will be needed to facilitate language learning. In addition to the adopted texts, we will need supplementary written resources including alternative texts, a variety of trade books, and magazines appropriate for the subjects covered. Writing materials other than ruled paper, such as notebooks, large chart paper, rolls of paper that can be cut to various sizes, and sentence strips will be needed. A variety of writing implements—

(continues)

Letter to an Administrator (*continued*)

pencils, markers, pens—will also be needed. Other materials that will make learning more visual are current classroom maps of the world and the United States, concrete objects for students to manipulate, and pictures of every item and concept that one can possibly imagine.

Assignment to classrooms. It is fortunate that our district has paraprofessionals who have passed the state-mandated test for working in the classrooms and are being trained to teach English language learners along with the rest of our staff. As a result, we need to consider carefully how our students are assigned to classrooms so that we can make the most effective use of our paraprofessionals.

I hope you can support us fully so that we may implement the new mandates in a way that is most effective for our students.

Survey for Reflection and Action

Survey the policies, procedures and accountability requirements that you have in place in your school district/school. Use a + when the policy is clearly written and implemented by all teachers, administrators and/or staff at your school, a √ when the policy is written but not clearly understood or implemented by everyone, and a − when there is no policy in place. Use a ? when you don't know. After you have completed the survey, look across your responses and identify strengths of your school district/school policies and procedures, and identify action steps to include in your school improvement plan.

The school district/school has a language policy for ELLs and an implementation plan that includes the following:

_____ A mission statement that (a) aligns the district's/school's policies, programs, and practices with all local, state, and federal mandates and (b) clearly articulates the district's/school's stance on languages other than English

_____ Procedures ensuring that ELLs have access to all programs and services that are available to all students, and that ELLs' needs are considered in all aspects of district/school programming (e.g., curriculum, instruction, assessments, promotion and retention, special needs services)

_____ Procedures governing the uses of languages in the school system, including issues of language choice, translators and interpreters, languages of tests

_____ Defining criteria of the type(s) of program(s)—ESL, bilingual education, heritage language—that is/are implemented in the district/school

_____ Procedures for the allocation of languages for instructional purposes at every grade level (i.e., how much English as well as native language instruction is included at different stages of language proficiency in each type of program)

_____ Procedures that enable the identification of students who are eligible for ESL/bilingual/heritage language services

_____ Procedures governing the assessment and placement of ELLs in appropriate program(s)

_____ Procedures for the recruitment, retention, and professional development of all teachers, administrators, and staff who work with ELLs

_____ Procedures governing all aspects of program implementation, including student movement across levels, testing accommodations, exit criteria based on multiple measures, promotion and graduation requirements, and ways to address ELLs' special needs

_____ Procedures governing the collection, analysis, and use of standardized and alternative assessment data on English language development

_____ Procedures governing the collection, analysis, and use of standardized and alternative assessment data on native language development (when native language development is a goal of the program)

_____ Procedures governing the collection, analysis, and use of standardized and alternative assessment data on the academic achievement of ELLs in the language(s) used for instructional purposes

_____ Procedures governing program monitoring and evaluation

_____ Procedures for the ways that summative and formative data are used to inform instruction, program, and professional development and to determine the effectiveness of different types of programs for ELLs

_____ Procedures for involving parents in all aspects of program development, implementation, and evaluation

_____ Procedures for articulating with community-based organizations and institutions of higher learning to support all aspects of program development, implementation, and evaluation

_____ Procedures governing how components of the language policy and implementation plan are reviewed and revised on a regular basis

_____ Procedures for how individual schools and the school district overall can obtain the resources they need to make implementation of the language policy a reality

Strengths of our school district/school policies and procedures _____

_____

Action steps _____

_____

References and Additional Resources

Abedi, J. (2004). The No Child Left Behind Act and English language learners: Assessment and accountability issues. *Educational Researcher, 33*(1), 1–14.

August, D., & Hakuta, K. (Eds.). (1997). Improving schooling for language-minority students: A research agenda. National Research Council. Washington, DC: National Academy Press.

Boston Globe, Nov. 3, 2002, p. A34.

Brisk, M. E. (in press). *Bilingual education: From compensatory to quality schooling* (2nd ed.). Mahwah, NJ: Erlbaum

Collier, V. P., & Thomas, W. P. (1989, Fall). How quickly can immigrants become proficient in school English? *Journal of Educational Issues of Language Minority Students, 5,* 26–39.

Corson, D. (1999). *Language policy in schools: A resource for teachers and administrators.* Mahwah, NJ: Erlbaum.

Crawford, J. (1992). *Hold your tongue: Bilingualism and the politics of English-only.* Reading, MA: Addison-Wesley.

Crawford, J. (1999). *Bilingual education: History, politics, theory and practice.* Los Angeles: Bilingual Education Services.

Crawford, J. (2000). At war with diversity: US language policy in an age of anxiety. Clevedon, UK: Multilingual Matters.

Crawford, J. (2004). *No Child Left Behind: Misguided approach to school accountability for English language learners.* Washington, DC: Center on Education Policy. Available at www.nabe.org.

Echevarria, J., Vogt, M., & Short, D. J. (2004). *Making content comprehensible for English learners: The SIOP model* (2nd ed.). New York: Allyn & Bacon.

Fishman, J. (1991). *Reversing language shift.* Clevedon, UK: Multilingual Matters.

Freeman, R. (2004). *Building on community bilingualism.* Philadelphia: Caslon.

Gottlieb, M. (2003*). Large-scale assessment of English language learners.* Alexandria, VA: Teachers of English to Speakers of Other Languages.

Hakuta, K. (2001). *The education of language-minority students.* Testimony to the U.S. Commission on Civil Rights. Washington, DC, Apr. 13.

Hakuta, K., & Beatty, A. (Eds.). (2000). *Testing English-language learners in U.S. schools: Report and workshop summary.* National Research Council. Washington, DC: National Academy Press.

Hakuta, K., Butler, Y. G., & Witt, D. (2000). *How long does it take for English learners to attain proficiency?* Santa Barbara, CA: Linguistic Minority Research Institute.

Hornberger, N. (2004, September/October). Nichols to NCLB: Local and global perspectives on U.S. language education policy. Paper presented at *Imagining Multilingual Schools: An International Symposium on Language in Education,* Teachers College, Columbia University, New York.

Kloss, H. (1977). *The American bilingual tradition.* Rowley, MA: Newbury House.

Menken, K. (2005). *When the test is what counts: How high-stakes testing affects language policy and the education of English language learners in high school.* Unpublished doctoral dissertation, Teachers College, Columbia University, New York.

National Association for Bilingual Education. (2004, Aug. 9). Comments on proposed amended regulations for Title I of the Elementary and Secondary Education Act of 1965. Washington, DC: Author.

National Clearinghouse for English Language Acquisition (NCELA). (2002). How has federal policy for language minority students evolved in the US? *AskNCELA , 3*. [Online] Available at http://www.ncela.gwu.edu/askncela/03history.htm. [Retrieved Jan. 10, 2003]

Pray, L. C., & MacSwan, J. (2002). *Different question, same answer: How long does it take for English learners to acquire proficiency?* Paper presented at the annual meeting of the American Educational Research Association, New Orleans, Apr. 4.

Ramírez, J. D., Yuen, S. D., & Ramey, D. R. (1991). *Final report: Longitudinal study of structured English immersion strategy, early-exit and late-exit transitional bilingual education programs for language-minority children.* San Mateo, CA: Aguirre International.

READ Institute. (1997). A 50-state survey of requirements for the education of language minority children. The Institute for Research in English Acquisition and Development. [Online] Available at http://www.ceousa.org/READ/50state.html. [Retrieved Mar. 17, 2005]

Ricento, T. (1995). A brief history of language restrictionism in the United States. In S. Dicker, R. Jackson, T. Ricento, & K. Romstedt (Eds.), *Official English? No! TESOL's recommendations for countering the official English movement in the U.S.* Washington, DC: TESOL.

U.S. Census Bureau. (2000). QT-P16 Language spoken at home: 2000. *Census 2000 Summary File 3*. Washington, DC: Author.

U.S. Department of Education. (2001). *The No Child Left Behind Act of 2001*. P.L. 107-110. Washington, DC: Author.

Wiley, T., & Wright, W. (2004, January/March). Against the undertow: Language-minority education policy and politics in the "age of accountability." *Educational Policy, 18*(1), 142–168.

Wright, W. E. (in press-a). English learners left behind in Arizona: The nullification of accommodations for ELLs in the intersection of federal and state language and assessment policies. *Bilingual Research Journal.*

Wright, W. E. (in press-b). The political spectacle of Proposition 203 in Arizona. *Educational Policy.*

Chapter 2

Linking the School and the Community

❦

_____ *Guiding Principles* _____

- We make sure that parents of English language learners know and understand the school district's/school's policies, programs, and practices regarding their children.
- Our policies, programs, practices, and assessments for English language learners have a clear enrichment orientation that sees linguistic and cultural diversity as resources to develop, not as problems to overcome.
- We ensure that parents of English language learners are actively involved in their children's education and in the school community.
- We collaborate with community-based organizations in ways that benefit all students, their families, the school, and the community.

Introduction

To say that parental involvement is critical to the success of any program has become an adage; so much so that we often say it without paying proper heed to what it actually means. For programs that serve students who have special characteristics, such as English language learners (ELLs), it is particularly important to think about the why and the how of parental involvement. Given the right kind of environment, parents of ELLs can be involved in the school, and they can become an administrator's and teacher's best allies in providing the support that ELLs need at home. Although it can take significant effort to establish a strong link between the school and the community, it is well worth the effort. Having a strong group of parents whose needs are heeded and who, in turn, support the school and their children's teachers is one of the best investments that an administrator can make.

Parents of ELLs are often farther away from the community of the school than any other parents within that community. However, their physical absence from the school does not mean they do not support their children's education. It may simply be a sign that the parents are reluctant or unable to come to school and to participate in their children's education in this way. Notions of parental involvement and how necessary parental involvement is vary significantly among families and across cultures. For some families, participation in a child's schooling may mean coming to the school building at least once a week. For others, it may mean making sure that the child has a quiet place in the home to complete homework.

The success of children as students is largely dependent on how closely parents pay attention to them as learners and as members of their classroom and school communities. Parents of children in U.S. schools are expected not only to keep track of the multitude of classroom and school activities, both academic and extracurricular, but also to respond to numerous queries that are sent home and to help with homework. For educated parents who are familiar with how U.S. schools function, the task is easier. For parents who themselves are not highly educated, the task is more challenging. For a parent who does not speak English proficiently, who is not familiar with the way that school works, or who may feel uncomfortable or inadequate in an unfamiliar culture, these not so simple tasks can take on gargantuan dimensions. In order for parents to become involved in and supportive of their children's education, they must understand the educational policies, programs, and practices available to their children at school, and they must feel welcome in the school.

From the ELL's perspective, linking the home and the school accomplishes another crucial goal: it provides some continuity between their home and school lives. ELLs need to see something familiar when they enter the school building and when they enter their classrooms, and they need to learn new concepts through a context that is recognizable. To learn new abstract concepts through a nonproficient language in a perplexing cultural context may be too many hurdles to overcome for many ELLs. Schools can support their ELLs by changing their general orientation toward the teaching of English to speakers of other languages. Administrators can lead/support the school's efforts to shift the perspective of educating ELLs from a compensatory to an enrichment approach: we do not need to compensate for the fact that ELLs are coming with lower than necessary skills in English; rather, we need to enrich their lives by adding English. This shift in orientation changes the school's perspective on cultural diversity, from one that views diversity as a deficit to one that views diversity as a difference. This simple change is essential to creating what some have called a positive sociocultural context for ELLs.

This chapter begins with the first step in ensuring the link between the school and the community: letting parents of ELLs know their rights. Insofar as many foreign-born parents do not know they have legal rights that give them decision-making power in their children's schooling, this is a critical first step. Answers to most of the rest of the questions in the chapter provide concrete strategies that administrators can use and adapt to create a positive sociocultural context at school that supports ELLs, integrates parents of ELLs, and is enriching to all students. The chapter concludes with a survey for reflection and action that administrators can use to review how their school relates to linguistic and cultural diversity, and to identify action steps the school can take to strengthen school-community links.

Question

What are the legal mandates for involving parents of English language learners?[1]

ELSE HAMAYAN AND ADELA WEINSTEIN

The first thing that parents of English language learners (ELLs) must realize is that schools must ensure that all ELLs develop English proficiency based on state expectations, and meet the same academic content and achievement standards that all children are expected to meet. In many states, this is achieved through specialized support in English as a second language (ESL) and through instruction of the content areas in the students' native language while they are developing proficiency in English. Unfortunately, several states do not provide instruction through the native language, which makes it quite difficult for ELLs to keep up with the English-speaking population in learning the academic content. More seriously, some states limit the length of time that ELLs may receive specialized support in ESL. However, regardless of the type of program available in a school district, the opportunity to achieve academic standards must be equitable for all students.

---

1. This information was adapted from *NCLB Action Briefs: Programs of English Language Learners*. Available at www.ncpie.org/nclbaction/english_language_learners.html.

Schools are also obligated to provide parental notification as to why their child is in need of placement in a specialized language instruction program. Many states have required such notifications to parents. More recently, under the No Child Left Behind (NCLB) Act, schools must inform parents of a child identified for participation in a Title III-funded program within a specified time. (At the time of publication of this book, that time limit was thirty days after the beginning of the school year. For a child who enters school after the beginning of the school year, the school must inform parents within two weeks of the child's placement in such a program.)

Parents also have the right to know that their children are being assessed in a language and a format that can elicit the most accurate information about what their children know and can do. Schools can make testing accommodations, such as developing an assessment in a student's native language, providing translation help, or conducting an oral test, if it is felt that those strategies will yield more accurate information about an ELL's academic achievement.

Title III funds are to be used to provide language instruction educational programs, defined as courses in which ELL students are placed for the purpose of attaining English proficiency, while meeting challenging state academic content and student academic achievement standards. According to federal law, these programs may make use of both English and the child's native language to enable the child to develop and attain English proficiency, but school districts are required to "use approaches and methodologies based on scientifically-based research."

States may require schools or school districts to involve parents and legal guardians of ELLs, as well as community members, in the program's decision-making process through the establishment of parent advisory committees. Under NCLB, each school or district using Title III funds must implement an effective means of outreach to parents of ELLs. They must inform parents about how they can be active participants in assisting their children to learn English, achieve at high levels in core academic subjects, and meet state standards. Not only do schools have the responsibility of sending parents information, they must communicate with parents in an understandable and uniform format, which means communicating the same information to all parents and in a method that is effective.

Schools receiving Title III funds must provide parents with information in an understandable and uniform format and, to the extent practicable, in a language that the parent can understand, about the following:

- The reasons for identifying their child as being limited English proficient and for placing their child in a language instruction educational program for limited English proficient (LEP) students.

- The child's current level of English proficiency, including how the level was assessed and the status of the child's academic achievement.
- The method of instruction that will be used in the program, including a description of all other available programs.
- How the program will meet the educational strengths and needs of the child.
- How the program will help the child learn English and meet academic achievement standards.
- How the program will meet the objectives of an individualized education program for a child with a disability.
- Program exit requirements, including when the transition will take place and when graduation from secondary school is expected.
- The parents' rights, including written guidance that gives parents the option of selecting from among different programs the school may offer if they wish to decline placement or have their child removed from a language instruction educational program.
- Any failure of the program to help the child make progress on annual measurable achievement objectives.

Administrators may suggest the following actions for parents:

- Get a copy of the school district's Title III plan and find out how parents and families are included in the development of objectives for ELLs, and the ways in which the district plans to include literacy opportunities for families.
- Ensure that the school district communicates with parents in a language they can understand.
- Become familiar with the various language instruction educational programs offered by the school district and the benefits and drawbacks of each.
- Make sure you know what resources are available in the school and in the community to support ELL students and their families.
- Title III provides funds for professional development. Make sure these funds are being used appropriately and effectively to help ELL students.
- Make sure that instructors of Title III programs are trained and certified to work with ELL students. Paraprofessionals may act as translators providing instructional support services but they must be under the direct supervision of a certified teacher.

Question

How do you communicate with parents of English language learners in ways that they can understand?

❦

MARLA HORI

The most critical thing to remember when communicating with parents of English language learner (ELLs) is that your approach must be as personal as possible. This means face to face, person to person, and using personal invitations when possible. Flyers and newsletters are the least effective means of communication. Administrators, teachers, or parents from the same language group should talk directly with ELL parents. This requires extra effort, but the payoff in terms of parental involvement as a result of better communication will make it worth while.

Being a partner in the educational process is a concept that is completely foreign to many ELL parents. It is simply not what "good parents" do in other countries. In most other countries, the school and the parents are not expected to work together as we do in the United States. ELL parents may not realize that we want to communicate with them, or that the schools value their ideas and input.

In order to communicate, we must first get the ELL parents into the school. Two keys to doing this successfully are to use school events with small settings and to personally invite ELL parents to help in some way or to attend an event.

Parents will most often come for performances involving their children, low-stress events that involve bringing food to school (potlucks, class lunches or parties, all-school picnics), or special events for the whole family, such as a Make-and-Take evening of some sort. The children motivate their parents to attend. These events then become opportunities for us to build personal relationships with the parents, which is especially important for administrators. If the setting is small, we use the event as an opportunity to share vital information about upcoming events such as summer school or parent conferences.

We have had much success with what we call Bridge Parents. We find at least one, preferably two, parents in each of our major language groups and ask them to help us reach into their like-language group. Two parents can support each other in their efforts. We give them a list of all the parents (names, phones, addresses) in the district who speak their language and ask them to be the leader of that group. It is important to honor and recognize this group of parents by publicly thanking them for their help, particularly within their language group. We have used this model to have coffees or teas at school for each language group. There is safety in numbers for people who speak a common language, and it tips the scales in the ELL parent's favor, as the administrators and teachers are always in the minority at these gatherings. We have held these coffees in our Bridge Parent's homes and also at school. It is a wonderful way for people to build community and talk with other parents in their first language about school programs, concerns, and issues.

Translators can often be found within the Bridge Parent group. Parents who become empowered in the groups are usually quite willing to help translate in a variety of settings or even to make a phone call to another parent on behalf of a teacher or the school.

The difficulty arises when confidential information needs to be translated, such as in a parent conference or in a special education meeting. We have had luck finding translators for confidential meetings by using teachers and staff who speak that language, or by using friends or relatives of that teacher or staff member. Our administrators and teachers have also networked with other professionals in our township to find someone to translate if we are unable to find someone within our district.

Question

How do you create a positive school environment for English language learners and their parents/ members of their household?

REBECCA FREEMAN AND ELSE HAMAYAN

Schools that see linguistic and cultural diversity as resources to be developed rather than as problems to be overcome offer more positive environments for English language learners (ELLs) and their families and members of their household. Schools with a positive sociocultural orientation make efforts to connect with and build on the linguistic and cultural expertise that ELLs and their families and communities bring with them to school. Although not all schools can fully promote additive bilingualism, every school can find creative ways to link the school with the community to support ELLs, welcome their families, and provide a more enriching educational experience for all students.

Administrators can lead this effort by encouraging their school leadership team (which should include parents and community members) to review the school's orientation toward linguistic and cultural diversity as reflected in their general school environment, policies, programs, curriculum, materials, instructional practices and assessments, and parental and community involvement. We focus here on the visibility of languages other than English in the general school environment and on the integration of culture into the curriculum.

An easy and obvious place to begin is to ask whether the languages that the ELLs, their parents, and the local communities speak are readily observable and audible at school. The relative visibility or invisibility of linguistic and cultural diversity sends a strong message to ELLs, their families, and the rest of the student body about the value of those languages and cultures at school. The following kinds of questions can help guide the leadership team: Is there evidence of languages other than English at school, for example, in student work on the walls in the hallways and in the classroom? Are there books in languages other than English in the library? Are students encouraged to use their home languages as resources in content area instruction? Are materials and resources available in the languages that the students speak at home or in the community? Does the school partner in any ways with community-based organizations? If so, what is the purpose and nature of these partnerships? When the leadership team identifies a problem, they can work together to address that problem given their resources and constraints. For example, if they see little to no representation of the more than thirty languages spoken by students in their school, they can brainstorm creative ways to bring those languages into the school, and they can reflect on what happens over time as a result of the changes they have made.

It is important for educators to think of a school's orientation toward linguistic and cultural diversity as an integral part of what they already do, rather than as one more thing that they have to do. For example, as educators review their curriculum (as part of the regular curriculum review process or in preparation for teaching), they can ask themselves how culture is conceptualized within their curriculum. There are different perspectives on integrating culture into school life. Culture may be thought of as (1) a lesson to be taught and studied, (2) a subject to be integrated into the curriculum, (3) a human-relations issue to be dealt with at school, (4) a school reform movement in education, or (5) a multilayered, multifaceted social framework within which schooling takes place (Banks, 1988). During the curriculum review, educators can look into the representation and evaluation of different linguistic and cultural groups and take steps to ensure that the curriculum they teach fully integrates the cultural contributions and perspectives of the diverse groups represented at their school and in society.

Integrating a resource orientation toward linguistic and cultural diversity into the curriculum does not mean a lack of attention to standards and accountability requirements. For example, schools can draw on what Moll (1995) calls "cultural funds of knowledge" from the home or the community as a link between ELLs' prior knowledge and they concepts and skills they need to develop at school. Students might use their family and community histories as a thematic center of an integrated unit. In social studies they might learn to conduct qualitative research into the community, and then write expository texts to share what they learned. In math, they might conduct quantitative studies of language use first among students in their class, and then throughout the school and larger community. In language arts, they might draw on their inquiry-based math and social studies projects as a foundation for writing persuasive texts that argue for solutions to problems that they identify in their homes, school, and community, and as a basis for social action.

An integrated multicultural curriculum can help link the school and the community. This approach can bring the languages and literacies used in students' homes and throughout the community into the school as resources to build on, help ELLs make connections between their prior knowledge and skills and the new abstract content area knowledge and skills that they need to develop at school, connect children with their families and other community members, enrich the lives of the English-speaking students as they explore the rich linguistic and cultural diversity in their neighborhood, and address challenging state standards and accountability requirements. Perhaps most important, linking the school and the community in this way prepares students to think critically about the world in which they live and to develop the tools they need to change that world.

Question

How do you integrate parents of English language learners and community members into your program/school?

🐝

MARITZA MEYERS

Our goal is to educate immigrant parents and give them the opportunity to move up the social ladder into an integrated society. Here are some suggestions for achieving this goal, first within the school community and then in the larger society.

Let the Native Language Play a Significant Role within the School

- Provide school personnel and resources in the native language by hiring, whenever possible, bilingual teachers, psychologists, counselors, social workers, secretaries, and community liaisons.
- Have postings throughout the school in the native language.
- When offering workshops for parents of English language learners (ELLs), make sure they are in the native language (with the exception of ESL classes, of course).
- Whenever possible, hire ELL parents. They can provide a valuable native language and native culture resource for the entire district.

Make it Easier for Parents to Attend Events at School

- Provide transportation for parents: Districts can provide bus transportation to schools during important events. Designated stops at various locations throughout the community will facilitate transportation to and from school functions.
- Offer child care services during parent workshops and meetings. Parents can attend the meetings while their children are being watched in another room.

- Provide meals at the meetings that are appropriate to the time of the meetings.
- Dedicate a room in the school to parents. That can become their "homeroom."

Offer Classes for Parents

Survey parents as to their need for various types of classes and workshops, which may include the following:

- ESL classes for a minimum of ten classes per session
- Literacy, technology and GED classes
- Citizenship classes
- Craft workshops where parents and children work separately for half of the session and come together during the second half of the session
- Cross-cultural communication. Do not shy away from dealing with cross-cultural issues; try to deal with cultural differences in an open and positive way.
- Instruction on at-home activities to support learning. Help parents improve their parenting skills so that children come to school better prepared.
- Programs and services available in the community such as clinics, city hall, public library, and community agencies.

Encourage Participation in School Governance

- Parent Advisory Committee: Form a committee of parents, teachers, administrators who serve as representatives for the school. The role and function of the committee can be determined by the program coordinator and a small subcommittee. The committee can promote partnerships between the district or school and other community organizations. Members will provide advisory input on any matters that the committee deems appropriate to the improvement of ELL education in the district.
- Parental attendance at Board of Education (BOE) meetings: Invite parents to attend BOE meetings. A facilitator can act as translator during the meeting and can then provide a brief summary of what transpired during the meeting.

Encourage Home Visits

A visit to the home by a teacher or school personnel provides great insight into students' home life, and can give educators the opportunity to see how ELLs use their home language and English (orally and in writing) in their everyday lives. These visits also benefit the parents since they will feel more comfortable with school staff on their own ground and thus feel more comfortable venturing into school.

Recruit Parents as Volunteers

Volunteering is an incredibly rewarding way for parents to feel ownership and shared responsibility in their child's education. It is also a great way for them to get to know the workings of a school intimately. Volunteering could take place during the school day or even after school or on occasional weekends. Some opportunities for volunteering include:

- In the classrooms, working one on one with students under the direction of a teacher
- On school trips or other special events
- In the front office or as a morning greeter
- In the lunchroom or library
- As a monitor of various clubs

Hold Activities that Integrate the English-speaking and ELL Community

The child is the common element that creates the opportunity for gatherings such as:

- Workshops where children and parents come together to participate in activities
- School shows at which all children perform. Showcase a performance in the native language.
- Cultural activities
- Exhibits
- Story-telling nights

R. C. Rodriguez

Involving parents of English language learners (ELLs) is a process (Epstein et al., 2002). First, ELL parents must have a good understanding of your program, its goals, and its objectives. More often than not ELL parents concentrate on their child learning the English language. As administrators we need to help them understand that the focus of schools serving ELL students is twofold, on academics and on English language learning. Second, we need to point out that time is of essence, especially for older students. Third, it is also important to educate ELL parents about the research that stands behind our approaches and programs. Addressing this challenge effectively can be an administrator's first step in integrating ELL parents within the campus environment.

The administrator can get started by extending an invitation for a day or evening meeting to parents so they can build a better understanding of program goals. These meetings are sometimes known as *cafesitos,* or "coffee with the principal." One good way to begin such a meeting is by using the KWL strategy used in many of our ESL classes. What do you *know* about our program and second language learning? What do you *want to know* about our program and second language learning? Finally, what did you *learn* about our program and second language learning? This approach allows misconceptions to be aired and addressed, and it helps parents form a true picture of their child's learning environment. During this same meeting a bilingual/ESL classroom observation can be planned, perhaps showcasing the campus program through a video that features other ELL parents speaking about the benefits of the program. It is worth noting that the most valuable tool we have in getting ELL parents involved is other ELL parents who have already formed a partnership with the school or district. These parents already have the trust and realization that their children will learn English and grow in all academic areas. These ELL parents become educators, and this becomes the second level of the integration process for ELL parents into the school or district: ELL parents teaching one another.

As our ELL parents begin to feel valued for what they bring to the learning environment of their children, the third level of school integration seems to occur naturally. This is the level you as an administrator seek to obtain: help and support in the school and classroom. It is at this level of the process that ELL parents often begin to suggest ideas and make requests for getting other ELL parents involved. Most frequently they ask to meet with other ELL parents from the same school. They also ask for English as a second language

(ESL) classes, computer classes taught in the native language or through ESL approaches, and ideas on how to assist in educating their children at home. Our ELL parents also enjoy make and take workshops.

Once this level of commitment is reached, most ELL parents are willing to move on to more sophisticated involvement with the school. It is important to note that not all ELL parents can fulfill these roles, as many are working parents or have other children at home. However, administrators are likely to find that even busy parents want to help, however they can. Here are some ways our ELL parents are integrating themselves into our schools.

Parents as Teachers at Home

ELL parents can help extend the learning day into the home. With help from educators and resource materials, ELL parents can learn to reinforce academic skills for their children at home. Several publishing companies offer take-home kits or materials that are parent-friendly and allow them to work individually with their children (see also Einhorn, 2001). When parents become closely involved in their children's learning process, they can provide valuable feedback to the teacher, and this in turn helps to integrate them into the school mainstream.

ELL Parents as Translators

When ELL parents are bilingual and received a formal education in their native country, they can assist you with translating instructional materials, documents, parent letters, newsletters, and brochures. When ELL parents assume the role of translator, one must be cautious of the following:

1. Allow enough time for translation: Translating is time-consuming. However, with proper time and planning, your translator can be a valuable resource.

2. Always have other native speakers review and edit the translation.

3. Be aware of regional dialects or language differences that could result in an ineffective translation.

ELL Parents as Tutors

We have found this type of parental involvement to be the most beneficial for both the school and the parent. Training and supervision are key to the success of this strategy. ELL parents can help with remediation, enrichment, and skills practice. Many tutorial resources and materials can be purchased today to help you focus on academic or linguistic goals and objectives. However, make sure that these materials are parent friendly.

Other ways of integrating parents into the mainstream are using the services of ELL parents as mentors, interpreters, meeting facilitators, campus volunteers, and advisory council members.

Recommendations

1. Review your district or campus policies and procedures before getting parents involved.

2. Observe all clearance policies your department of human resources may have in place.

3. Obtain funding for these programs through Title III or Title I funds, grants, and community partnerships.

4. Make it a point to learn about the cultures and languages represented on your campus.

ROBERT FUGATE

At Greenfield Elementary School, parents of English language learners (ELLs) participate in an after-school English as a second language (ESL) class once a week. The class is designed to teach the parents writing and computer skills, as well as basic English language skills. During the class, the parents write a cookbook of their own recipes in their first languages and then translating them into English. While the parents are working in the computer lab, their children are participating in a homework/study skills workshop led by high school students volunteering their time. Each week after the parent class a potluck dinner is held, and the parents participate in a drawing for door prizes. The door prizes and the dinner are necessary incentives to attract as much parent participation as possible. During the dinner, the parents talk with one another. This helps them feel less isolated in their community and more comfortable in coming to the school.

As most of the parents participating in the class are Spanish speakers, some bilingual instruction is necessary to meet their individual language needs. The parents' educational levels also vary from those who do not read and write in their first language to those with much education and first language literacy. Because the parents have varying levels of education and English language proficiency, the parents with the most proficient English language skills act as interpreters for the parents with lower proficiency. This allows all parents appropriate comfort levels to participate actively in the class and not to feel intimidated by the language barrier. It also fosters a sense of camaraderie among the parents; they know they are not alone.

Additional benefits of the class are the parents' comfort in coming to the school for programs, teacher conferences, and visiting their children at lunch. They know that the staff members at Greenfield Elementary School are sensitive to their needs and to the language barriers. The ESL teachers serve as liaisons between the classroom teachers and the parents. They also do some interpreting, as needed. Another benefit for the parents is their children seeing their own parents as language learners in their own school. This has led to building a language learning community at the school where children and parents are stakeholders. During the time the class has met, the parents' comfort with the English language has grown, along with their proficiency and literacy levels.

The parent ESL class is possible as the result of a grant that provides funds for all materials and people necessary to make it work. The program is sponsored by the Chesterfield Public Education Foundation and administered by the Chesterfield County Public Schools Department of Business and Government Relations in collaboration with the Instruction Division.

Question

What do parents of English language learners contribute to your school? What kinds of roles do they play?

JUDITH KWIAT YTURRIAGO

Parents of English language learners (ELLs) serve on the district's Bilingual Parent Advisory Committee (BPAC) as mandated by the Illinois Administrative School Code, and they contribute in many ways to the education of their children. Parents on the BPAC review the district's applications for grants and help with the implementation of activities outlined in the grants. BPAC parents also organize classes of Spanish as a second language for English-speaking families and other social and community activities. BPAC parents review standardized assessment data and participate in developing an action plan for the various types of programs for ELLs, aimed at raising academic performance based on that data. Parents have been advocates for the two-way immersion (TWI) program by lobbying the school board for the expansion of the program from 1999 until the present. The district would not have a TWI program were it not for the parents voicing their criticisms of the transitional bilingual program at school board meetings.

Parents also volunteer in classrooms to assist the teachers, to read to children, and to tutor children other than their own. They also volunteer to participate in a myriad of PTA activities such as organizing and working in book fairs, fund-raisers, carnivals, and family literacy nights. Parents translate for the school newsletters and mentor new families to the school. Parents attend PTA functions, curriculum nights, and family literacy nights.

Parents in our district are also learners: they take adult (ESL) English as a second language and GED (General Education Diploma) classes offered through the local high school 's adult continuing education department. By doing so, they model lifelong learning for their children. More than forty families have participated over the course of two years. Similar activities are planned for this year.

Parents are encouraged to plan independent family learning activities. In addition to the local school efforts, the district has a family center located in the administration center where child care services are available while parents learn how to use computers, the Internet, and other life skills. ESL classes are also offered at the family center for parents who find it difficult to go to the high school.

Question

What can you tell parents of English language learners about language use at home?

JUDITH KWIAT YTURRIAGO

Parents of English language learners (ELLs) in School District 65 are constantly urged to speak their native languages at home and to read to their children in their native languages. This message is repeated each year as new and former parents meet with teachers and administrators. At Washington School, one of the four two-way immersion schools in our district, the parents have had the opportunity to participate in a state-funded family literacy grant for two consecutive years. Parents participated in afternoon and evening activities aimed at helping them learn to use the libraries in town and in the school. Parents also were able to learn new skills for helping their children with their schoolwork. All this was done with the intent that parents would become better able to help their children at home in their native language.

This philosophy is based on the notion that children who are supported at home are more likely to succeed in school than those who do not receive much help with homework and those who are not read to. Parents of ELLs, who themselves are not very proficient in English, are better able to give that support to their children in the native language than in English. In fact, when ELL parents feel obligated to speak English to their children, both the quantity of language used in conversations diminishes and its quality suffers drastically.

In addition to the educational benefits of getting support in the native language, there are some cognitive benefits as well (Bialystock & Hakuta, 1994). Children who are raised bilingually tend to be stronger students. We are never worried that these ELLs will not have enough English. The English language is so powerful in the larger society that, if anything, we have to find ways of getting children to stop using it at home!

Finally, we see some affective benefits to families using their native language at home as much as possible. The dynamics of parent-child relationships and the roles that parents and children play at home are sacred and should not be upset in any way. When the lingua franca at home becomes English, the children, who surpass their parents in English language proficiency, sometimes take on roles that are not typical of children. Parents lose the ability to communicate openly and fluently with their own children. That is something we need to avoid.

This is why we encourage parents to help their children with the homework (whether it is in English or the native language) in their own language. It is why we encourage parents who do not read in their own language to tell stories to their children in their native language. We encourage our teachers to send home wordless books that parents can use to tell more stories in the native language. It is a small gesture that has tremendous returns for our students.

Letter to an administrator:
From the parent of an English language learner

Dear Mrs. Clark,

Since my daughter Lupe started school back in September, I've wanted to write to you. I do not know if you were aware in the beginning of the school year when we met with Lupe's teacher how nervous we were. When we are asked to attend places where English is spoken, we get very nervous. We do not know if we are able to understand everything or how we are to do things. We do not know when we need to be seated or need to stand, nor do we know when to shake hands or what we are going to do when we need to ask a question. In the town we live in Guatemala, we would regularly attend the school's activities. So, we knew the school well. But we do not know what to expect here. You can't imagine how relieved we were when we arrived at the school and we were received by Mrs. Gomez, who spoke Spanish and translated for us and the Camargos. I would have liked to walk through the entire building to get to know the school but at least we were able to visit Lupe's classroom and get an idea where she goes daily.

I was very surprised when we were not able to speak to Lupe's teacher, Mrs. Gibbons, individually. In Guatemala we all knew the teachers and the teachers knew the parents. This way the teachers knew where the students came from. We do not know anyone here nor does anyone know us. Even though it would take a long time for the teacher to speak to each parent, we would have liked to tell Mrs. Gibbons how much we value education and how our family spends time at home and that we attend mass with our neighbors, who are from Guatemala and Mexico.

I also wanted to tell Mrs. Gibbons of a young man who lives down the street from our home and who will be helping Lupe with her English. So not to worry, even though we do not speak English, it will not affect Lupe from doing well with her homework.

I want to share with you, Mrs. Clark, how surprised I was when Mrs. Ward, the teacher from the other kindergarten, asked us to read books to our children each day. My parents never read books to me nor did my husband's parent's read to him. We feel very bad because we are not able to read books in English to Lupe. We do not have any books in English. I was lucky; my neighbor Mrs. Alvarez was able to show me how to use the library. I learned how to check out books in English for my daughter. But Mrs. Gibbons has been very kind to us; when I told her that it was very difficult for us to read books in English, she said it would be marvelous to be able to read books in Spanish to our daughter. That way Lupe can share with her classmates the books she has read in Spanish. I was even more surprised when I found out that Mrs. Gibbons did not even speak Spanish.

I enjoy attending the coffee talks that are organized by Mrs. Gomez every two weeks but I am sorry I am not able to attend each time because it becomes difficult for me to take the time off from work. It is very important for us to know how Lupe is progressing. We would like to know any information pertaining to Lupe's progress.

Thank you very much for everything you are doing for our daughter.

Sincerely,
Alicia Garcia Amaya

Survey for Reflection and Action

The following survey is based on the guiding principles articulated in the introduction to the chapter. Read the following statements and indicate the degree to which you agree or disagree: DK = don't know; 1 = strongly disagree; 2 = disagree; 3 = agree; 4 = strongly agree. Identify your program strengths and needs, and develop appropriate strategies for action.

Parents of ELLs know and understand our policies, programs, and practices.

Parents of ELLs at our school know and understand our policies regarding ELLs (e.g., re student identification, placement, and exit criteria; assessments and accommodations; promotion, retention, and graduation criteria). DK 1 2 3 4

Parents know and understand the program options (e.g., bilingual, ESL, heritage language, special education, gifted and talented, extracurricular) at our school. DK 1 2 3 4

Parents know and understand instructional practices at our school (e.g., curricular programs and materials, classroom norms and expectations). DK 1 2 3 4

Our school sees linguistic and cultural diversity as resources to be developed.

There is observable and audible evidence of the linguistic and cultural diversity of our students and surrounding community in our general school environment. DK 1 2 3 4

There is evidence of the linguistic and cultural diversity of our students and surrounding community in our policies. DK 1 2 3 4

There is evidence of the linguistic and cultural diversity of our students and surrounding community in our programs. DK 1 2 3 4

Teachers regularly draw on the linguistic and
cultural diversity of the students in their classes
in order to make the curriculum meaningful and
relevant to students' lives.   DK 1 2 3 4

School staff draw on and work with the linguistic and
cultural resources of community-based organizations
to enrich the lives of all students.   DK 1 2 3 4

Parents of ELLs are actively involved in their children's education.

Parents of ELLs understand and
support the educational initiatives at our school
(e.g., they support their children's home language
and literacy development, provide a supportive
environment for homework, come to parent-teacher
conferences, help with school activities).   DK 1 2 3 4

ELL parents are involved in the decision making at
our school (e.g., they participate in home-school
association, serve on school leadership teams,
act as community liaisons).   DK 1 2 3 4

Strengths of our efforts to link the school—home—community

_____

_____

_____

_____

Action Steps _____

_____

_____

_____

References and Additional Resources

Auerbach, E. (with Barahona, B., Midy, J., Vaquerano, F., Zambrano, A., & Arnaud, J.) (1996). *From the community to the community: A guidebook for participatory literacy training.* Mahwah, NJ: Erlbaum.

Banks, J. A. (1988). Approaches to multicultural curriculum reform. *Multicultural Leader, 1*(2).

Bialystock, E., & Hakuta, K. (1994). *In other words: The science and psychology of second language acquisition.* New York: Basic Books.

Einhorn, K. (2001). *ESL activities and mini-books for every classroom.* New York: Scholastic.

Epstein, J., Sanders, M., Simon, B., Salinas, K., Jansorn, N., & Voorhis, F. (2002). *School, family and community partnerships: Your handbook for action* (2nd ed.). Thousand Oaks, CA: Corwin Press.

Freire, P., & Macedo, D. (1987). *Literacy: Reading the word and the world.* South Hadley, MA: Bergin & Garvey.

Henze, R., Katz, A., Norte, E., Sather, S. E., & Walker, E. (2002). *Leading for diversity: How school leaders promote positive interethnic relations.* Thousand Oaks, CA: Corwin Press.

Moll, L. (1995). Bilingual classroom studies and community analysis. In O. García & C. Baker (Eds.), *Policy and practice in bilingual education* (pp. 273–280). Clevedon, UK: Multilingual Matters.

Nieto, S. (2003). *Affirming diversity: The sociopolitical context of multicultural education.* White Plains, NY: Longman.

Olsen, L., Bhattacharya, J., Chow, M., Jaramillo, A., Tobiassen, D. P., & Solorio, J. (2001). *And still we speak: Stories of communities sustaining and reclaiming language and culture.* Oakland, CA: California Tomorrow.

Street, B. (2005). *Literacies across educational contexts.* Philadelphia: Caslon.

Chapter 3

How Children Learn in Two Languages

℘

_____ *Guiding Principles* _____

- We make our pedagogical decisions based on the fact that it takes time for English language learners to acquire the academic language and literacies they need for school success.
- Because a strong first language (including first language literacy) provides a solid foundation for cognitive development, academic achievement, and language and literacy development in English, we draw on and support an English language learner's first language to the greatest degree possible at our school.
- Our programs and practices reflect an understanding of and sensitivity to the ways that culture influences all aspects of learning and teaching at school.
- Our program for English language learners allows for variation in the ways that these students acquire English and achieve academically at school.

Introduction

Questions regarding how children learn in two languages must be at the base of any educational decision made about English language learners (ELLs) at school. It is essential that program planning, curricula, and instructional strategies be based explicitly on what we know about how students learn a second language, how they develop literacies in a second language, and how they develop cognitively and learn academic content through a second language. Yet many schools end up with policies and regulations that go against what is known about the most effective ways for children to develop proficiency in English, the language of instruction, while they are developing cognitively and acquiring knowledge and skills in the curriculum content areas through their second language. For example, some districts restrict the time that an ELL may receive specialized English as a second language (ESL) services to one year. Yet, we know that it takes many children eight to ten years to develop the full range of English proficiency necessary to succeed in school. Other districts prevent ELLs from learning the mainstream curriculum through their proficient native language while they are developing proficiency in English. Yet, we know that students with little or no proficiency in English develop cognitively and learn new abstract content area concepts more effectively through their native language.

Regardless of whether the program for ELLs provides support in the native language, as in transitional bilingual programs, aims for bilingual proficiency, as in dual language programs, or shelters content area instruction in English, as in sheltered English programs or in mainstream classes that serve ELLs, administrators must pay heed to how children learn best in two languages. Not to do so is counterproductive at best.

This chapter briefly introduces administrators to research on how children learn in two languages so that they can make principled decisions about the programs they develop and implement for the ELLs at their schools. Although there is considerable confusion and controversy in schools today about ELLs, quite a bit is known about how children learn in two languages. We know why it takes so long for ELLs to develop the academic language and literacies they need for academic success. We know that knowledge and skills developed in the native language in oral and literacy domains transfer to English, the second language. We know that students can more readily learn abstract, cognitively challenging content area concepts through a proficient language, and that ELLs must continue to develop cognitively while they are acquiring English in order to achieve academically at school. We know that concepts learned in the native language do not need to be learned again in the second language. We know that it is easier to learn to read in a language that one is orally proficient in. This has significant implications for how we teach content area concepts to ELLs, and when and how we introduce second language literacy to these students. We also know that it is easier to develop proficiency in a second language, and to learn in that language, in a familiar cultural context. Thus, cultural relevance must be central to the ELL classroom and school.

The responses offered by the experts in this chapter and throughout this guide are based on research on how younger and older students learn in two languages. To help administrators apply these research findings to their class-rooms and educational programs, the chapter concludes with a survey for reflection and action. Administrators can use this survey in their schools to determine whether their policies, programs, practices, and assessments are theoretically sound, and to address any discrepancies they find.

Question

How long does it take for an English language learner to become proficient in a second language?

JIM CUMMINS

This question seems fairly straightforward until we probe a little deeper into what we mean by proficient and what aspects of second language proficiency we are talking about.

What is language proficiency?

As all administrators who have to deal with state standards and high-stakes assessments know, the term *proficient* can refer to widely different levels of actual competence, depending on the test and state standards. What counts as proficient in one state on a reading assessment, for example, may be far from proficient in another state. For purposes of thinking about English language learners' (ELLs') academic progress in English, however, we can define proficient in relation to the level of English competency of their native English-speaking peers. So the question can be rephrased as, How long does it take ELLs to catch up to their native English-speaking peers in English proficiency?

This brings us to the issue of what we mean by English proficiency. Although we commonly talk about "learning English" as though English proficiency were a unitary construct, we can all intuitively recognize some clear distinctions within that notion of English proficiency. These distinctions are apparent whether we are talking about native speakers of a language or second language learners. Specifically, we know that *conversational fluency* is quite different from *academic proficiency* in a language. The fast talkers in our classes are not necessarily the best readers. We also know that there are major differences between many of the technical or rule-governed aspects of a language, such as the rules for sound-symbol relationships (phonics), spelling, grammar, and so on, and the kinds of skills involved in reading comprehension. Thus, we can begin to distinguish three very different aspects of language proficiency: *conversational fluency, discrete language skills,* and *academic language proficiency.*

How long does it take for ELLs to catch up academically?

Very different time periods are required for ELLs to catch up to their peers in each of the three dimensions of proficiency. It usually takes about one to two years for students to become reasonably fluent in conversational English. About the same time is typically required for many ELLs in the early grades to acquire basic decoding skills in English to a level similar to that of their English-speaking classmates of similar socioeconomic background. However, research studies conducted in several countries show that second language learners usually need at least five years to catch up to native English speakers in academic English. Sometimes the catch-up period is much longer. Research conducted in Israel, for example, showed that Russian and Ethiopian immigrant students required about nine years to catch up to their peers in Hebrew academic skills.

These observations bring us to the next question: What exactly *is* academic English, and why does it take so long to catch up in this dimension of language?

Why does it take so long?

Academic English is the language of school success. As students progress through the grades, they are required to read increasingly complex texts in the content areas of the curriculum (science, math, social studies, literature). Academic language becomes increasingly complex after grades three and four. The complexity of academic language reflects:

- The difficulty of the concepts that students are required to understand.

- The vocabulary load in content texts, which may include many low-frequency and technical words (primarily from Latin and Greek sources) that are rarely used in typical conversation.

- Increasingly sophisticated grammatical constructions that, again, are almost never used in everyday conversational contexts. By the upper grades of elementary school, students encounter the frequent use of the passive voice, embedded clauses, and extended noun phrases.

Not only are students required to read this language, they must also use it in writing reports and essays, and in other forms of homework.

One reason that catching up in academic English is challenging for ELLs, then, is the complexity of academic language. A second reason is that they are trying to catch up to a moving target. Native English-speaking students are not standing still waiting for ELLs to catch up. Every year, they make gains in reading, writing, and vocabulary abilities. So ELLs have to run faster to bridge the gap. In fact, in order to catch up within six years, ELLs must make fifteen months' gain in every ten-month school year. The average student makes just ten months' gain in every ten-month school year.

How can we support students in acquiring academic English?

Understanding the nature of academic language points to some of the ways we can help students acquire it. If academic language is found in texts rather than in typical conversations, then we have to ensure that students are given ample opportunities and encouragement to read extensively. Thus, an administrative priority should be to ensure that school and classroom libraries are well stocked with engaging books. Encouraging students to write for authentic purposes is also crucial. Even recently arrived ELLs can create dual language books by writing stories or accounts of their experiences, initially in their first language and then working with peers, teachers, volunteers, older bilingual students, and even technology (Babel Fish or Google language tools) to translate and adapt their writing into English. (Two good Web sites with examples are http://thornwood.peelschools.org/Dual/ and http://www.multiliteracies.ca). Finally, some technology tools may be useful. An example is the the e-Lective Language Learning program, which provides supports to enable students to access the curriculum and to harvest the language of academic texts (www.e-Lective.net).

Question

What is the role of culture in language learning?

EUGENE GARCÍA

During the past decade, many educational theorists became interested in sociocultural theory, an international intellectual movement that brings together the disciplines of psychology, semiotics, education, sociology, and anthropology. This movement draws on work done earlier in the twentieth century by the Russian theorists L. S. Vygotsky and Mikhail Bakhtin and relates it to the thought of such theoreticians and philosophers of education as William James, John Dewey, C. S. Pierce, and Jean Piaget. The aim is to find a unified way of understanding issues of language, cognition, culture, human development, and teaching and learning.

The importance of sociocultural theory for education is its proposal that individual learning and social interaction are inextricably connected. Sociocultural theorists argue that the psychology of the individual learner is deeply shaped by social interaction; in essence, both student and teacher are engaged in the process of constructing their minds through social activity. In this view, knowledge is not a given set of fixed ideas that are passed from teacher to student. Rather, knowledge is created in the interaction between teacher and student. Higher-order mental processes, the tendency to look at things in certain ways, and values themselves are produced by shared activity and dialogue (Rogoff, 2003).

Our social lives, often considered to be the major products of culture and language, are instead for sociocultural theorists the major ingredients of cognition. Social experience is inseparable from thought. Moment by moment we construct reality. That process of construction, and the understanding it generates, depends on our previous understandings and our previous social experiences. The focus of sociocultural theory holds particular import for education, partly because education has been a major interest of many of its founding writers, but mostly because educational practice and theory need a unifying theory of teaching and learning.

Educators of culturally diverse students will find this theoretical framework helpful because it conceives of learning as an interaction between individual learners and an embedding context. That embedding context may be as immediate as the social environment of the classroom or as broad as the traditions and institutions that constitute the history of student and family. Both contexts and many more come into play whenever teachers and students interact. Important contexts for teaching and learning range from close, detailed instruction of individual learners and concern for the social organization of classrooms to a consideration of the cultural and linguistic attributes of teachers, students, and peers. These contexts interweave, and we can follow their strands to gain a new understanding of the relationship between language and culture.

☙

ELSE HAMAYAN

English language learners (ELLs) are faced with three significant challenges in school: they must learn new concepts (often quite abstract, especially above third grade), they must learn in a language in which they are not proficient, and they must learn in a cultural context that may be quite unfamiliar to them. This last challenge is the one that most educators pay the least attention to because it is not an explicit aspect of schooling and education (Cole, 1996).

Every ELL brings subtle cultural norms and values with him- or herself to school. Many of these norms and values go beyond the superficial displays of folktales, fashion, food, and festivals, which are merely the tip of the iceberg (Figure 3–1). They consist of the ways in which each of us interacts with and makes sense of our surroundings, or what may lie just below the surface in the iceberg model. These norms and values govern how we do what we do. Notions of modesty, a preference for competition or cooperation, and approaches to problem solving, lie well below the visible surface. However, they permeate every aspect of the lives of ELLs at school. It is precisely for this reason that administrators need to consider cultural diversity in every aspect of the program that they establish for ELLs.

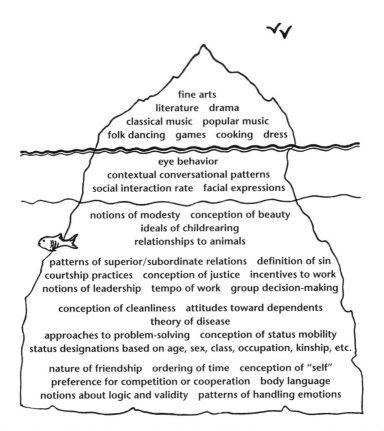

Figure 3-1.   The iceberg model of culture (Illinois Resource Center, 1997).

As Eugene García stated in the immediately preceding discussion, culture is tightly interwoven with language learning and use. It is also a critical factor in learning in general. The way we interpret and interact with our environment can facilitate or inhibit learning. One way in which culture plays a role in the learning process relates to how well a student functions within the culture of the classroom. Students who are comfortable with the culture of the classroom and who behave according to the norms that govern the classroom are more relaxed learners than students who feel as though their behavior is off the mark. Often, students who are not acculturated into the culture of the classroom are not even able to articulate what it is that makes them different from the others. Students who stand too close to others or those whose norms of modesty are different than those of the general school population simply know they are uncomfortable, or that they are making others uncomfortable. As a consequence, they are likely to function at a lower level than their potential allows, and they may not be able to devote their full attention to learning.

Another way in which culture plays a role in learning is that culture serves as a key to understanding new concepts. An unfamiliar cultural context in which a new concept is being introduced can stand in the way of demystifying that concept. For example, during shared reading time, a story about a young child who is rewarded for showing great independence may be very confusing to a student who has been taught that reliance on parents and older siblings is not only acceptable but highly regarded. A classroom activity that is structured around competition and "winning" may be very hard to complete for a student who has learned to shun competitiveness and to value collaboration.

Our task as administrators is first to be aware of the diversity that exists among all students and to see that diversity as a source of enrichment for everyone in the school community. Second, we need to be open to learning, most easily from the students and their families, what their norms and values are. Next, we must think of ways of incorporating cultural diversity, in all of its complexity, into the everyday working of the school. In summary, the culture of the student must enter into the minds and hearts of teachers and administrators if the culture of school is to enter into the minds and hearts of the students.

Question

How do English language learners acquire a second language at school?

FRED GENESEE

ffective English language and literacy instruction for English language learners (ELLs) takes multiple factors into account—factors in and outside school, as well as factors linked to ELLs' first language and English. Many of these factors are within the control of educators and should be considered seriously when planning English language and literacy instruction for ELLs.

My focus here is on factors within the school, but it is important to recognize that language experiences outside school can also facilitate English language and literacy development in school. In particular, literacy experiences in the home (such as being read to at home) and well-developed literacy-related skills that have been acquired in the home (such as knowledge of letters and letter-sound relations, decoding skills) facilitate ELLs' acquisition of literacy in English in school. This is true whether these experiences and skills are based on the home language or English. Thus, educators should encourage and support parents in providing literacy-related experiences and skills in the home, either in students' home language or in English. This can be done through home-based projects in which teachers send materials home to parents to work on with their children. The focus should be on language for literacy and higher-order cognitive purposes, not simply talk—for example, developing a wide range of vocabulary, knowledge of letters and letter-sound relationships, awareness of the purposes of writing, and the ability to thinking critically and inferentially about ideas and what is written. Many parents will need guidance in how to accomplish this, but this is entirely realistic if given help from the school. Encourage enriched experiences in the home language if parents are most competent in that language; otherwise, encourage literacy in English at home.

The development of literacy in English as a second language is similar in some important and fundamental respects to the development of literacy in English as a first language (Genesee et al., in press). Both types of literacy development are influenced by learners' oral language skills, their acquisition of skills that are particularly relevant to reading and writing (depth of vocabulary, knowledge of letters and relationships between sounds and letters), and their use of metacognitive skills linked to reading (such as phonological awareness, comprehension monitoring strategies, or inferring the meaning of unfamiliar words from context). Thus, teachers can use many of the instructional strategies that are useful with native English speakers with ELLs as long as they adapt them to the language level and needs of ELL students. At the same time, ELLs have a reservoir of skills, strategies and knowledge that are linked to their home language. This reservoir of first language (L1) resources can help them bootstrap into English reading and writing, especially during the early stages of learning to read and write. This is true whether students are in English-only programs or in bilingual programs.

Educators should encourage and even train ELLs to see links between English and their home language and to draw on skills and knowledge acquired in the home language to comprehend or produce written text in English (such as knowledge of cognates or strategies for figuring out the meaning of unknown words in L1). Teachers should recognize that L1 influences on second language (L2) reading and writing are positive signs. When ELLs transfer their knowledge of L1 sounds or letters to English reading and writing or when they use cognates from L1 to interpret novel L2 words, they are actively using resources at their disposal to crack into the English system. Effective reading/writing instruction must take a multidimensional approach, focusing on the technicalities of reading/writing (such as decoding, spelling, and organization) while also teaching students to use strategies for comprehending, inferring, and so forth (such as using context and inferencing, monitoring comprehension, and invoking prior knowledge) and exposing ELLs to authentic texts that are adapted to their developmental needs.

PATRICK H. SMITH

Although much can be done to help learners master the language skills necessary for school success, increasing pressure for results can make the task seem a daunting one. In this section, I focus on three fundamental principles: (1) understanding the basics of second language acquisition, (2) building on what learners can already do with language, and (3) providing opportunities for meaningful language use. School administrators who become knowledgeable in these areas can serve as educational leaders for English language learning.

Understanding the Basics of Second Language Acquisition

Because learning and using our first language is part of our biological programming as humans, how we do these things is largely hidden from us. The automaticity of first language (L1) acquisition also blinds us to the facts of second language (L2) learning (Hall, in prep.). Let us look at the key differences. Unlike first language acquisition, which virtually everyone masters without conscious reflection over a relatively fixed period of time, developing advanced proficiency in a second language often requires conscious effort, can occur in different sequences for different learners, and usually occurs over a greater time span. Another fundamental difference is that unlike L1 acquisition, L2 acquisition does not result in uniform outcomes: some people learn L2 more completely than others. This is especially true for academic language proficiency and literacy. Perhaps most important, the quality and nature of the linguistic input do not seem to matter as much in L1 acquisition. No matter who talks to them, how, or how much, babies develop a first language. But to develop advanced proficiency in a second language we need a great deal of consistent and comprehensible linguistic input.[1] Finally, because second language learning frequently happens later in a person's life than first language learning, second language learners are generally more cognitively mature. Because they are older, they also have greater linguistic knowledge and social experiences to draw on as they develop a new language in school. Understanding these fundamental differences between first and second language acquisition—and sharing this knowledge with teachers, parents, and learners—is critical knowledge for administrators who want to foster English language learning.

Building on What Students Can Already Do with Language

A second fundamental principle is to build on what students can already do with language. While some aspects of language, including cognates, transfer across languages automatically, reading and other abilities require explicit guidance from skilled teachers. This is particularly true of speaking and writing because of the premium placed on conventional forms. This attention to form can be taught through specialized ESL strategies and by using the stu-

---

1. There are some important parallels here for English speakers, especially those who speak vernacular varieties of English, in their acquisition of standard academic English.

dents' first language as a basis for building new language skills. Because literacy and other academic language abilities are differently understood across cultural contexts, knowledge about students' first languages and the ways schooling is organized in students' countries of origin is an especially useful tool for educators (Smith, Jiménez, & Martínez-León, 2003).

Provide Opportunities for Meaningful Language Use

Third, in order to develop oral and written language success, learners must use English to convey meaning. One way to do this is through curriculum that pairs learners with more proficient speakers. Integrating English learners with native speakers of English in communicative tasks provides possibilities for language and cultural modeling, providing that all students are cognitively challenged.

❧

Else Hamayan and Rebecca Freeman

Second language acquisition is a developmental process that takes time, especially the development of academic English and literacies in English. There is also considerable variation in the ways that English language learners (ELLs) acquire the spoken and written English that they need in order to participate and achieve at school. This variation depends both on the language and literacy expertise that the ELL brings to school and on the language and literacy contexts that the ELL participates in at school, home, and in other places in his or her everyday life.

While we know that second language and literacy development is not a linear process that is the same for all students, we also know that there is considerable uniformity in the stages that ELLs go through (Krashen & Terrell,1983). Five stages have been identified: preproduction, early production, speech emergence, intermediate fluency, and fluency. As Table 3–1 summarizes, each level of English production is associated with student characteristics that can be observed, descriptions of how students learn at that level of proficiency, and the most effective language for literacy development and content area instruction.

When many mainstream teachers and administrators learn about Krashen's (1982) notion of a "silent period" (the preproduction stage), they often breathe a sigh of relief as they begin to understand why some of their ELLs don't talk to them for what may seem an uncomfortably long time. According to Krashen, what language learners need at this stage is a focus on meaningful

Table 3-1. Learning English: The stages (Illinois Resource Center [1999]; adapted from Krashen and Terrell [1983]).

Level of English Production	Student Characteristics and Needs	How Students Learn	Most Effective Language for Instruction
Preproduction	Silent period: no speaking Responds to instructions and commands (e.g., "put on your coat") Needs environments where they can understand teachers and peers	Learns by listening and watching Points, gestures, draws, or recreates something to show understanding	First language
Early Production	Speaks using one or two words Gives "yes" or "no" answers May mix languages (this is a normal part of language development) Needs environments where s/he can understand teachers and peers	Learns by listening, watching, and speaking using one or two words Points, gestures, draws, recreates, or responds to questions with one or two word answers to show understanding	First language
Speech Emergence	Speaks using more than one or two words to express a thought and can retell a story or event Responds to open-ended questions Ready for formal reading and writing instruction in English Needs environments where s/he can understand teachers and peers	Begins to ask questions Utilizes basic literacy skills Participates in discussions and responds to questions using emerging syntactic structures (grammar)	First language
Intermediate Fluency	Ready for more advanced reading and writing instruction in English Needs considerable help with vocabulary development in math, science, social studies Needs environments where s/he can understand teachers and peers	Utilizes more advanced literacy skills Builds on content learned through discussions using more advanced syntactic structures	Sheltered English and first language
Fluency	Language and learning skills are comparable to those of a native English speaker		English and first language

communication or comprehensible input in a low-anxiety environment without being forced to produce the language. This is what Krashen and Terrell (1983) called the natural approach. The key here is comprehensibility: when beginning language learners are immersed in an environment that is rich in oral and written language, and when they can make sense of that language, they acquire that language.

Educators also need to recognize that there is considerable variation in how long it takes for different ELLs to move through the preproduction (silent period), early production, and speech emergence phases. This is very similar to infants and young children acquiring their mother tongue. Some children begin talking at the age of one; others do not start to talk until they are well into their second year of age. Jim Cummins earlier in this chapter noted that it typically takes ELLs about one to two years to develop what he calls conversational fluency, or what is called intermediate fluency in Table 3–1. Some learners exhibit a longer silent period than others, and the same student may talk more in some contexts than others or more about some topics than others. Individual factors such as age, learning style, personality, motivation, background knowledge, and contextual factors, and what Eugene García calls sociocultural factors, such as the relationship between the participants in the interaction, and the setting in which the interaction takes place, can all influence the quality and quantity of ELLs' talk.

ELLs at school need to do more than just acquire English; they also need to learn complex content-area concepts so that they can achieve academically, and the pressure is on for these students to perform at grade level in English. Although intuitively it may make sense to think that spending more time in English and less time in the native language at school would enable ELLs to acquire the academic English they need for school success more quickly, this is actually not the case. According to comparative longitudinal research on ELLs in different types of programs in the United States (e.g., Lindholm-Leary, 2000; Thomas & Collier, 1997, 2002; Collier & Thomas, 2004), the most effective language for literacy and content-area instruction when students are beginning to acquire English is their native language. Virginia Collier also emphasizes that "the main reason for teaching instructional material in L1 is the crucial role that cognitive development in L1 plays, and the fact that cognitive development in L1 needs to continue nonstop through around age 12 to ensure academic and cognitive success in L2" (personal communication, 2005).

Finally, intermediate fluency is a very broad category. Educators must be careful not to assume that when students *sound* like they can speak English (that is, they have what Cummins calls conversational fluency, or what here is called intermediate fluency), they have acquired the oral and written academic English they need to participate and achieve without support in the all-English mainstream classroom. Sheltered instructional strategies in English (such as using an approach like the Sheltered Instruction Observation Protocol model) with native language support is most effective for complex content area instruction (Echeverria, Vogt, & Short, 2004) for ELLs at this stage in their second language development.

In sum, this stage model allows educators to begin to understand in a very general way characteristics of ELLs at different stages of second language acquisition, and it suggests which languages are most effective for literacy and content area learning At the same time, educators must be sure to observe their particular ELLs closely to understand and document how their ELLs are acquiring English at school, and how they best can support these processes.

Question

How does first language literacy development relate to second language literacy development?

Ｔ

DIANE AUGUST

Ｒesearchers have explored the relationships between first language literacy and second language literacy for word-based components (word recognition, vocabulary, and spelling) and text-based components (reading comprehension, strategy use, and writing). Taken as a whole, researchers find evidence of both negative and positive transfer (Fashola et al., 1996; Gholamain & Geva, 1999; Jimenez, García, & Pearson, 1996;. Lanauze & Snow, 1999; Nagy, McClure, & Mir, 1997; Reese et al., 2000). More specifically, the following has been found across a wide range of ages:

- Word recognition skills acquired in a first language transfer to the second language.

- There is positive transfer of vocabulary knowledge for words that are cognates.

- Children use spelling knowledge in the first language when they spell in their second language, and errors associated with first language spelling disappear as students become more proficient in their second language.

- There is evidence of cross-language transfer of reading comprehension in bilinguals of all ages, even when the languages have different types of alphabets.

- For comprehension, there is also transfer from student's second language to their first; bilingual students who read strategically in one language also read strategically in their other language. Moreover, the more students use strategies in reading, the higher their reading performance.

- For writing, the studies suggest there are cross-language relationships for writing, but levels of first language and second language proficiency may mediate these relationships.

The studies as a whole indicate that it is important to consider factors other than the components of interest in thinking about cross-language relationships. The nature of the written systems involved—the kind of alphabet and its orthographic complexity—and how alike they are in how they influence children's ability to take advantage of their first language for some components of literacy. For example, several studies suggest that there is transfer for spelling only in cases where the two languages are somewhat alike. The proficiency of the learners in both their first and second language is an important variable. For example, in the area of metacognition, some research suggests that children need to have attained a threshold of second language proficiency before they can apply first language strategies to the second language. In the area of writing, there appears to be transfer for older students, but only for those who are orally proficient in their first language but not in their second. Finally, while many studies have found transfer from the first language to the second, others have found that there is also transfer from the second language to the first. For example, in the area of writing, students instructed exclusively in their second language may apply the second language writing skills when writing in their first language.

Question

Does learning in the native language delay the acquisition of English?

ELSE HAMAYAN AND REBECCA FREEMAN

The quick answer to this question is yes and no. For the longer answer, we can turn to what is known about early childhood bilingualism, and then separately to what is known about the acquisition of a second language at a later time.

Let us start with early childhood bilingualism, by which we mean learning two languages from birth or in the first year of life. There is some evidence that children who grow up with two languages show some delay in language production. When language does appear, there may be mixing of the two languages, at least in the early stages of language development. However, both of these occurrences, delay and mixing, have no long-term effects and are not related in any way to observable developmental issues. Given high-quality exposure to both languages, children who grow up bilingually develop proficiency in both languages. Proficiency in the two languages may develop equally or to different levels depending on the continuity of exposure to and use of the two languages, as well as a few other variables (Bialystock, 2001; Genesee, 2003, 2005).

There is evidence that this type of early additive bilingualism, in which both languages are valued and nurtured in a quality environment, is advantageous for children. Bilingual children show earlier concept development than their monolingual peers, and they also show more creativity in problem-solving tasks. Whether these occurrences have any long-term effects is questionable. However, if nothing else, this jump-start that bilingual children experience may lead to high expectations and a positive self-image, both desirable conditions for young children (Hakuta, 1986).

As for later acquisition of a second language, some delay in learning the new language may be observed in the earlier stages of second language development if the learner is continuing formal instruction in the native language. Students who are taught in their native language while beginning to learn English as a second language may develop proficiency in the second language at a slower rate than students who are immersed in English with little or no support in their native language. However, this early boost quickly levels off, and students who receive intense instruction in English as a second language early without support for their native language often begin to fall behind, and many do not attain a high enough level of proficiency to survive in an academic setting where English is the language of instruction. This subtractive type of bilingualism has adverse effects on second language acquisition. Conversely, students who continue to learn through their native language may have a slow start in learning English as a second language; however, their development in English continues steadily until they reach a high level of proficiency that allows them to learn new abstract concepts through that language.

Letter to an Administrator:
From an educational consultant

——Original Message——

From: Else Hamayan [ehamayan@thecenterweb.org]
To: Ed Rathman
Subject: RE: Workshop planning

Dear Ed,

Thanks for inviting me to work with your teachers over the next couple of months. I'm thrilled that both mainstream and ESL teachers will be participating in the workshops.

Ed, I hesitated to write to you about this, but I consider you a friend, so I hope that you will understand that what I am about to say is coming from someone who wants to support your staff in the best way possible. As you know, I talked to several people from your school about the professional development program we are about to offer. I was dismayed to hear from almost every person I talked to, including you, a request to focus on teaching strategies at the expense of the theoretical foundation underlying those strategies. The sentence I kept hearing was: "We don't want theory. Just give us the strategies." I have to tell you that my heart sinks every time I hear that, and I do hear it from administrators and teachers in many districts.

I can give your teachers all the strategies that I know as effective for ELLs. But I would be remiss if I didn't allow those teachers to develop a clear sense of <u>why</u> we do things the way we do. I believe that the most important thing a teacher can do is to ask WHY. In fact, as a consultant, I am most satisfied when teachers in my workshops ask me that question repeatedly…. Well, let's just say, a couple of times ☺

The strategies we use are clearly based on what we know about how children and adolescents learn. The theoretical foundations that our teaching strategies are based on include general learning theory, but more pertinently, theories of second language learning and bilingualism. I firmly believe that we do not teach, as lore suggests, based on how we were taught as children, but rather, based on how we believe children learn. Without that belief/knowledge, we wouldn't be able to adapt our teaching to the specific needs of students, to teach what we feel are the most important big ideas in a lesson, or to understand how children are progressing.

Ed, I hope you can support me in this. Since this professional development you are planning for your staff is not a one-shot deal, and we do have a little time to spend in thinking about the WHY, how about letting me focus a little on the theory behind the strategies? You know that my workshops are activity-centered and involve the participants. We will not use the word "theory" in any material we give to the teachers, and I think they will really enjoy understanding the why of instructional strategies.

Let me know what you think. Best regards,
Else

Survey for Reflection and Action

This survey is based on the guiding principles articulated in the introduction to this chapter. Use this survey to review how your policies, programs, practices, and assessments reflect fundamental assumptions about how children learn in two languages. Use a + when your school is clearly aligned with the guiding principles, a √ when your school is working to address this area, and a − when you find no evidence of this underlying assumption. Use the results of this survey to guide decisions about your policies, program and professional development, and classroom practices.

We understand that second language acquisition, especially the acquisition of the academic language and literacies needed to participate and achieve at school, is a developmental process that takes time.

_____ Our policies for English language learners (ELLs) reflect an understanding of how ELLs acquire English for social and academic purposes.

_____ Our bilingual and/or ESL programs allow ELLs the time that they need to develop social and academic language and literacies.

_____ Our classroom practices provide opportunities for ELLs to participate in comprehensible content-area instruction while they are acquiring English.

_____ Our assessments allow ELLs to demonstrate content area knowledge and skills while they are in the process of developing proficiency in English.

We understand that a strong first language background, including literacy in the first language, provides a solid foundation for language and literacy development in English.

_____ Our policies support the maintenance and development of ELLs' first language to the greatest degree possible.

_____ Our bilingual and/or ESL programs support the maintenance and development of ELLs' first language to the greatest degree possible.

_____ Our practices support the maintenance and development of ELLs' first language to the greatest degree possible.

_____ Our assessments support the maintenance and development of ELLs' first language to the greatest degree possible.

We understand that culture influences all aspects of language learning and use.

_____ Our policies reflect an understanding of and sensitivity to the cultural backgrounds of all of the students in our school and community.

_____ Our educational programs reflect an understanding of and sensitivity to the cultural backgrounds of all of the students in our school and community.

_____ Our classroom practices reflect an understanding of and sensitivity to the cultural backgrounds of all of the students in our school and community.

_____ Our assessments reflect an understanding of and sensitivity to the cultural backgrounds of all of the students in our school and community.

We understand that there is considerable variation in the ways that ELLs acquire English.

_____ Our policies allow for variation in the ways that ELLs are expected to acquire English and achieve academically at school.

_____ Our programs are designed to address the variation that we find among the ELLs in our school in ways that build on the linguistic, cultural, and educational resources that ELLs bring with them to school.

_____ Our instructional practices build on the diverse strengths of the ELLs in our classes as we differentiate instruction to address their varied language, literacy, and learning needs.

_____ Our assessments provide us with valid and reliable evidence of what ELLs know and can do in the content areas regardless of their English language proficiency level.

_____ Our assessments provide us with valid and reliable evidence of our ELLs' English language and literacy development.

Strengths of our understanding of how children learn in two languages

_____

Action Steps _____

_____

References and Additional Resources

Baker, C. (2005). *Foundations of bilingual education and bilingualism*. Clevedon, UK: Multilingual Matters.

Bialystock, E. (2001). *Bilingualism in development: Language, literacy and cognition*. Cambridge, UK: Cambridge University Press.

Cole, M. (1996). *Cultural psychology: A once and future discipline*. Cambridge, MA: Belknap Press of Harvard University Press.

Collier, V.P., & Thomas, W.P. (2004). The astounding effectiveness of dual language education for all. *NABE Journal of Research and Practice, 2*(1), 1–20. http://njrp.tamu.edu/2004.htm.

Cummins, J. (2000). *Language, power and pedagogy: Bilingual children in the crossfire*. Clevedon, UK: Multilingual Matters.

Echevarria, J. E., Vogt, M., & Short, D.J. (2004). *Making content comprehensible for English language learners: The SIOP mode* (2nd ed.). Boston: Pearson.

Fashola, O. S., Drum, P. A., Mayer, R. E., & Kang, S.-J. (1996). A cognitive theory of orthographic transitioning: Predictable errors in how Spanish-speaking children spell English words. *American Educational Research Journal, 33*(4), 825–843.

García, G. G., & Beltrán, D. (2003). Revisioning the blueprint: Building for the academic success of English learners. In G. G. García (Ed.), *English learners: Reaching the highest level of English literacy* (pp. 197–226). Newark, DE: International Reading Association.

Genesee, F. (2003). Rethinking bilingual acquisition. In J. M. deWaele (Ed.), *Bilingualism: Challenges and directions for future research* (pp. 158–182). Clevedon, UK: Multilingual Matters.

Genesee, F., & Nicoladis, E. (2005). Bilingual first language acquisition. In E. Hoff & M. Shatz (Eds.), *Handbook of Language Development*. Oxford, UK: Blackwell.

Genesee, F., Lindholm-Leary, K. J., Saunders, W., & Christian, D. (in press). *Educating English language learners: A synthesis of empirical evidence*. New York: Cambridge University Press.

Gholamain, M., & Geva, E. (1999). Orthographic and cognitive factors in the concurrent development of basic reading skills in English and Persian. *Language Learning, 49*(2), 183–217.

Hakuta, K. (1986). *Mirror of language: The debate on bilingualism*. New York: Basic Books.

Hall, C. J. (in prep.). *The language spell*.

Illinois Resource Center (1997). *The iceberg model of culture*. Desplaines, IL: Illinois Resource Center.

Illinois Resource Center (1999). *Learning English: The stages*. Desplaines, IL: Illinois Resource Center.

Jimenez, R. T., García, G. E., & Pearson, D. P. (1996). The reading strategies of bilingual Latina/o students who are successful English readers: Opportunities and obstacles. *Reading Research Quarterly, 31*(1), 90–112.

Krashen, S. (1982). *Principles and practices in second language acquisition*. Oxford, UK: Pergamon Press.

Krashen, S., &. Terrell, D. (1983). *The natural approach: Language acquisition in the classroom*. Hayward, CA: Alemany Press.

Lanauze, M., & Snow, C. E. (1999). The relation between first- and second-language writing skills: Evidence from Puerto Rican elementary school children in bilingual programs. *Linguistics and Education, 4,* 323–339

Lightbrown, P. M., & Spada, N. (2003). *How languages are learned.* Oxford, UK: Oxford University

Lindholm-Leary, K. (2001). *Dual language education.* Clevedon, UK: Multilingual Matters.

Nagy, W. E., McClure, E. F., & Mir, M. (1997). Linguistic transfer and the use of context by Spanish-English bilinguals. *Applied Psycholinguistics, 18*(4), 431–452.

Peregoy, S. F., & Boyle, O. F. (2005). *Reading, writing, and learning in ESL: A resource book for K-12 teachers.* Boston: Pearson Education.

Reese, L., Garnier, H., Gallimore, R., & Goldenberg, C. (2000). Longitudinal analysis of the antecedents of emergent Spanish literacy and middle-school English reading achievement of Spanish-speaking students. *American Educational Research Journal, 37*(3), 633–662.

Rogoff, B. (1990). *The cultural nature of human development.* New York: Oxford University Press.

Smith, P. H., Jiménez, R. T., & Martínez-León, N. (2003). Other countries' literacies: What U.S. educators can learn from Mexican schools. *Reading Teacher, 56*(8), 772–781.

Thomas, W.P., & Collier, V.P. (2002). *A national study of school effectiveness for language minority students' long-term academic achievement.* Santa Cruz, CA: Center for Research, Education, Diversity and Excellence, University of California, Santa Cruz. http://www.crede.ucsc.edu/research/llaa/1.1_final.html.

Thomas, W.P., & Collier, V.P. (1997). *School effectiveness for language minority students.* National Clearinghouse for Bilingual Education (NCBE) Resource Collection Series, No.9. http://www.ncela.gwu.edu/pubs/resource/effectiveness/.

Chapter 4

Program Development

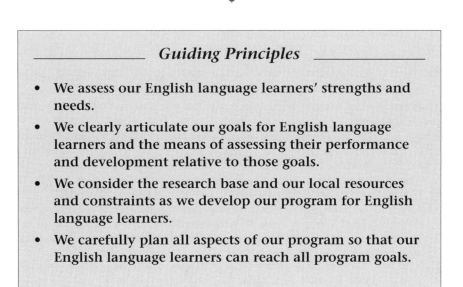

Guiding Principles

- We assess our English language learners' strengths and needs.
- We clearly articulate our goals for English language learners and the means of assessing their performance and development relative to those goals.
- We consider the research base and our local resources and constraints as we develop our program for English language learners.
- We carefully plan all aspects of our program so that our English language learners can reach all program goals.

Introduction

Although English language learners (ELLs) must ultimately reach the same high educational standards that all students must reach, there is no one-size-fits-all program model that schools can uncritically implement to accomplish this goal. Schools vary tremendously in terms of the student and community populations they serve, local goals for ELLs, and the school's human and material resources and constraints. Administrators must assess the specific strengths and needs of their students and school. They can then turn to more than thirty years of research on and practice in a range of English as a second language (ESL) and bilingual programs that have been developed for ELLs. This research base yields strong converging evidence about critical features of effective programs. Administrators can draw on this research base to inform their decisions about the specific programs that they develop for their school and community contexts.

The goal is for schools to develop educationally sound programs that everyone (parents, teachers, district personnel, community members) understands and supports, and to implement those programs effectively so they can deliver results for ELLs. Program coherence is key. Unfortunately, too few schools develop coherent programs for their ELLs, and too many ELLs lag behind their English-speaking counterparts. This chapter guides administrators' efforts to meet this challenge and develop programs that are appropriate for the ELLs in their schools.

The chapter begins with general questions about prototypical bilingual and ESL programs that we find in U.S. public schools today, and about the research base on the effectiveness of these different kinds of programs. The majority of the chapter addresses more specific questions about program development. The responses that experienced educators provide to these questions give insight into the decision-making processes of effective leaders in diverse school and community contexts. The chapter concludes with a survey for reflection and action that administrators can use to review the effectiveness of the programs for ELLs that they have developed for their schools, or to guide the development of more appropriate programs. This survey is intended to help educators ensure that their programs for ELLs are educationally sound. Administrators can use the results of this survey to identify their program strengths and action steps, and they can draw on the expertise in this chapter to improve their programs as necessary.

Question

What kinds of programs are available for English language learners?

DONNA CHRISTIAN

As English language learners (ELLs) face the challenge of mastering English and acquiring academic skills and knowledge for success in school, schools are challenged with designing programs to help them achieve these goals. ELLs are not homogeneous; they vary in socioeconomic status, community background, the variety of English or other languages they speak, and in many other ways. Furthermore, they enter U.S. schools at every grade level and throughout the academic year. Although students who enter at the elementary level have more time to acquire language and academic skills than do ELLs who enter at the secondary level, they still need appropriate and challenging instruction from the very beginning, through the first or second language, or both.

A variety of program alternatives have been developed to meet the diverse and complex needs of ELLs. Some incorporate content instruction in the native language.

- *Two-way immersion* programs serve ELLs who speak a common native language along with native English speakers. For both groups of students, the goals are to develop high levels of first and second language proficiency, academic development, and cross-cultural understanding. All students experience an environment in which both languages are valued and developed, and academic content is learned through two languages. These are typically full K–6 or K–12 instructional programs.[1]

- *Developmental bilingual* programs also aim for of high levels of proficiency in English and the students' native language, with strong academic development, but the students served are primarily ELLs. Students generally participate in these programs for five to six years and receive academic instruction in both languages. The model has also been referred to as "late-exit" or maintenance bilingual education.[2]

- In *transitional bilingual* programs (also known as "early-exit" bilingual education), academic instruction in the students' native language is provided while they learn English (to varying extents and for varying lengths of time). As their English proficiency develops, students move to all-English, mainstream classes, typically after one to three years.

- *Newcomer* programs are specially designed programs for recent arrivals to the United States who have no or low English proficiency

---

1. Two-way immersion programs are also sometimes referred to as *dual language programs*. This guide takes a broad view of dual language education as a bilingual program that promotes bilingualism and biliteracy (that is, additive bilingualism), academic achievement in two languages, and positive cross-cultural understanding for its target populations. Under this broad view, a two-way immersion program is one type of dual language education.

2. Developmental bilingual programs are also sometimes referred to as *one-way developmental bilingual programs*. This guide considers one-way developmental bilingual programs to be a type of dual language education because they share the goals of additive bilingualism with other types of dual language programs. One-way developmental bilingual programs differ from two-way immersion programs in terms of target populations.

and often limited literacy in their native language. The goal is to accelerate their acquisition of language and academic skills and to orient them to the United States and U.S. schools. Students typically participate in such programs for one to one and a half years. Although newcomer programs exist in elementary schools, they are more prevalent at the secondary level. Some programs follow a bilingual approach; others focus on sheltered instruction in English.

Other program models offer primarily English instruction to ELLs. This choice is often made when ELLs in a school come from many different language backgrounds.

- In *English as a second language (ESL)* programs (also known as English language development [ELD] programs), ELLs may receive content instruction from other sources while they participate in the ESL program, or they may be in self-contained classrooms. They receive developmentally appropriate English language instruction tailored for their level of English proficiency. Students generally participate in ESL programs for one to five years, depending on their initial level of proficiency and rate of progress.

- Another ESL-oriented program model is *sheltered instruction,* which offers ELLs grade-level, core content courses taught in English using instructional strategies that make the content concepts accessible to ELLs and that promote the development of academic English. Most sheltered instruction programs are designed to meet all the requirements for credit toward grade-level promotion or graduation. Students remain in them for two to three years. The term *sheltered instruction* may also be used to describe pedagogy rather than a program design. Sheltered instruction practices and individual sheltered instruction courses can be and often are implemented in conjunction with other program alternatives.

Program alternatives for ELLs differ on several dimensions. Some work toward bilingualism (two-way immersion, developmental bilingual), while others emphasize proficiency in English (ESL, sheltered instruction). The focal student populations vary, particularly in the homogeneity of their language backgrounds, and the length of participation also differs, with some programs short term or transitional (one to four years) and others longer in duration (six or more years). Finally, the necessary resources vary from model to model in features such as teacher qualifications (language skills and professional preparation) and the extent of bilingual curricula and materials needed.

Question

What are the most effective kinds of programs for English language learners?

KATHRYN LINDHOLM-LEARY

The academic achievement of English language learners (ELLs) has received considerable attention, particularly with respect to the underachievement of ELLs. Most of the research in this area addresses policy issues relating to the best way to educate ELLs and consists primarily of evaluations of various program models. In a recent comprehensive synthesis of the empirically based research on the achievement of ELLs (Genesee et al., in press), there was strong convergent evidence that the educational success of ELLs is positively related to sustained instruction through the student's first language. Almost all evaluations of students at the end of elementary school and in middle and high school show that the educational outcomes of bilingually educated students, especially in late-exit and two-way programs, were at least comparable to, and usually higher than, their comparison peers. There was no study of middle school or high school students that found that bilingually educated students were less successful than comparison group students. In addition, most long-term studies report that the longer the ELL students stayed in the program, the more positive were the outcomes. Students who participated in an assortment of different programs and those who received no educational intervention (that is, they were put into mainstream English classes with no additional assistance) performed at the lowest achievement levels and had the highest dropout rates. These results hold true whether one examines outcomes in reading or mathematics achievement, GPA, attendance, high school completion, or attitudes toward school and self.

The studies reviewed in the synthesis also indicated that students who achieved full oral and literate (reading and writing) proficiency in both languages had higher achievement scores, GPAs, and educational expectations than their monolingual English-speaking peers. In addition, there were significant positive correlations between subject matter in the two languages, so that students who scored high on measures of reading (or math) achievement in Spanish also performed at high levels on measures of reading (or math) achievement in English. These results suggest that educational programs for

ELLs should seek to develop their full bilingual and biliterate competencies in order to take advantage of these interdependencies across languages.

Thus, the best models for ELL students are those that are specially designed to provide the students with sustained and consistent instruction through the first language (at least through sixth grade), with the goals of full oral and literate bilingual proficiencies. Further, a program that is enriched, consistent, provides a challenging curriculum, and incorporates language development components and appropriate assessment approaches is also endorsed by research on factors associated with effective programs for ELLs.

Question

What is the best way to promote the English language development and academic achievement in English of English language learners when you don't have a bilingual program?

❦

FRED GENESEE

Success in oral language (including language for academic purposes) and literacy is more likely in structured programs such as English as a second language (ESL), sheltered instruction, or bilingual programs that are designed to meet English language learners' (ELLs') particular second language learning needs rather than in mainstream classrooms that make no special provisions for their particular language and academic needs. In other words, simply mainstreaming ELLs in English-only classes is not likely to be successful for most students. Moreover, ELLs who participate in enriched, cognitively challenging programs that are consistent and coherent across grades achieve significantly higher literacy and academic results than ELLs who participate in a hodgepodge or incoherent set of programmatic interventions from grade to grade. School administrators must work with their teaching and curriculum personnel to develop programs that are sensitive to ELLs' particular linguistic and cultural backgrounds so that they are coherent across grade levels. This calls for team work and plenty of time for planning.

When it comes to academic achievement, instructional approaches that are most successful with ELLs are those that modify the use of English to ensure that academic content is comprehensible and, at the same time, develop the English language skills that ELLs need to succeed in academic domains. Sheltered instruction (SI) is one such approach. In SI, teachers teach the core curriculum in English but modify it to meet the language development needs of English language learners. Specific strategies are used to teach particular content areas so that the material is comprehensible while at the same time promoting English language development (see Echevarria, Vogt, & Short, 2004, for more details). While SI shares many features of high-quality instruction for native English speakers, it is characterized by careful attention to ELLs' distinctive second language development needs and aims to bridge the achievement gap between mainstream and ELLs.

When it comes to literacy development, interactive and direct instructional strategies work well. Interactive instruction emphasizes learning through interaction with other learners and more competent readers and writers (the teacher, other students in the class, older students) and also engagement in learning to use written language. The goals of interactive approaches include general literacy outcomes (enjoyment in reading/writing, autonomy as a reader/writer, familiarity with authentic written language) as well as the acquisition of specific reading and writing skills (decoding, paragraphing, punctuation) and strategies (using context to discover the meaning of unfamiliar words in text). Instructional conversations is an example of an effective interactive instructional approach (Saunders & Goldenberg, 1999). Direct instruction emphasizes explicit and focused instruction of specific reading/writing skills and strategies, such as decoding, vocabulary, or comprehension skills. Instruction that combines interactive with direct approaches has much to recommend it since it involves teaching specific reading and writing skills within carefully designed, interactive contexts. Interaction between learners and between learners and their teachers creates a learning context in which adaptation to and accommodation of individual differences and preferences among ELLs can be accomplished. Carefully planned interactions in the classroom can be both the medium for delivering appropriate instruction about literacy and academic material and the message, insofar as the very language that is used during interactive instruction, if planned carefully, embodies many key features of language for literacy and broader academic purposes. Direct instruction of specific skills ensures student mastery of important reading and writing skills that are often embedded and even obscured in complex literacy or academic tasks. Presenting direct instruction in interactive learning environments ensures that it is meaningful, contextualized, and individualized. Research indicates that a focus on both specific reading/writing skills and meaningful use of reading/writing for communication, intellectual engagement, and personal enjoyment is important for the success of ELLs.

Question

What is the difference between English as a second language (ESL) and sheltered instruction/SDAIE?

WAYNE E. WRIGHT

English as a second language (ESL) and specially designed academic instruction in English (SDAIE) are both critical components of any program model for English language learners (ELLs). Federal law requires schools to help ELLs (1) develop English proficiency, and (2) meet state academic content standards. ESL instruction focuses on the first of these requirements, while SDAIE focuses on the second. SDAIE is also referred to as sheltered instruction.

The purpose of ESL instruction is to help ELLs become proficient in English. Interactive listening, speaking, reading, and writing activities help students acquire the vocabulary and structure of the language and develop communicative competence for social and academic settings. ESL is sometimes referred to as English language development (ELD), particularly at the elementary level. ESL is a separate content area, just as math or science is a separate content area, and has its own standards and curriculum. The short-term goals of ESL instruction are to help students move up at least one proficiency level on their state's English language proficiency assessment. The ultimate goal is redesignation as fluent English proficient, meaning students no longer require extra assistance and can succeed in a regular, mainstream classroom.

SDAIE instruction focuses on the teaching of content area subjects—language arts, math, science, and so forth—in English using a wide range of strategies and techniques that help make the instruction comprehensible for

ELLs. The ultimate goal of SDAIE is for ELLs to master the same content-area standards as all other students do.

Elementary ELLs, whether in bilingual or English-only program models, need at least thirty minutes of direct ESL instruction each day. Some schools and districts create their own ESL curriculum, while others adopt a commercially produced ESL/ELD program. In English-only program models, all other content areas are taught in English using SDAIE strategies. In bilingual programs, some content areas are taught in the students' first language and the others are taught in English using SDAIE strategies. In transitional bilingual programs, as ELLs develop proficiency in English, the amount of SDAIE content-area instruction increases as students gradually transition to mainstream instruction in English. At the secondary level ELLs need SDAIE content-area courses and at least one period of ESL each day.

ESL instruction is for ELLs only. In classes that include both ELLs and non-ELLs, teachers need to structure their classrooms in a manner that allows them some time to work separately with the ELLs each day. SDAIE instruction, however, includes many strategies and techniques that are appropriate and effective for all students.

While ESL focuses on teaching English and SDAIE focuses on teaching content, there is some overlap. Students will learn some content during ESL, and effective SDAIE instruction will help students gain greater proficiency in English. In fact, the Sheltered Instruction Observation Protocol (SIOP) model—a popular model for SDAIE instruction—emphasizes the need for content-area lessons to have both language and content-area objectives (Echevarria, Vogt, & Short, 2004). Nonetheless, these language objectives should *supplement,* not *supplant,* daily ESL instruction. This overlap is advantageous for ELLs. For example, an SDAIE science lesson on the water cycle is made more comprehensible when preceded by an ESL lesson on talking about the weather.

Some assume that ELLs no longer need ESL instruction once they achieve a basic level of English, and that SDAIE instruction alone will help them become proficient. However, if schools stop providing direct ESL instruction, many ELLs may not progress beyond their current level for several years and will fall further behind as the content-area instruction demands increase each year. Many ELLs who sound fluent learn to decode print yet fail to comprehend what they read because they lack vocabulary and an understanding of complex sentence structures. Thus, ELL students need both ESL and SDAIE instruction each year until they are redesignated as fully English proficient. Administrators can ensure their ELLs learn English and meet state content standards by ensuring their teachers obtain proper training and provide effective instruction in both ESL and SDAIE.

Question

What is the best bilingual model of instruction?

Kathryn Lindholm-Leary

Two-way bilingual immersion (TWBI) education is a program that has the potential to promote the multilingual and multicultural competencies necessary for the new global business job market while eradicating the significant achievement gap between English speakers and English language learners (ELLs). The appeal of two-way programs is that they combine successful education models in an integrated classroom composed of both English proficient (EP) speakers and ELLs, with the goals of full bilingualism and biliteracy, grade-level academic achievement for both groups, and multicultural competencies.

TWBI programs provide ELLs and native EP speakers with academic instruction that is presented through two languages in an integrated environment. The major goals are the following: (1) Students will develop high levels of oral language and literacy in English and the non-English language. (2) Academic achievement will be at or above grade level as measured in both languages. (3) Students will have positive attitudes toward school and themselves, and will exhibit positive cross-cultural attitudes and multicultural competencies.

The definition of TWBI programs (or dual language programs) encompasses four critical features: (1) The program involves instruction through two languages, where the non-English language is used for a significant portion (at least 50 percent) of the student's instructional day. (2) The program involves periods of instruction during which only one language is used (that is, there is no translation or language mixing). (3) Both ELLs and EPs are participants in a fairly balanced proportion. (4) The students are integrated for most content instruction. TWBI programs have surged in popularity over the past twenty years (from 37 programs in 1987 to 320 programs in public schools in twenty-five states and the District of Columbia).

Several investigators have examined the reading and math achievement of students in TWBI at late elementary or secondary levels to determine the long-term impact of these programs. These studies are consistent in showing that overall, ELLs made significant progress in both languages: they scored at least to well above grade level measured in both languages by middle school, and they performed at comparable or superior levels compared to same-language comparison peers. On both norm-referenced and criterion-referenced standardized tests of reading and math achievement in English, previously ELL students scored not only significantly higher than ELLs in the state, but they also performed on a par with native English-speaking students in English-only classrooms (Howard, Sugarman, & Christian, 2003; Lindholm-Leary, 2001, 2005).

Studies have also examined students' attitudes toward school and the TWBI program. In studies of secondary students who had been in a TWBI program in elementary school, results showed that students had very positive attitudes toward school and the TWBI program. Most students believed that learning through two languages helped them learn to think better, made them smarter, and helped them do better in school. Students also felt valued in the TWBI program, were glad they participated in it, and would recommend it to other students.

In sum, the TWBI program has been carefully developed according to the theoretical and empirically based literatures on effective schools and second language learning to more adequately address the cultural, ethnic, and linguistic diversity represented in today's classrooms. However, like mainstream classes, not all TWBI program classes are high quality; the quality and effectiveness of the TWBI model implementation can vary tremendously from school to school. Results demonstrate that well-implemented TWBI programs are successful in promoting high educational outcomes for both ELLs and EP students; that is, students demonstrate bilingual proficiency, biliteracy, achievement at or above grade level, and positive attitudes.

Question

How do you decide what kind of program for English language learners is appropriate for your school?

Ester de Jong

Effective programs for English language learners (ELLs) are developed in response to the community's specific context. The tremendous variation within and among ELL populations makes it impossible to approach the schooling of ELLs with a "one-size-fits-all" approach. Instead, districts and schools should adopt a flexible approach to address the diversity that exists in their student population. Flexibility does not imply random decisions. The district and the schools should articulate their program choice according to a consistent program philosophy, grounded in principles of effective programs for ELLs.

ELLs are not a homogeneous group; rather, they have become increasingly more diverse. The number of students is one variable. For example, when a district has multiple language groups with few speakers of each language, it is difficult to implement a bilingual program. If, on the other hand, much of the ELL population comes from the same language background, bilingual education is a feasible option. Similarly, students with strong first language (L1) literacy skills and highly educated parents have significantly different needs from students with interrupted schooling or limited L1 literacy skills. When both student populations exist side by side in the district, different programs should be implemented in recognition of these different needs.

To avoid random or conflicting policies, it is important that district leaders make themselves familiar with common program options for ELLs (such as two-way immersion programs, developmental bilingual education, self-contained English as a second language [ESL] programs, and pull-out ESL classes) and their theoretical underpinnings, strengths, outcomes, and implementation challenges. Further, school and district leaders must find out about the needs of the ELLs in the school and the district. Once the ELL population has been identified (through a home language survey, language and literacy assessments, or academic skills assessment), schools and the district must develop a plan to address their needs. This plan should involve the whole school because the responsibility for ELLs lies with all staff. Schools must develop a shared vision for the education of all students that reflects the linguistic and cultural diversity in the school.

Regardless of the particular program model chosen, an effective whole-school plan for educating ELLs and fluent English speakers reflects the following principles:

- An effective program for ELLs builds on and extends the linguistic and cultural resources that ELLs bring to school. They are enrichment programs; not remedial programs.

- An effective program for ELLs sets linguistic, cultural, and academic goals for ELLs that are shared by the whole school, and it allocates resources accordingly.

- An effective program for ELLs hires quality, bilingual personnel who implement a curriculum that reflects high expectations and the multilingual and multicultural realities of the students and who use instructional strategies that have been shown to be effective to support ELLs' content, language, and literacy development.

- An effective program for ELLs uses assessments that are ongoing and fair for linguistically and cultural diverse students. It is involved in a cycle of self-examination and reflection about how the program is meeting its linguistic, cultural, and academic goals.

- An effective program for ELLs develops strong and positive home/community-school relationships that are responsive to parents' needs and strengths.

Diep Nguyen

Several factors should be considered in deciding on the best program for English language learners (ELLs) in your district.

1. The most important factor to consider is the profile of your students as a group. A complete group profile includes pertinent information about the ELLs' immigration, sociocultural, linguistic, and educational history, such as level of educational background, English as a second language (ESL) proficiency, native language proficiency, and ethnic background. For example, if you have large numbers of students from the same language background (such as Spanish or Chinese) and equally large numbers of English speaking students who want to become bilingual, a two-way immersion program is a good option to consider. If the students are mostly immigrants from one language background, a one-way developmental or maintenance bilingual program may be appropriate. If there are substantial numbers of ELLs who speak different languages, a sheltered ESL program may be feasible, ideally with native language support. If there are only a few ELLs at the school, a pull-out or push-in ESL program may be the only option (in this case, the administrator must make sure that mainstream teachers who have ELLs in their classes understand how to use sheltered instructional strategies). The first principle of good programming is *know your students*.

2. The second factor to consider is the sociopolitical climate of your community. In other words, the community context in which you

operate a program has great influence on its success and failure. Your program design and approaches need to meet the needs of your students and be accepted by the community. For example, while some communities may be ready to embrace dual language programs, in other communities a transitional bilingual program or ESL program may be a better first option. Review the political climate in your community constantly in order to gauge their readiness for more innovative approaches. Spend time getting to know your community and to educate parents and colleagues about different options for ELL students before launching a program. The second principle at work here is *know your community.*

3. Regardless of the program model chosen, the measure of true effectiveness of the program lies at the instructional (teacher-student) level in each classroom. Consider your resources (both human and material) carefully before adopting a model. Issues that need to be considered include staff expertise and competence, administrative buy-in, materials variety and availability, and evidence of the effectiveness of similar programs elsewhere. Visit school districts that have effective programs, spend time in the host classrooms to find evidence of their instructional program's effectiveness, and ask questions that will help you decide if a particular model is a match for your school district. It is important to be realistic about the resources you have. The third principle is *count your resources.*

4. Basic research on teaching and learning, as well as evaluation studies conducted on existing programs, provides valuable information when it is time to make decisions about the core values and design of your own program. To ensure that instructional effectiveness is at the heart of your design, spend time with others reviewing research on program effectiveness and best practices. Seek out experts in the field who have either studied or implemented these models and ask them for advice on your choice. The fourth operating principle here is *be informed, be in the know.*

5. Finally, adopt the general approach based on sound research and best practices. However, tailor the design to meet the needs of your students using your local resources. Don't be afraid to differentiate your program options for your students. In other words, wherever appropriate, use different program options for different subgroups of students at your local school district. The fifth operating principle here is *differentiate your program.*

Most of all, be sure to create a flexible and student-focused system of instructional services for all your ELL students. In the end, it is less about the program than it is about the quality of instructional services that you can make available for your students. Think about the program as the frame or skeleton that supports instruction, which is the real meat of ELL education. Remember that it's all about quality education for all students.

Question

How do you plan for language development?

☙

JOHN HILLIARD AND ELSE HAMAYAN

Decisions regarding the use of English and the students' native language must be made carefully and with great deliberation. These decisions must focus on how the students' two languages or, at a minimum, how supported forms of English are to be used in instruction. Language allocation decisions must be considered at three levels (Figure 4–1):

1. The programmatic level: How much instruction over the course of the entire program will be delivered in which language?

2. The curricular level: Who, where, when, and what will be delivered in the two languages or in a sheltered English versus a mainstream environment?

3. The instructional level: What actually happens linguistically between teacher and students during instruction?

These decisions must be planned over the long term that the student is in a particular school rather than year by year or, worse, randomly. In fact, the language development plan in one school will hopefully connect with the next level of schooling that the student will attend.

At the programmatic level, the allocation of languages for instruction in a bilingual program has to be determined in terms of the proportion of time spent in each language during each year of participation. In a dual language program, students receive either 50 percent of their instruction in English and 50 percent in the other language, or they start out with a larger percent-

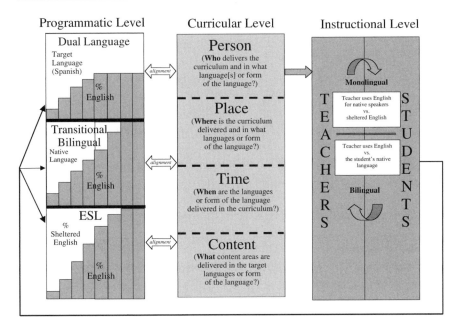

Figure 4-1. Language allocation and use in programs for second language learners.

age in the language other than English and gradually receive more instruction through English until the proportion is 50:50. In a transitional bilingual program, students receive a higher proportion of their instruction initially in their native language, which is gradually phased out for an all-English education. In the case of an English-only program, the decision has to focus on the amount of time spent in a sheltered English environment versus a mainstream setting. If possible, as much of the instruction should be delivered initially through sheltered strategies until the students are proficient enough to survive in the mainstream classroom without special support. At a minimum, the more abstract the content area, the more important it is for that teacher to shelter the instruction.

At the curricular level, in a dual language or transitional bilingual program, we need to determine which language is used for what. In an English-only program where not all teachers are skilled in sheltering instruction, the decision has to do with which content areas are taught through a sheltered format and which components of the school day are spent in the mainstream classroom. It is natural for these decisions to be influenced by contextual factors such as the availability of resources, both human and material, as well as scheduling issues. However, it is critical that these decisions be made from the learner's perspective and that they make developmental and pedagogical sense. In dual language programs, the program design dictates that support for the minority student's language be maintained at a level of no less than 50 percent. In transitional bilingual programs where there are no such programmatic constants, it is important to maintain support in the native language for as long as the students need it. Instruction in the native language must be diminished gradually rather than being offered haphazardly from year to year. Similarly, for students who are receiving instruction only in English, those content areas that are more cognitively demanding must be taught through sheltered strategies, and that support must be reduced gradually, based on student need, rather than be dropped abruptly.

At the instructional level, teachers must adhere to the language of instruction (or, if it is an ESL program, to the sheltering of English) very carefully. Otherwise, the long-term language development plan will be altered and may not follow a path that makes sense for the learner.

It is only through careful long-term planning that ELLs' development of English language proficiency, acquisition of academic content area knowledge, and, ideally, maintenance of their native language can continue to evolve through the students' entire experience in school, from kindergarten until graduation from high school.

Question

How do you promote first/home language literacy development when you can't have a bilingual program?

DIEP NGUYEN

Depending on the community that you serve, efforts to support native/home language literacy can range from informal classroom efforts to formal programs of family literacy to provide the opportunities for parents and other community members to use what they know to teach the students to read and write in their respective native languages. We describe some efforts that have been fruitful in our district.

- The simplest way of supporting native language literacy is to inform parents of the importance of these skills for their children and ask them to invest their time in teaching their children to read and write in their native language. Many parents of English language learners (ELLs) look to educators to guide them in making language choices for their children. Parents need to know that we, as educators, believe in and encourage the use of native language literacy at home.

- The most informal way of supporting home language literacy is to allow and encourage students to express themselves in their native language in writing when appropriate. To accomplish this task, the teacher may have to solicit a parent volunteer who can respond to the students' writing and assist the teacher in the translation/interpretation of the students' work into English when necessary.

- Another informal way of supporting native language literacy in an all-English environment is to sponsor before- or after-school clubs or groups where students can practice native language literacy through reading clubs or writing clubs supervised and led by a bilingual adult (staff or parent volunteers).

- Many immigrant communities, while believing that native language maintenance is not a required responsibility of the public schools, have an earnest desire to teach their own language to their children. Many communities have after-school classes or weekend schools to each their native language to children. We can support these efforts by offering classroom space for these programs during after-school hours gratis or for a nominal fee.

- The most proactive approach is to sponsor family literacy programs after school at which parents can work with teachers in activities that enrich and teach native language literacy skills for students. Successful family literacy programs always include three educational components: (1) the parents learn to become reading and writing instructors with their children, (2) parents and children have ample opportunities to read and write together, and (3) there is a direct link between the literacy practices in the program and the instructional goals for reading and writing for the students during the school day. However, it is important to be sensitive to the cultural "ways with words" (Heath, 1983) of the students you serve so that you can establish family literacy programs that are culturally responsive to the language traditions of families. We try to involve key parent leaders and community members who can help use the "funds of knowledge" (Moll, 1995) within the community to create a family literacy that truly belongs to and serves the intended students and their families.

☙

Rebecca Freeman

Although research demonstrates the effectiveness of additive bilingual programs, or programs that support the development of English language learners' (ELLs') first language while they add English, not all schools can implement dual language programs. Unfortunately, most programs for ELLs lead to subtractive bilingualism, or the loss of the ELLs' first language as they acquire English. Although subtractive bilingualism is the typical outcome for students in English-only programs and transitional bilingual programs, this does not have to be the case. Schools can work to promote additive bilingualism for their ELLs even when they cannot offer a dual language program.

When schools have a substantial population of ELLs or English speakers who come from the same home language background, a heritage language program may be feasible (Freeman, 2004). According to Guadalupe Valdés (2000), the term "heritage language speaker" is used to refer to students who

- are raised in a home where a language other than English is spoken,

- understand and/or speak the heritage language, and

- are to some degree bilingual in English and in the heritage language.

Heritage language programs target heritage language speakers (who may or may not be designated as ELLs) and they offer the heritage language as a core subject area such as language arts or a world language class. A primary goal of these enrichment programs is to enable heritage language speakers to broaden their linguistic repertoires in their heritage language. Heritage language teachers need to be specially trained so that they know how to build on the linguistic and cultural resources that heritage language speakers bring with them from home, and so that they can provide opportunities for these students to learn to use their heritage language for a wider range of oral and written purposes. Because these students collectively have such a wide range of expertise in their heritage languages, teachers must know how to differentiate their instruction.

Spanish for Spanish/Native Speaker (SNS) programs are the most common heritage language programs in U.S. schools today. Most of these programs are offered at the high school level (see, for example, the SNS curriculum developed by North Carolina Dept. of Public Instruction, 2003). We can also find some examples of programs that support the maintenance and development of other heritage languages (such as native American languages and other immigrant/community languages), and some of these programs begin in the early elementary grades. Community-based heritage language programs are often found in churches, Saturday schools, or other community institutions. Schools can make efforts to link with existing community-based programs to strengthen possibilities for heritage language development for students, their families, and the community overall (Peyton, Ranard, & McGinnis, 2001).

Schools that offer transitional bilingual programs are well positioned to offer heritage language programs to their former ELLs. That is, when former ELLs meet the exit criteria to be redesignated as fully English proficient and are transitioned into the all-English academic mainstream, they can be offered classes that promote the maintenance and development of their oral and written expertise in their home language. In this way, transitional bilingual programs, the most common type of bilingual program in the United States today, do not have to lead to subtractive bilingualism (which is associated with lower academic achievement). By offering a heritage language program, perhaps as a world language or as part of the language arts curriculum, schools can provide their former ELLs with structured opportunities to maintain and develop their home language after they enter the all-English academic mainstream.

Question

What are the critical features of programs for English language learners?

Nancy L. Commins

Programs for English language learners (ELLs) differ according to the number of students served, the languages they speak, the available human and material resources and—quite important—public policy and the political will of the community. In some programs all instruction is in English, while others use students' primary language for the reinforcement of content area concepts or for initial literacy instruction. In ideal circumstances, programs aim for full academic bilingualism through in-depth and ongoing development of both literacy and content in students' primary language and English (Miramontes, Nadeau, & Commins, 1997).

The goal of each kind of program must be to produce academically proficient English speakers. The availability of primary language instruction will affect:

- The length of time it takes for second language learners to function academically at the same level as native English speakers

- The extent to which teachers will need to modify their instruction to make the curriculum understandable to all students

- Students' potential for lifetime bilingualism

The less access students have to learning through their primary language, the longer it will take to reach full English proficiency (Thomas & Collier, 2002). All-English programs, far from being the easy solution, take more concerted efforts on behalf of all the teaching staff to ensure that second language learners achieve success. In addition, students in all-English programs are much more likely to lose their first language.

While programs for second language learners can vary dramatically, they all should be guided by certain basic principles and understandings. It is very important that students receive planned daily instruction in English as a second language and that teachers do whatever is necessary to make instruction understandable through all learning modalities. The following critical features can guide educators' efforts to address the needs of their ELLs, regardless of program type.

Create a Climate of Belonging

- Utilize materials that value students' home language and culture.

- Reach out to parents and community members.

- Encourage parents to interact with their children in their strongest language (usually not English).

Implement Standards-based Instruction

- Organize instruction around a common body of knowledge, with attention to differentiation in the methods of delivery.

- Identify enduring understandings and essential vocabulary and highlight them in instruction.

- Gather curriculum materials at a wide range of reading levels.

Use Data to Inform and Shape Instruction

- Find out who the learners are and what they bring to instruction.
- Assess students' academic and literacy skills in their primary language, whether or not it is used in instruction.
- Use multiple forms of assessment to document students' progress, as well as attainment of benchmarks.

Elevate Oral Language Practice

- Provide constant opportunities for interaction in order to increase student talk and decrease teacher talk.
- Determine the language structures required for participation in instructional activities, and provide students with opportunities to practice them aloud.

Deliver Meaning-based Literacy Instruction

- Use text to represent ideas and concepts that students understand and can say.
- Incorporate language experience approaches.
- Make conscious connections between the big ideas from the content areas and what students will read and write during literacy instruction.

Prepare the Physical Environment to Tie Meaning to Text

- Use every inch of the classroom as a resource for students in their independent work.
- Make it apparent through words and pictures posted on the walls what students are learning about.

Collaborate with Professional Colleagues

- Take a schoolwide perspective on meeting students' needs.
- Work in grade-level or content area teams.
- Find time to articulate across grade levels: topics and genres, enduring concepts, shared resources, expectations, and assessments.

Letter to an administrator: From a graduate student

Dear Dr. Torres,

I am a graduate student in Educational Linguistics and I'm planning to write a dissertation on language education and policy in your school district. I am contacting you for two reasons: (1) I need your permission to collect the data I need to complete my research and (2) I believe that we can collaborate to benefit your English language learners (ELLs). The dissertation uses ethnographic and sociolinguistic research methods, which means that a long-term engagement is desired to acquire an insider's perspective. I am particularly interested in how ELLs are educated and the educational language policies and plans which sculpt their education. In turn, I am an action-oriented researcher, which means that I am not only interested in observing and studying, but also in helping and acting. This means that I can be used as a resource for projects with students, teachers, and other administrators.

I would like to emphasize that my interest in doing research in your schools stems from my commitment to educational opportunity and equity for English language learners. This is a formidable task, and we need all the help we can get. By working together—students, parents, teachers, administrators, and educational linguistic researchers (even neophyte ones like myself)—we can continue to build sound educational programs for ELLs.

As a trained educational linguist, I have skills that your schools can take advantage of, but because I'm still a doctoral student, I come cheap. In fact, I am willing to work for free. There are a variety of projects on which we could work together. Language policies, like Title III of the No Child Left Behind Act, greatly affect language education and the lives of administrators. I have read this policy and studied how other school districts interpret and respond to its demands. Standardized tests have become increasingly important, yet many schools are struggling to find time to administer the tests and monitor the results. I could help on both ends: test administration and monitoring. I would be willing to administer tests and I could help with the organization and analysis of the test data. Also, I could work with teachers on programmatic and curricular decisions.

These are just a few examples of ways we could work together. I know I have a lot to learn about the intricacies of language education and policy in your school district and I would greatly appreciate your sharing this world with me. In return, I would like to share the knowledge and skills I have gained as a language teacher and educational linguistics researcher.

Sincerely,
Robert Thompson

Survey for Reflection and Action

This survey is based on the guiding principles articulated in the introduction to the chapter. Read the following statements and indicate the degree to which you agree or disagree: DK = don't know; 1 = strongly disagree; 2 = disagree; 3 = agree; 4 = strongly agree. Identify your program strengths and needs, and develop appropriate strategies for action.

We assess the strengths and needs of target populations

Everyone at the school who comes into contact with English language learners (ELLs) (administrators, ESL and/or bilingual teachers, mainstream teachers, support staff, parents) has a clear understanding of the following:

- Number of ELLs at the school (attention to language(s) represented)   DK 1 2 3 4

- ELLs' proficiency in English (listening, speaking, reading and writing)   DK 1 2 3 4

- ELLs' proficiency in their home language(s) (listening, speaking, reading, writing)   DK 1 2 3 4

- ELLs' educational history/academic background   DK 1 2 3 4

- ELLs' cultural background   DK 1 2 3 4

- Number of English speakers who speak a language other than English at home (i.e., heritage language speakers)   DK 1 2 3 4

- Heritage language speakers' proficiency in heritage language (listening, speaking, reading, writing)   DK 1 2 3 4

We clearly articulate goals for students

Each of the relevant constituents (students, teachers, administrators, support staff, parents, community members) has a clear and coherent understanding of the goals for the target populations, including

- English language development for ELLs (social and academic language development)   DK 1 2 3 4

- Academic achievement for ELLs (in language(s) used for instructional purposes)   DK 1 2 3 4

- First language and literacy development
  for ELLs   DK 1 2 3 4

- Positive cross-cultural understanding and
  communication for all students   DK 1 2 3 4

- Heritage language and literacy development
  for heritage language speakers   DK 1 2 3 4

- Second language/literacy development
  for English speakers   DK 1 2 3 4

- Each of the relevant constituents supports
  the goals of the program   DK 1 2 3 4

We carefully plan the program for ELLs

The program for ELLs is theoretically sound and aligned with research on program effectiveness. Specifically, the program includes the following critical features:

- Comprehensible standards-based content area
  instruction using sheltered instructional
  strategies in English and/or instruction in
  the ELLs' L1 (for ELLs' academic achievement
  across content areas)   DK 1 2 3 4

- A well-articulated standards-based ESL program
  (for ELLs' English language development)   DK 1 2 3 4

- A positive sociocultural environment that sees
  linguistic and cultural diversity as assets or
  resources to be developed, not as deficits or
  problems to be overcome   DK 1 2 3 4

- Support for the maintenance and development
  of ELLs' L1   DK 1 2 3 4

- Support for the maintenance and development
  of heritage language speakers' home/heritage
  language   DK 1 2 3 4

For bilingual programs

- There is a clearly articulated language plan
  that specifies how the two languages are to
  be used for instructional purposes. This plan

is aligned with research on the bilingual
education model implemented in that context
(i.e., TWI, DBE, TBE). DK 1 2 3 4

- All of the constituents (students, educators,
  parents, community members) have a clear
  and coherent understanding of how the
  program is structured so that the target
  populations can reach their goals. DK 1 2 3 4

We ensure that the program has adequate resources for implementation

The program for ELLs has the resources necessary for effective implementation, including

- Appropriate curriculum in the language(s) used
  for instruction DK 1 2 3 4

- Appropriate materials in the language(s) used
  for instruction DK 1 2 3 4

- Qualified personnel with appropriate professional
  development DK 1 2 3 4

- Valid and reliable formative and summative
  assessments of student performance and
  development relative to the goals of the program
  in the language(s) used for instruction DK 1 2 3 4

We use data to drive decision making

- Administrators use valid and reliable summative
  and formative data to inform program development. DK 1 2 3 4

- The program delivers results, based on valid and
  reliable accountability data. DK 1 2 3 4

Program Development Strengths _____

_____

Action Steps _____

_____

References and Additional Resources

Brisk, M. E. (1998). *Bilingual education: From compensatory to quality schooling.* Mahwah, NJ: Erlbaum.

Cloud, N., Genesee, F., & Hamayan, E. (2000). *Dual language instruction: A handbook for enriched education.* Boston: Heinle & Heinle.

Collier, V.P., & Thomas, W.P. (2004). The astounding effectiveness of dual language education for all. *NABE Journal of Research and Practice, 2*(1), 1-20. http://njrp.tamu.edu/2004.htm.

Diaz-Rico, L. T., & Week, K. Z. (2006). *The cross-cultural language and academic development handbook: A complete K–12 reference guide* (3rd ed.). Boston: Pearson/Allyn & Bacon.

Echevarria, J., Vogt, M. E., & Short, D. (2004). *Making content comprehensible for English language learners: The SIOP model* (2nd ed.). Boston: Allyn & Bacon.

Freeman, R. (2004). *Building on community bilingualism.* Philadelphia: Caslon.

Genesee, F. (Ed.). (1999). *Program alternatives for linguistically diverse students* (Educational Practice Report No. 1). Santa Cruz, CA, and Washington, DC: Center for Research on Education, Diversity & Excellence. [Online] Available at http://www.cal.org/crede/pubs/edpractice/EPR1.htm.

Genesee, F., Lindholm-Leary, K. J., Saunders, W., & Christian, D. (in press). *Educating English language learners: A synthesis of empirical evidence.* New York: Cambridge University Press.

Heath, S. B. (1981). *Ways with words: Language, life, and work in communities and classrooms.* New York: Cambridge University Press.

Howard, E., & Christian, D. (2002). *Two-way immersion 101: Designing and implementing a two-way immersion program at the elementary level* (Educational Practice Report No. 9). Santa Cruz, CA, and Washington, DC: Center for Research on Education, Diversity & Excellence.

Howard, E. R., Sugarman, J., & Christian, D. (2003). *Trends in two-way immersion education: A review of the research.* Washington, DC: Center for Applied Linguistics.

Lindholm-Leary, K. J. (2001). *Dual language education.* Avon, UK: Multilingual Matters.

Lindholm-Leary, K. J. (2005). Two-way bilingual immersion programs. *Educational Leadership.*

Miramontes, O. F., Nadeau, A., & Commins, N. L. (1997). *Restructuring schools for linguistic diversity: Linking decision making to effective programs.* New York: Teachers College Press.

Moll, L. (1995). Bilingual classroom studies and community analysis: Some recent trends. *Educational Researcher 21*(2), 20–24.

North Carolina Department of Public Instruction. (2003). *Spanish for Native Speakers Curriculum.* [Online] Available at www.learnnc.org/dpi/instserv.nsf/category9.

Ovando,C., Collier, V., & Combs, M. C. (2003). *Bilingual & ESL classrooms: Teaching in a multicultural context* (3rd ed.). Boston: McGraw-Hill.

Peregoy, S. F., & Boyle, O. F. (2005). *Reading, writing and learning in ESL: A resource book for K–12 teachers.* Menlo Park, CA: Addison-Wesley.

Peyton, J. K., Ranard, D. A., & McGinnis, S. (2001). *Heritage languages in America: Preserving a national resource.* McHenry, IL: Center for Applied Linguistics and Delta Systems.

Saunders, W., & Goldenberg, C. (1999). The effects of instructional conversations and literature logs on the story comprehension and thematic understanding of English proficient and limited English proficient students. *Elementary School Journal, 99*(4), 277–301.

Short, D. J., & Boyson, B. (2004). *Creating access: Language and academic programs for secondary school newcomers.* McHenry, IL, and Washington, DC: Delta Systems and Center for Applied Linguistics.

Thomas, W.P, & Collier, V. P. (2002). *A national study of school effectiveness for language minority students' long term academic achievement.* Santa Cruz: Center for Research, Education, Diversity, and Excellence, University of California, Santa Cruz. http://www.crede.ucsc.edu/research/llaa/1.1_final.html.

Thomas, W.P., & Collier, V.P. (1997). *School effectiveness for language minority students.* National Clearinghouse for Bilingual Education (NCBE) Resource Collection Series, No.9. http://www.ncela.gwu.edu/pubs/resource/effectiveness/.

Valdes, G. (2000). *Spanish for native speakers: AATSP Professional Development Series Handbook for Teachers K–16* (pp. 1–20). Orlando, FL: Harcourt College.

Webb, J. B., & Miller, B. L. (2000). *Teaching heritage languages: Voices from the classroom.* New York: American Council for Teachers of Foreign Languages.

Chapter 5

Program Implementation and Evaluation

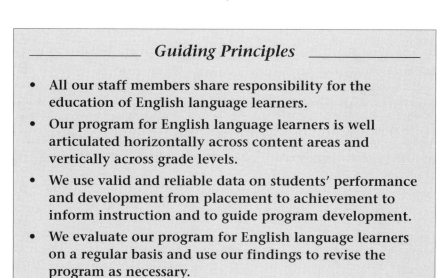

Guiding Principles

- All our staff members share responsibility for the education of English language learners.

- Our program for English language learners is well articulated horizontally across content areas and vertically across grade levels.

- We use valid and reliable data on students' performance and development from placement to achievement to inform instruction and to guide program development.

- We evaluate our program for English language learners on a regular basis and use our findings to revise the program as necessary.

Introduction

Programs for English language learners (ELLs) must be well implemented in order for ELLs to reach all program goals. Research demonstrates that it takes time for ELLs to develop academic English and to achieve academically in all content areas, and that everyone who works with ELLs in the school must share responsibility for these students. Each professional at the school must understand how his or her part fits into the larger system, and they must be afforded opportunities to collaborate with other professionals in the school community so that ELLs have access to the educational opportunities to which they are legally entitled.

Administrators are key to effective implementation. They provide the leadership and the structure to ensure that the professionals working together in their school have the knowledge, skills, and opportunities to effectively implement their program for ELLs. Administrators set the tone for collaboration in the school district or school. Once they have developed a theoretically sound educational program and ensured they have all the necessary human and material resources they need, they must ensure that their program for English language learners is well implemented and that it delivers results. This requires a coherent instructional approach across classes, a shared language among educators, an authentic assessment plan, and the ongoing use of data to drive all decisions concerning the education of ELLs, from placement to achievement.

This chapter is organized around questions that administrators are asking about program implementation and evaluation. The answers that experts provide offer insight into effective implementation of programs for ELLs in a wide range of contexts. The chapter concludes with a survey for reflection and action that administrators can use to review how well their program for ELLs is implemented, and to identify action steps they may need to take to improve their program.

Question

How do you ensure that everyone in the school shares the responsibility for educating English language learners, not just those who are specialists in the field?

CYNTHIA MOSCA

A crucial responsibility of administrators is ensuring that everyone in a school and in a school district, regardless of the person's position or specialization, shares the responsibility of educating English language learners (ELLs). In our school district, we have tried to get everyone on board by committing to three major strategies that have become part of the school culture.

The first strategy has to do with the school improvement plan, the second revolves around the provision of support in the mainstream classroom, and the third strategy concerns professional development.

Each of our schools has a school improvement plan (SIP) written by the staff and community of the school. Each SIP has one goal that specifically addresses the academic achievement of ELLs within the school community. That section of the SIP includes activities that help attain the goals and a method for measuring the success of the goal. Requiring each school to pay special attention to the needs of their ELL population within the SIP has proved to be quite effective. Having one goal that addresses the needs of ELLs brings those students into the foreground and promotes shared responsibility by all staff.

The second way that we obtain shared responsibility is by providing specialized support in the mainstream classroom. In grades four through six, English as a second language (ESL) teachers push into all English classrooms during reading to give extra support to students who are particularly struggling with reading. This is made possible by offering reading throughout the day so that ESL and reading specialists can be scheduled into every room on a regular basis. When the ESL teacher goes into that reading class, he or she serves reading groups that include ELLs and that also may include students who are not ELLs. Giving ESL teachers the more general role of support for all students leads to the perception that an ESL teacher can help all students. More important, it leads to the perception among reading teachers that they also have equal responsibility for all the students in the classroom, including those who are ELL.

The third way in which all staff are helped to develop a sense of responsibility for ELL students is through professional development. We offer opportunities for specialized course work to all of our teachers, and we especially encourage mainstream classroom teachers to take the courses. These courses lead to an ESL (or bilingual, for those teachers who have proficiency in another language) approval. We make it as easy as possible for these teachers to complete the course work by having cohorts go through the requirements right in their own schools. Whenever possible, we offer financial support for tuition.

With these strategies, we attempt to draw all school staff into the responsibility of educating ELLs so that they begin to see themselves as primarily accountable for these students. Without this shared responsibility, ELLs would be relegated to the remote corners of the school community, which does not help build the best learning environment for them.

Question

How do you articulate your program so that it provides the intensity, continuity, and length of time that English language learners need to acquire academic English?

CYNTHIA MOSCA

A program for English language learners (ELLs) must be articulated in a school or school district in both a formal and an informal way. Formal ways of articulation are based on conscious and explicit decisions that a group of staff made at some point in the development of the program. Formal articulation strategies are typically part of the textual history and culture of the school or school district: they are usually written down and are adhered to rather formally. Informal articulation strategies, on the other hand, happen more on the spur of the moment and may change slightly from year to year, depending on current needs and conditions.

In the school district where I direct the program for ELLs, the following formal articulation strategies are in place:

- Monthly meetings with central office administrators to provide updates for program issues, state mandates, personnel, and certification issues.

- Monthly meetings with school administrators on the same issues as above.

- Monthly school improvement plan (SIP) meetings. Each central office administrator is assigned to one school to serve as part of the SIP team.

- Scheduled meetings at a district or school level for institute days, early release days, or building curriculum meetings on particular issues regarding ELLs. For example, a meeting on the new English language proficiency standards was held with all staff at each school by the school's principal. The principals were trained initially by the ELL department. They were provided with a PowerPoint presentation and a strategies handbook to give to the staff.

- New teacher orientation. All new teachers participate in an interactive presentation on the ELLs who are served in our district. Out of 13,000 students, 6,000 receive some type of service from an ELL teacher (bilingual or ESL). All classrooms in our district have students who are or were ELLs.

- New teacher mentoring program. At least one of the mentoring meetings is dedicated to strategies for English acquisition.

- Scheduled meetings as requested by school administrators in order to meet with selected groups of teachers for the purpose of clarifying issues related to the education of ELLs.

The informal articulation strategies that are used in our district ensure ongoing professional development in relation to ELL issues for all teachers. They also help to establish an atmosphere of easy and open communication between staff who specialize in ELL education and those who deal with the general student population:

- Two courses per year leading to an ESL endorsement are offered to all staff through the Illinois Resource Center, the statewide resource center for ELL education. Currently we have two cohorts of teachers who are participating in the course work.

- All staff members are offered the opportunity to attend the state bilingual conference.

- District communication is extremely open. All staff members are free to ask questions and seek clarification at any time through personal contact, telephone, or e-mail.

- Voluntary after school meetings on specific issues are held regularly.

With these strategies in place, we ensure that ELLs are seen as the responsibility of all teachers, administrators, and departments. Without this shared responsibility, ELLs would be less likely to receive quality support in an integrated way and for as long as they need it.

MARITZA MEYERS

It is crucial for an effective program for English language learners (ELLs) to be well coordinated and for all staff to be on the same page. Classroom teachers, Title I teachers, reading specialists, resource room teachers, ESL teachers, school psychologists, counselors, and administrators need time and a vehicle to properly coordinate the various services that ELLs receive. It is important for professionals to meet on a regular basis to plan a cohesive instructional program for the students, with each utilizing his or her expertise to enhance instruction. To meet the needs of ELLs, the administrator of ELL programs has the responsibility of establishing and disseminating an organized agenda that would articulate the different components of ELLs' education. This agenda should be written as a formal document and should be given to all individuals who come into contact with ELLs; it can serve as a focus for discussions about ELLs. The document can include the following:

- Long- and short-term goals that ensure acquisition of academic language: This part of the document specifies the best ways to assess these students, how to provide the best opportunities for them to experience enriched academic language and content learning, and how to ensure standards-based learning.

- A language development plan: This plan specifies how ELLs are to reach the goals and objectives set for them. The plan addresses literacy goals and ways to reach those goals explicitly. It also describes the allocation of language of instruction in the various programs available to ELLs.

- Long-term content learning: This part of the document specifies approaches known to be effective for content area instruction. It specifies how language and literacy objectives are to be incorporated into content area lessons.

- Guidelines for hiring practices, which include a forum of teachers and parents working together: A collaborative hiring process allows stakeholders in a school to be involved in hiring the best possible candidate to work with students. Further, collaborative vision-sharing leads to increased levels of commitment and knowledge regarding school and programs goals.

- Description of a mentoring system for teachers that is intended to provide greater consistency and quality of instruction for ELLs: This mentoring program provides support to all teachers in relation to issues of ELL education.

- A commitment to ongoing professional development for all teachers, administrators, and parents in respect to ELL education: This training program provides on-site training and coaching in the classroom and includes participation in local, state, and national conferences, as well as visits to successful schools

An agenda such as the one just described promotes a common understanding of how ELLs are to be educated in the district. It helps stakeholders identify and discuss pathways and goals. It provides an opportunity for parents, community members, teachers, administrators, and other stakeholders to come together to plan and maintain a quality program. However, just having an agenda or a physical document is not enough to elicit meaningful discussion and participation. It is important for the administrator to share information via letters, Internet, meetings, and workshops on an ongoing basis. Any major decisions should be made collaboratively, and opportunities must be provided, especially to teachers, to discuss practices, student progress, effective lessons, and program goals.

Question

How do you ensure that the mainstream teachers and English as a second language teachers collaborate with each other to effectively address the content and language needs of the English language learners?

JANA ECHEVARRIA

In our extensive work developing the Sheltered Instruction Observation Protocol (SIOP) model with teachers who have English language learners (ELLs) in their classrooms, one thing has become clear: English as a second language (ESL) specialists alone cannot adequately meet the needs of the ever-growing numbers of these students (Echevarria, Vogt, & Short, 2004). All school personnel share in the responsibility of educating ELLs. While the ESL teacher offers valuable expertise in language development, the mainstream teacher also must understand the importance of tending to the second language acquisition needs of ELLs while delivering content to these students. The best way to accomplish this goal is to have a good, collaborative relationship between the ESL teacher and the mainstream teacher.

From our work, we have found that there are essentially three overarching factors that contribute to productive collaboration: training, time, and relationships. First, many administrators have reported that when their staff have all been trained in the same approach for teaching ELLs, the school "speaks the same language," which contributes greatly to good collaboration. Too often, teachers are compartmentalized into areas such as special education, language arts, mainstream, ESL, and so forth, and each area receives different kinds of professional development experiences. Fragmented professional development can be an impediment to collaboration and can contribute to feelings of territoriality.

Once teachers, specialists, and administrators approach the education of ELLs in a coherent way, the next factor for making sure collaboration takes place is to provide time in which to collaborate. This sounds easy. However, extra time is sorely lacking in a school day. While recognizing the limitations on time, let me mention a couple of ways that administrators have found to allow teachers time for collaboration. In elementary schools, there may be an ELL team that meets to discuss issues and then takes the information back to their grade-level meetings. Many of those issues also are discussed during monthly staff meetings. If the collaboration is as specific as lesson planning and coordination of instruction, some schools find funds to provide substitutes for planning days or extra pay for after-school planning sessions. In secondary schools, conference periods are coordinated so that the ESL and mainstream teacher share planning time. In other cases, coverage is provided during a given period to free up time to collaborate. Again, collaboration takes less time when staff members share the same approach to instruction and the same terminology.

Finally, collaboration is a voluntary process, since one really cannot be forced to collaborate, even if mandated by the administration. An issue that impedes effective collaboration is territoriality. Administrators can serve an important role and help defuse this issue by valuing each teacher and clearly communicating that a team approach is called for. The ESL teacher needs to understand that he or she brings a wealth of knowledge to the setting and will continue to have an important role as the leader on ELL issues. The mainstream teacher likewise needs to understand that each student is as important as the next and that utilizing all available resources is in everyone's best interest. The ESL teacher may start by developing a strong relationship with several teachers who are willing to collaborate. Then, at staff meetings, these teachers may be invited to talk about the benefits of their collaboration to students and mainstream teachers alike.

Collaboration has become a buzzword in education. It is much easier to talk about than to implement. However, we have seen that over time the relationships necessary for effective collaboration can develop, as long as the administration is committed to making it happen.

❦

Lynne Díaz-Rico

Educating English language learners (ELLs) requires the collaborative effort of classroom teachers and English as a second language (ESL) specialists. In this process, it is essential that site administrators be strong leaders who keep the staff's vision focused on the goal of providing high-quality education for ELLs, in part by helping staff members develop the skills and practices needed to implement this goal.

To provide high-quality instruction, educators face four key challenges: sustaining high academic expectations, tracking success in English proficiency while monitoring fair grading practices, ensuring a high level of teamwork, and promoting a supportive environment for students' primary language and culture. A description of each challenge follows, along with recommended solutions.

Research has shown that students take at least three to five years to acquire the academic language needed to master the elementary curriculum. While they are acquiring this academic English, ELLs must also keep pace with native English speakers' academic performance. Educators walk a tightrope: How does one make content understandable to a non-English speaker without the language-support activities themselves slowing the curricular pace? How can ELLs maintain access to the same level of information and produce the same quality of performance that is expected of high achievers? Techniques of specially designed academic instruction in English (SDAIE) or sheltered instruction include the use of modified teacher speech (clear enunciation, simple sentence structures, reduced use of slang and idioms, increased use of gestures), modified instructional delivery (use of primary language resource materials, peer coaches, visuals), and modified texts (teacher-created text outlines, simplified text, and audio recordings of text available in learning centers). Each lesson in a content domain should have both language development objectives and content goals. The site administrator monitors instruction closely so that language development takes place while academic standards are met.

An integrated connection between placement scores in English proficiency and subsequent instruction ensures that the ELL is properly placed according to language skills. A tracking folder that follows the ELL from placement to achievement and includes a checklist of proficiency goals level by level provides a structured means for accountability in English language acquisition. As part of sustaining high academic expectations, the site administrator bears the responsibility of monitoring the report card grades received by ELLs so that these grades are neither artificially inflated because of lower expectations nor deflated due to unfair competition with native English speakers.

A high level of collaborative teamwork is needed to ensure that ELLs succeed to the same degree as do their native-English-speaking peers. If the school has an ESL coordinator, the role of this specialist is to model SDAIE/ sheltered techniques for mainstream teachers, to administer proficiency tests and maintain records, to help create materials for SDAIE-enhanced content delivery, and to educate parents in their role of instructional support. (In a high-quality program, there is no expectation for the ESL coordinator to "pull out" ELLs for instruction away from the mainstream classroom.) A mutually respectful, collaborative relationship between classroom teachers and the ESL specialist has several key elements: The collaboration should be based on shared goals, parity of status, shared responsibility for key decisions, shared resources, shared accountability for outcomes, and a sense of emergent trust (Friend & Cook, 2000). These elements are best fostered when the administrator also models these elements. If problems arise, the administrator's role is to facilitate open lines of communication and problem solving.

In a school setting that promotes inclusion, much support is evident for maintaining students' primary language and affirming the culture in which that language lives. School staff who are bilingual, welcome signs and announcements in the primary languages, time set aside within the curriculum for instruction in the foreign or heritage language, financial support for translators or community liaison workers, and a full range of primary language resource materials in a central library or classroom resource centers— these efforts send the community the message that English language instruction is an additive rather than subtractive influence on students' native language skills. A commitment to linguistic multi-competence ("everyone is bilingual") is a vote for collaboration not only between teachers and specialists, but also between the school and community. The administrator sets the tone by actively and enthusiastically embracing diversity, and making it possible for collaboration to flourish.

Question

How should English language learners be grouped for instruction?

ESTER DE JONG

As a general rule, districts should strive to group English language learners (ELLs) age-appropriately by grade level and organize their services in such a way that ELLs will have access to grade-appropriate content and language instruction. Grouping ELLs becomes a complex issue as practical issues such as the number of ELLs, available resources, and the desired program model interact with program philosophy and good intentions. Some issues are outlined below.

Prioritizing services around *language proficiency levels* helps ESL/bilingual teachers develop targeted lessons for a particular proficiency level. Handling a wide range of proficiency levels can be challenging, particularly if the teacher cannot communicate in the students' native language. Grouping ELLs by proficiency level must take age differences into consideration, avoiding too large an age gap within one class (for example, a first grader and a second grader can be placed together but a first grader and a third grader should not be placed together). If grouping by language proficiency level involves multiple grades, content learning tends to be sacrificed. Depending on the program type, language proficiency grouping may also isolate students at the same level by not exposing them to more proficient students.

The choice to group students by *language background* is also influenced by program type. Bilingual services require a certain amount of clustering by language background to create optimal opportunities for the use of the native language for content and literacy instruction. It is important that, within the context of bilingual programs, schools create systematic and frequent opportunities to interact with native English speakers. English as a second language (ESL) programs, on the other hand, can be organized either for one-language groups or for mixed language groups. In this context, grouping students from the same language group together is sometimes considered disadvantageous because it may discourage use of the target language. Some argue that heterogeneous language grouping facilitates English language learning because it creates a communicative need to use English. While the latter is often the case, the issue is more complex. First, whether students exclusively use their first language during second language classes is not only a function of the ELLs. It also depends on the language environment created by the teacher and the larger school culture. Second, grouping students by language background can be advantageous in the ESL classroom if the teacher knows how to capitalize on the bilingual resources available for both content and language learning. Using the native language as a scaffold can accelerate ELLs' academic language development. Regardless of the grouping chosen, schools should consider native/non-native speaker interactions in addition to groupings that involve only ELLs.

Grade level placement is often the most appropriate grouping practice. It is important that ELLs be placed with students who are academically and socially their peers. ELLs should never be placed in a lower grade simply because their English is limited. At the same time, the diverse backgrounds of ELLs requires districts and schools to develop policies regarding the placement of overage students (older students with academic and literacy skills that are well below grade level, students whose schooling has been interrupted or limited), as well as students who enter the school district during the school year. However, grade-level placement must also be considered in connection to available services. A multi-age or combination-grade classroom can be an appropriate placement if this arrangement allows the school to provide bilingual/ESL services.

Regardless of their grouping practices, districts should be aware of the advantages and disadvantages of different grouping options, take steps to counter the potential negative effects of certain grouping practices, articulate their grouping practices clearly as part of their school plan, and demonstrate how grouping practices promote excellence and meet academic, language, and sociocultural goals for all students, including ELLs.

☙

NANCY L. COMMINS[1]

Sound instructional programs in linguistically diverse schools purposefully plan for differentiation along multiple dimensions. One is the language background of the learners in the group (Commins & Miramontes, in press). Three groupings are possible: *heterogeneous groups,* where teachers work with students who are both native and second language speakers of the language of instruction; *second language groups,* where all the students in front of the

---

1. This response is based on ongoing work with Silvia Latimer and Sheila Shannon.

teacher are working in their second language; and *primary language groups,* where every student in front of the teacher is a native speaker of the language of instruction. Each setting offers opportunities for linguistic and academic development not necessarily available in the others. Together they can provide the full range of instruction that students need to become academically proficient in English.

Heterogeneous groups. English language learners typically spend the most time in heterogeneous groups. They benefit in these settings when they can experience "authentic" communication with fluent English-speaking models and are exposed to a rigorous academic program. Because of the presence of native English speakers, teachers usually adhere more closely to grade-level or subject area curriculum and expectations.

Heterogeneous groups, however, can be quite stressful for second language learners. When teachers plan with native speakers in mind, it is easy to overlook the language demands of instructional activities and texts, making the pace and content of the lessons beyond the grasp of many. Having to compete with more proficient native speakers can inhibit second language learners' attempts to express themselves in English.

Second language groups. Second language groups allow ELLs to work on both the structure of English and the academic content side by side with students with similar language needs. When teachers focus on making information understandable and allow for language practice, students usually feel more comfortable and tend to participate more actively in these groups than in heterogeneous groups.

However, it is not wise to segregate students into special classes all day. If their teachers are trained only as language teachers, students' access to the concepts of the academic curriculum may be limited. If their teachers are content teachers, they may not be familiar with strategies appropriate to a second language setting. In any case, their opportunities to hear and use English with native models in an academic setting will be limited.

Primary language groups. This third setting, available in programs that incorporate students' primary language into instruction, can allow students to go deeper into concepts, work on higher-order thinking skills, and make use of a full range of text materials. Although there are great benefits to primary language instruction, if students spend their day learning only in their first language, they will effectively be denied the opportunity to learn a second language. Grouping solely by first language may also contribute to a segregation of students along racial and ethnic lines.

Why is this planning with language background in mind important? This kind of planning allows teachers to utilize the instructional strategies most appropriate for the learners in front of them. These understandings also shed light on how students experience instruction across their day. Ideally, second language learners should have opportunities to work in each kind of group each day. In all-English programs, at a minimum both homogeneous second language and heterogeneous groupings should be part of daily instruction.

Accomplishing these goals necessitates schoolwide planning to organize the adult human resources and allow the grouping and regrouping of students both within and across classrooms. This kind of planning also allows schools to maximize limited resources, such as primary language speakers or second language specialists.

Question

How should you assess the language proficiency of English language learners?

MARGO GOTTLIEB

A good assessment of the language proficiency of English language learners (ELLs) should include an assessment of both English (L2) and the native language (L1), regardless of the type of program the student is in. An assessment in English language proficiency is necessary because it forms the basis of all instructional decisions. An assessment of the native language is necessary in programs where the native language is used for instruction, but it is also highly desirable even if the student is not receiving any part of the instruction in his or her native language. One reason for this is that ELLs' language proficiency, in both L1 and L2, runs along a continuum. Some ELLs come with very little or no proficiency in English and others arrive with skills that allow them to survive in the mainstream classroom with some support. L1 proficiency can be even more varied for ELLs: Some ELLs have fully developed L1 across the language domains. Others may be strong in their L1 oral language but may not have had prior experiences with literacy. Thus, assessment of both languages would yield the most complete picture of who the students are and what they are able to do.

English Proficiency

Federal and state laws usually define how English proficiency is to be assessed. Most recently, the No Child Left Behind Act has set general parameters for the development and implementation of English language proficiency assessment for ELLs. Among its required features, these measures must:

- Represent the four language domains: listening, speaking, reading, and writing (that also generate a derived comprehension score from listening and reading).
- Be anchored in state academic content standards.
- Reflect the language of language arts, mathematics, and science.
- Be divided into grade-level clusters.
- Have descriptive performance levels.

States have had to adopt ESL proficiency standards and to establish an assessment tool that reflects those standards.

Native Language Proficiency

To date, there are no standardized measures of native language (L1) proficiency that parallel the new generation of standards-based, content-driven tools of English language (L2) proficiency. Therefore, school districts with dual language or developmental bilingual students must design strong classroom assessments in L1. In that way, ELLs' L1 proficiency can be initially determined and monitored side by side with their L2 proficiency.

The overall design of classroom assessment for L1 proficiency and the collection of data need to be structured in a fashion similar to L2 proficiency in order to yield meaningful results that can be reported and used in comparable ways. Because there are variations among classrooms, L1 proficiency assessment must be systematic and reliable. If results are to be generalized to a program level, standard ways of interpreting and reporting data need to be in place. Therefore, administrators, working with teachers, need to select, modify, or develop rubrics or scoring guides that will capture how students perform in a uniform way. In addition, an assessment schedule should be devised so that data collection on specific tasks (such as oral or writing samples) occurs within a designated time frame. Table 5–1 illustrates how to track the relative language proficiency of students in dual language settings by using the same performance definitions for both L1 and L2 levels of language proficiency.

In programs where the native language is not used for instruction, an attempt should be made to gather as much information as possible about the students' L1 proficiency, especially in regard to literacy. A student who is literate in his or her native language is a different kind of learner than a student who has few or no literacy skills.

Table 5-1. Mapping language proficiency assessment in L1 and L2

Levels of Language Proficiency	Oral Language Development				Literacy Development			
	Listening		Speaking		Reading		Writing	
	L1	L2	L1	L2	L1	L2	L1	L2
5								
4								
3								
2								
1								

Defensible data are the cornerstone to establishing the effectiveness of any program for ELLs. For this group of students, L1 and L2 proficiency assessment data help document student progress and attainment of language proficiency standards. And because language proficiency works in tandem with academic achievement, reliable and valid assessment allows administrators to gain insight into the viability of their program at a school or district level.

Question

How should you assess the academic achievement of English language learners?

MARGO GOTTLIEB

The academic achievement of English language learners (ELLs) needs to be assessed in both the classroom and a large-scale setting. At the classroom level, it is important for teachers to gather data on a systematic, ongoing basis to ascertain student achievement for each content area. When teachers assess the academic achievement of ELLs, they must keep in mind that English language proficiency often confounds what we can learn about student performance, especially if instruction is being delivered in English. As a general rule, assessment should be done in the language of instruction. In fact, it should be embedded in instruction and should be performance-based rather than being a separate activity or test at the end of an instructional unit. Children can be assessed while they are engaged in hands-on activities and working on long-term projects, perhaps ones that integrate technology so that they can use multiple resources to access content and create meaning.

Information about ELLs that comes from the classroom is one source of information that tells teachers and other stakeholders, such as parents, how students are achieving academically. To make the information consistent and reliable, classroom assessment must be standards-based. Teachers can use existing state academic content area standards to help them gauge where the students are (keeping in mind that the standards are designed for native speakers of English) and as a starting place for developing rubrics. Instruction in English always needs to be modified for ELLs, and since assessment is bound to instruction, the rubrics must take into consideration the language proficiency that is necessary for completing the assessment tasks.

Looking at large-scale measures, most states and districts are administering tests in English as stipulated by the No Child Left Behind (NCLB) Act. However, federal requirements are being interpreted too narrowly if assessment of ELLs occurs only in English. NCLB clearly states that students can indeed be measured in a language other than English. However, at this time there are only a few national tests that are available in Spanish, and they are not standards-based. Some states have translated their individual assessments or produced versions in plain English, but no state has designed an academic achievement test that accounts for the unique characteristics of ELLs. Even when academic achievement tests allow for accommodations, such as longer time to complete the assessment, the use of dictionaries, and directions given orally, students generally are unable to show what they know and can do until they reach a certain threshold level of English language proficiency. Thus, the data from academic achievement testing of ELLs are not very meaningful. Many students will appear not to be attaining the required criteria or standards, and consequently, their schools and districts are likely to be penalized for not demonstrating adequate yearly progress.

For this reason, the assessment information that comes from teachers is critical, yet it is not part of state accountability systems. In some states there are attempts to develop more classroom-relevant, alternative assessments for ELL academic achievement. These alternative assessments ideally should be based on English language proficiency standards, state academic content standards, and Spanish language arts standards (for the 75 percent of ELLs in the United States who are Spanish speaking). In Illinois, for example, we may eventually utilize various formats that yield more reliable and valid results than multiple-choice responses. We plan to include items that have significant visual support, such as providing a circular graphic organizer and having the students label the parts of a cycle. This way, students will not have to sort through and decipher a lot of extraneous information in order to select the right answer out of a list of four or five choices.

In conclusion, we need to drastically improve the ways in which we assess the academic achievement of ELLs because that is their key to school success. As long as ELLs' academic achievement is viewed as an absolute rather than as growth over time, the success stories will be few. We must strive to seek alternative means, both at the classroom level and at large-scale levels, to collect and report what our students can do in the core content areas.

Question

When should English language learners exit their bilingual/English as a second language program?

ESTER DE JONG

The mere existence of an exit process as an integral part of a bilingual/English as a second language (ESL) program often sends a powerful (negative) message to English language learners (ELLs) and their teachers that their program is "less than" the standard curriculum classroom. If schools fail to value and count ELLs' learning through their native language or in ESL classes until ELLs have left the bilingual/ESL program, the school overlooks the educational value of these programs and their important role in reaching academic, language, and sociocultural goals for their students. Administrators must purposefully work with their staff to avoid such perceptions and counter the potential marginalization that results from those perceptions. They can show that the bilingual/ESL program plays a positive role in the school, treat the program with equal status to the standard curriculum program, and promote high-quality, grade-appropriate instruction.

The purpose of exit policies is to develop guidelines for exiting ELLs that will ensure the success of ELLs in a standard curriculum classroom after ELLs no longer receive specialized services. It is inappropriate to set guidelines that merely aim at bare linguistic and social survival in the standard curriculum.

After all, ELLs must master sufficient English not only to socialize with their peers and to participate in English language arts classes but also to succeed in math, science, social studies, and other content area classes. This implies that schools and districts must set exit guidelines that reflect high expectations. The following are some key considerations for developing exit guidelines:

1. Exit policies should reflect our understanding of the second language learning as a complex and nonlinear process that takes time. Therefore,
   - Exit policies should be flexible, accommodating individual students' needs and histories and allowing for a gradual transitioning from bilingual/ESL programs to standard curriculum programs.
   - Exit policies should not be based on time factors (such as an arbitrary mandate that after one year, students should exit the program) but on the actual proficiency levels attained by ELLs.
   - Exit policies should make clear that the academic language development of ELLs will need continued support in the standard curriculum classroom after they exit.

2. Exit policies should reflect ELLs' age-appropriate social and academic language proficiency levels. Therefore,
   - Exit policies should include an assessment of oral as well as literacy skills.
   - Exit policies should include assessment of the language skills necessary for content area learning (math, science, social studies, and other subjects).
   - Exit criteria should reflect the demands of the grade level and should therefore vary from grade to grade (or from grade cluster to grade cluster).

3. Exit policies should use appropriate language and content assessments for ELLs, including authentic, classroom-based assessments that provide meaningful information about how the ELL is able to function socially and academically in the classroom at age-appropriate levels.

4. Exit policies need to take the level of preparedness of the standard curriculum classroom staff into consideration. Standard curriculum staff must have the skills to provide appropriate support for ELLs who have exited from the program to promote academic success. Therefore,
   - Professional development with respect to teaching ELLs must be offered to all staff.

- Exit policies must be sensitive to the standard curriculum teaching expertise

5. Exit policies should be developed collaboratively between bilingual/ESL and standard curriculum teachers so that expectations for proficiency levels and academic preparedness are clear and consistent.

6. Exit policies and the decision-making process should be articulated clearly to all staff, students, and parents.

Finally, administrators must realize that the exit process affects class size and hence student assignment. They must plan ahead to ensure that the standard curriculum classrooms that receive the students do not become overcrowded classrooms. Some grade levels will be more heavily affected than others because of the large number of incoming students. Receiving classrooms should be given sufficient space to include the ELLs who have exited from bilingual/ESL programs. This requires making the exit process an expected, integral part of the school culture.

Question

What should happen to English language learners after they leave the bilingual/English as a second language program designed for them?

☙

ESTER DE JONG

For many years, the responsibility of teaching English language learners (ELLs) was placed squarely at the feet of the bilingual or English as a second language (ESL) program. Once the bilingual student left the program, he or she became invisible. The expectation was that once the ELL left the bilingual/ESL program, that student's problems were "fixed," and the student could be treated just like a native English speaker without any further accommodations to the curriculum or instructional practices. This practice is harmful for several reasons. First, it may take five to seven years (or more) for ELLs to catch up academically to their fluent English-speaking peers. Even with the support of a bilingual/ESL program, it is likely that they will need continued support after they have exited. Second, treating ELLs as native English speakers denies the bilingual and bicultural realities that continue to exist after ELLs leave their bilingual/ESL program. Third, the responsibility of educating ELLs should be that of the entire school, so that policies and practices will benefit all students in the school, including ELLs. One implication is that after ELLs exit their program, standard curriculum teachers must have the skills to provide the necessary continuing support ELLs need to meet the academic, language, and sociocultural goals of the school. Another implication is that accountability for ELLs cannot stop after the students exit the bilingual/ESL program.

Many districts consider the length of time that students remain in a bilingual/ESL program (exit rates) as major indicator of program effectiveness. However, there is little evidence that an early exit guarantees subsequent academic success for the student. Rather, data from states such as California and Florida suggest that former ELLs continue to lag behind their English-fluent peers and that this gap widens as the grade level increases. Once ELLs leave the bilingual/ESL program, therefore, it is important that schools and districts continue monitoring their academic achievement.

First, a process can be set up whereby the standard curriculum teacher reports on a regular basis on how the exited ELLs are performing in their classroom to parents and school leadership. Any issues that arise in the course of the transition from the bilingual/ESL classroom to the standard curriculum classroom can be immediately addressed by the standard curriculum teacher, the former ESL/bilingual teacher, and support personnel. Second, the school and the district should systematically collect specific information regarding the achievement of exited (or former) ELLs. There are two general ways of doing so.

1. Districts can administer follow-up surveys or other assessments that are administered in the school/district. A follow-up survey can examine social integration, academic performance, and the extent to which the ELL is able to demonstrate grade-appropriate academic English skills.

2. Districts should disaggregate academic achievement data for exited ELLs as a special subgroup. This procedure requires that districts be able to track ELLs after they have exited the program. Tracking can be done by assigning an exit code to the individual student. For example, the Florida Department of Education uses the code LF for students who exited within the last two years and LZ for students who exited more than two years ago. Such an exit code could also

include program-type data, if districts are interested in documenting programmatic outcomes. Districts may also elect to include the nature of the exit process as part of the exit code. For example, parents sometimes take their child out of the bilingual/ESL program before the teachers considered the student ready. This situation differs from an exit process in which the staff agree that bilingual/ESL services can end. Collecting these data allows district to examine whether there exists a gap between former ELLs and fluent English speakers. If a gap exists, it may point to inequalities within the system that should be addressed by the school staff as part of whole-school reform efforts.

Question

How do you use data on student performance to make decisions about the implementation of your program for English language learners?

Diep Nguyen

Student performance data should be used for both short-term and long-term program implementation decisions. Different sets of data, both formal and informal, when combined appropriately can guide daily program decisions as well as long-term changes.

Using Data to Make Daily Program Operational Decisions

Patterns that emerge from classroom assessment data, when disaggregated, can help determine whether individual or groups of students meet learning goals and expectations. Using data to make daily program operational decisions prevents educators from making sweeping overgeneralizations about the success and needs of English language learners (ELLs). Yearly results from a language measure such as the Idea Proficiency Test (IPT) or the Language Assessment Scale (LAS) can be analyzed to gauge the yearly progress of ELL students in particular classrooms, schools, and second-language programs. This analysis will guide program decisions for the following year in terms of classroom instruction, staff development needs, and the needs for targeted assistance for a specific group of students. In our school district, each January, ELL students' IPT results and their overall ESL levels are incorporated to construct the staffing plan and program adjustments for the next school year at each school.

Students' portfolios are extremely helpful because they provide evidence of progress and learning that helps to transition a student out of a transitional bilingual program or ESL program or identify additional assistance that a student may need. Exit criteria that are based on student's performances, as evidenced in a comprehensive student assessment portfolio, are essential in order to ensure that (1) the student meets standards required for transition, (2) the student will be successful in an all-English mainstream classroom environment once exited, and (3) there is a consistency in students' evaluation from teacher to teacher and from school to school.

Student performance data are also useful in order to identify subgroups of students who may need additional targeted assistance in a particular content subject. In School District 54, for example, to recommend particular students for the Reading and Math Targeted Assistance Program, teachers use the student's IPT results, their profile as indicated by the Qualitative Reading Inventory (QRI) and other classroom assessments. With these data submitted by the teachers, the targeted assistance program can be designed to target each student's specific areas of weaknesses in reading or math for instruction. The data gathered on each student's reading performance are used to construct groups of students for instruction, as well as to make decisions about the targeted assistance program design and evaluation.

Using Large-scale, Longitudinal Data to Make Long-term Changes, Publicly Report on Program Updates and Validate a Program

While making small program adjustments can be based on yearly data of students' performances, school districts also need to collect multiyear data to study patterns of growth and the long-term effects of second language programs. The types of data currently used for this purpose are often large-scale tests that are tied to accountability and standards of instruction. However, triangulating large-scale quantitative analysis with qualitative data collected from classroom assessments will yield richer evidence of learning from students. Furthermore, results from quantitative analysis, when compared to qualitative evidence, can be used to create internal validity for the study.

Another helpful strategy when collecting and analyzing longitudinal data is to involve an outside evaluator or researcher as a partner in the study. This person can bring his or her expertise in assessment to the task and provides a valuable outsider's point of view when it is time for data analysis and interpretation. The combination of emic (insider) and etic (outsider) perspectives not only protects the "contextualized objectivity and thus defensibility" of the results but, more important, contributes to the overall quality and depth of the study (see Gottlieb & Nguyen, in preparation, for further discussion).

Since large-scale assessments are often required by the state and federal government, the choice and purposes of each assessment are guided by political agendas as much as by educational goals. Each assessment must be reexamined at the local school level before investing in its results to construct the local school's longitudinal data pool. For example, if a state assessment is due to sunset in a year or two, it is best not to include that data set in the longitudinal study. The integrity of each data subset is extremely important in order to ensure the reliability and validity of the longitudinal study. It is also appropriate to note here that not all data need to be included in the study. The inclusion of particular data sets must be guided by the goals of each program and the questions that drive each longitudinal study.

Question

What should an evaluation of a program for English language learners include?

Karen Sakash

A program evaluation is used to determine to what degree a program is achieving its intended outcomes. If a program is on track, with English language learners (ELLs) achieving academic and English proficiency and all program components flourishing, then such evidence can be used to rally support, including funding, of an ELL program. Alternatively, evidence-based decisions for program modifications are often recommended through evaluations.

Program evaluation planning often prevents difficulties that might arise later. A good program evaluation is driven by clear goals for each program component and is continual throughout the duration of a program, always leading to thoughtful improvements and often leading to further defining goals and objectives. Clear goals can be turned into relevant questions regarding the efficacy of program components, and these questions are explored and answered through a variety of valid and reliable evaluation techniques, including assessment instruments, participant surveys, questionnaires, interviews, focus groups, or observation tools. These techniques provide both qualitative and quantitative data. Data are gathered using multiple measures on both student achievement and other program components such as parent participation, professional development for ELL and mainstream teachers, program management, and resource acquisition and allocation.

Evaluation data should be relevant, important, credible, and timely. Some examples of key questions that lead to the selection of evaluation measures are: What effect is the program having on its participants? Are ELLs making progress toward achieving state standards? Are ELLs learning in the core subject areas? Are mainstream and ELL teachers developing new knowledge and skills to better serve ELLs in the classroom? To what degree are parents involved in the education of their children?

Persons who design and implement program evaluations can be internal, if the expertise exists in a school district, or they can be external to the district if a program is grant-funded and it is stipulated that an external review is required by the funding agency. In either case a program director must work very closely with the evaluator to communicate clearly about the program, oversee data collection efforts, and make sure the administrative tasks of the program evaluation are handled professionally and efficiently. Sophisticated research designs are not necessary for effective evaluation studies that are oriented toward program improvement, but interpretable feedback is. A program evaluator often works with the program director to understand the audience for the evaluation, which may include parents, teachers, other administrators, members of the school board, the media, or state and federal program officers.

Usually a comprehensive written report is submitted to the program director and sometimes an oral report is provided to representatives from the district prior to the written report. The report typically includes a one- to three-page executive summary that can be used for briefing others about the successes of the program and the areas that need further refinement. A written report should minimally consist of these sections:

- An overview of the program, its context, goals, and objectives.
- The evaluation design and methodology used, including a description of instruments used for gathering data, and data collection and analysis procedures (attachments of actual surveys and instruments used are usually included).

- A description and analysis of the findings/outcomes of each program component.
- Recommendations to continue or revise program components.

A useful evaluation highlights the successes of the program and provides direction in planning for the future. Challenges are sometimes identified and suggestions for meeting these challenges are offered. Communication is key between a program evaluator and an administrator, and an effective evaluation includes input from all major constituencies in the program.

Letter to an administrator:
From a former English language learner

Dear Mr. Casey,

How are you? I don't know if you still remember me, but this is Mary Nguyen, class of 1976. I visited Ms. Harvey last week as I passed through Mount Hope. As we were reminiscing about my high school days, she told me that you would like to hear from me and that you have often asked about what has become of this little refugee girl from Vietnam that attended your school several years ago.

I am writing this letter to say hello, but also to send you and all the teachers at Mount Hope High School a sincere thank you for the education you provided me as I learned to adjust to my new country.

You will be glad to know that I have become a bilingual teacher and now I am working to help other immigrant and refugee students make the same arduous transition into American schools. I am also speaking to other teachers about how to best meet the needs of English language learners and sharing with them what I learned personally from you and your staff in 1975–76. I have come a long way since those days when I came into your office and you asked me what my name was and I did not know enough English to answer. I think that's why I ended up being called Mary Nguyen. I call myself by my original name these days, Diep Nguyen, a name that I identify most with. But please call me whichever name is comfortable for you. I don't mind a bit.

Did you remember talking to a core group of teachers and designating them to be my main support team, along with Ms. Harvey, who was my bilingual teacher? It turned out to be the best thing you did. I remembered that whenever I had concerns or questions in any subject, all I had to do was talk to Ms. Harvey, and the next day my content teachers would have known about it and found ways to change their instruction for me.

(continues)

Letter to an Administrator (*continued*)

They also gave me alternative assignments that were challenging but not impossible. I remember doing my English assignments every day with Ms. Harvey so that I'd be ready for the English 1 class. Although we did not call it bilingual education in those days, the fact that Ms. Harvey was able to explain the subjects in a language I understood (French was my second language after Vietnamese) made a huge difference in my learning and passing all the requirements for graduation. What I appreciate most is the fact that she was my designated guide and mentor who could support me both academically and emotionally as I learned English at an exponential speed that year.

I also remember very fondly Mrs. Keatly, my government teacher, who arranged for me to enter a speech contest that year. She had high expectations for her refugee student, and I remember working so hard to rise to her challenge. Although I did not win, that contest showed me that I could succeed if I worked hard. I am truly thankful for the efforts you and the staff put in that year to make sure that I experienced success.

Now, as I do my work with other students and teachers, I often share the story of how you and a small group of teachers in a small high school in West Virginia made me who I am today. Thank you for taking the time and the care to educate me.

Please do stay in touch. I'd love to hear from you.

Fondly,
D.N.

Survey for Reflection and Action

This survey is based on the guiding principles about program implementation and evaluation that were articulated in the introduction to the chapter. Read the following statements about your ELL program implementation and evaluation. Indicate the extent to which each of the following applies to your school: DK = don't know; 1 = strongly disagree; 2 = disagree; 3 = agree; 4 = strongly agree. Use your school-based assessment of your ELL program implementation and evaluation strengths and needs to determine what, if any, actions you should take to improve the services that you provide for your ELLs.

We understand that English language learners are everyone's responsibility

- Everyone who works with ELLs in our school (mainstream teachers, administrators, support staff, bilingual and ESL teachers, parents) understands their responsibility to the ELLs at our school, and shares in that responsibility.   DK 1 2 3 4

- Teachers have opportunities to plan together and collaborate with each other on a regular basis so that they can effectively address their ELLs' language, literacy and learning needs over time.   DK 1 2 3 4

The program for ELLs is well-articulated

- ELLs have access to comprehensible, standards-based instruction in all content areas so they can achieve academically while they learn English.   DK 1 2 3 4

- ELLs have access to regularly scheduled, standards-driven, content-based ESL instruction so that they can acquire the oral and written academic English they need to achieve in all content areas.   DK 1 2 3 4

- The program allows ELLs the time they need to reach all program goals.   DK 1 2 3 4

- The program for ELLs is an enrichment program, not a remedial program; that is, ELLs' native languages and cultures are seen as resources to be developed, not as problems to be overcome.   DK 1 2 3 4

Educators use appropriate data to drive decision making

- ELLs are immediately identified and placed into appropriate programs based on valid and reliable assessment of their language, literacy, and learning strengths and needs.   DK 1 2 3 4

- Valid and reliable data on student performance and development relative to all program goals are regularly collected.   DK 1 2 3 4

- Student performance data are used to inform instruction.   DK 1 2 3 4

- ELLs' performance and development is monitored after they are redesignated as proficient in English.   DK 1 2 3 4

- The program is regularly monitored and evaluated.   DK 1 2 3 4

- Appropriate data are used to guide program development.   DK 1 2 3 4

Program implementation and evaluation strengths _____

_____

Action steps _____

_____

References and Additional Resources

Commins, N. L., & Miramontes, O. (in press). *Linguistic diversity & teaching*. Mahwah, NJ: Erlbaum.

Echevarria, J., Vogt, M. E., & Short, D. J. (2004). *Making content comprehensible for English language learners: The SIOP model* (2nd ed.). Boston: Allyn & Bacon.

Friend, M., & Cook, L. (2000). *Interactions: Collaboration skills for adult professionals* (3rd ed.). White Plains, NY: Longman.

Gottlieb, M. (2005). *Assessing English language learners: Bridges from language proficiency to academic achievement*. Thousand Oaks, CA: Corwin Press.

Gottlieb, M., & Nguyen, D. (in preparation). *Using evidence to drive decisionmaking in programs for language learners*. Philadelphia: Caslon.

Miramontes, O. F., Nadeau, A., & Commins, N. L. (1997). *Restructuring schools for linguistic diversity: Linking decision making to effective programs*. New York: Teachers College Press.

National Study of School Evaluation. (2002). *Program evaluation: English as a second language* (Indicators of Schools of Quality Program Evaluation Series). Schaumberg, IL: Author

Chapter 6

Classroom Instruction and Assessment

❦

Guiding Principles _____

- We maintain high expectations for the academic achievement and English language development of English language learners.

- We create an enriching environment for all of our students that draws on the linguistic and cultural resources that English language learners bring with them to school.

- We address varied needs of our English language learners by differentiating and scaffolding instruction.

- We use classroom-based assessments of the performance and development of English language learners to drive instruction.

Introduction

Classroom instruction and authentic assessment of students' performance and development are critical to providing an effective education to English language learners (ELLs). Although administrators do not need to have an in-depth knowledge of how to teach and assess ELLs themselves, they do need to have a basic understanding of best practices in the field. Effective leaders must be prepared to make informed observations of classes that serve ELLs and to have grounded conversations with all of their constituents (students, parents, teachers, administrators, district officials, community members) about classroom practices in their schools. When conversations about the education of ELLs are based on observations of actual classroom practice and evidenced by valid and reliable assessments of student performance data, administrators can focus and sustain their professional and program development efforts.

When monolingual mainstream administrators and teachers begin to learn sheltered instructional strategies that they can use in their classroom to address the diverse language and learning needs of their ELLs, many say, "these are just best practices" (in other words, practices like those they have learned for monolingual English-speaking students). However, experts in the field agree that effective instructional strategies for ELLs involve more than best practices for monolingual English speakers; they are informed by an understanding of second language acquisition, academic language and literacy development in English as a second language, and how culture influences language education at school. Educators of ELLs, regardless of the program they are offering, must also have a good understanding of bilingualism and the development of students' native language while they are acquiring a second language. Equipped with a theoretical understanding of how children learn in two languages at school, educators can make informed decisions about instructional strategies for ELLs in their classes.

Effective educators of ELLs assess the particular language, literacy, and learning strengths and needs of their ELLs in relation to all of the students in their classes. They plan instruction to build on the linguistic and cultural resources that ELLs bring with them to school, including their knowledge of their first language and their literacies in that language. These educators clearly articulate content and language and literacy objectives that are appropriate for the particular learners in their classes, and they organize language-rich, print-rich, highly interactive classroom practices that use a repertoire of strategies to reach their goals. Effective educators of ELLs, whether they work in ESL, bilingual, or mainstream classes, use classroom-based assessments of their ELLs' language and literacy development and academic achievement to guide them in making decisions about instruction, the curriculum, and the program.

This chapter addresses administrators' questions about these aspects of the instruction of ELLs and concludes with a survey for reflection and action. This survey focuses attention on areas of effective classroom practices that are emphasized by the experts in this chapter and provides a common language for all of the school staff to discuss practice. Administrators can use this survey to begin their classroom observations and subsequent instructional conversations with teachers. As educators identify particular strengths and challenges in their classroom practice, we encourage them to revise the survey as necessary to focus and sustain their observations and actions.

Question

What are the best instructional approaches for English language learners?

YVONNE S. FREEMAN AND DAVID FREEMAN

English language learners (ELLs) are expected to learn English, and they are expected to keep up with native English-speaking classmates in the content areas, including language arts, social studies, science, and math. Teachers can best meet these challenges by teaching English through content and organizing curriculum around themes (Freeman & Freeman, 2001).

Reasons to Teach Language Through Content

1. Students get both language and content.
    Research in second language acquisition shows that students develop proficiency in a second language when they receive comprehensible input—messages they understand (Krashen, 2000). If the input is a science or a social studies lesson, then the students acquire both English and academic content knowledge at the same time.

2. Language is kept in its natural context.
    When language is taught through content, the language is kept in its natural context. Each content area has its own vocabulary and its own way of presenting information, so that, for example, students learn the language of science as they study lessons about weather patterns and temperatures.

3. Students have reasons to use language for real purposes.
    When teachers teach language through content, students use English words and structures as they write, read, and talk in the course of investigating interesting content area topics.

Reasons to Organize Curriculum Around Themes

Elementary teachers often organize around themes. At the secondary level, teams of teachers can coordinate curriculum to provide thematic instruction

(García, 2002). Organizing curriculum around meaningful themes provides several benefits for ELLs:

1. Students see the big picture, so they can make sense of English language instruction. Teaching around themes makes it easier for ELLs to follow the lessons. The students know the general topic, so they can better connect activities to key concepts. Knowing the theme also makes it easier to understand the details of each lesson.

2. Content areas are interrelated, so that teachers connect the different content areas during the day. The math lesson can reinforce and expand the concepts and language introduced in the science lesson, and the story a teacher reads can further unify and develop academic content and vocabulary. Students also become familiar with the structure of texts in different academic subjects.

3. Vocabulary is repeated naturally as it appears in different content area studies. Students acquire English as the result of hearing and seeing the same words in different contexts. The same terms come up in the discussion of a story, in a social studies discussion, and in a science chapter when the whole curriculum is based on a theme.

4. Through themes based on big questions, teachers can connect curriculum to students' lives. In fact, ELLs, with their varied backgrounds, often serve as a rich resource for the class. When curriculum touches students' lives, they become more involved and they learn more.

5. Because the curriculum makes sense, ELLs are more fully engaged and experience more success. Because students know the topic and are becoming familiar with the vocabulary, they invest more energy in trying to follow the lessons. As they more fully engage with lessons, they acquire more English and develop higher levels of content area knowledge and skills.

6. Since themes deal with universal human topics, all students can be involved, and lessons and activities can be adjusted to different levels of English language proficiency. All the students are studying the same theme, but the kinds of activities they do and their responses differ depending on their level of English proficiency.

Question

What can the mainstream classroom teacher do to teach English language learners effectively while they are in the mainstream class?

DEBORAH J. SHORT

Mainstream teachers who have English language learners (ELLs) in their classrooms need to plan their lessons and deliver instruction in such a way that the students receive high-level content material in a sheltered context. The SIOP (Sheltered Instruction Observation Protocol) model (Echevarria, Vogt, & Short, 2004) is a proven, research-based approach for sheltered instruction that helps ELLs develop oral language proficiency while building academic English literacy skills and content area knowledge. To implement the SIOP model appropriately, teachers need to understand how academic English is used in their subject area. The SIOP model consists of eight components:

Preparation: Teachers need to develop language and content objectives linked to standards. They also need to plan for meaningful activities that spark purposeful communication about the subject's academic concepts with oral and written language practice. Use of supplementary or adapted materials can help students who struggle with textbooks.

Building Background: Lessons need to connect new concepts with the students' personal experiences, cultural backgrounds, and past learning. Teachers must teach key vocabulary and concepts directly and provide opportunities for students to use this vocabulary orally and in writing throughout the lesson and unit.

Comprehensible Input: Teachers must become skilled in using the following sheltered techniques to make language and content more meaningful:

- Gestures, pantomime, demonstrations, and role-playing
- Pictures, real objects, and other visual aids
- Graphic organizers, manipulatives, and the chunking of text
- Restating, repeating, speaking at a speed appropriate to the proficiency level of the students, reducing use of idioms, and simplifying the sentence structure

Teachers also need to explain academic tasks clearly, both orally and in writing, while modeling or providing examples so that students know the steps they should take and can envision the desired result.

Strategies: Teachers must provide students with explicit instruction and practice in learning strategies. They must scaffold instruction, beginning at a level that encourages student success and providing support to move students to a higher level of understanding. They may scaffold information with techniques such as anticipation guides and graphic organizers, as well as with systematic questioning and verbal cues.

Interaction: Teachers must provide frequent opportunities for interaction so that students can practice important skills such as elaborating, negotiating meaning, clarifying information, persuading, and evaluating. Students should interact with each other and with the teacher. Cooperative learning groups offer effective ways for students to share information, solve problems, and prepare products that integrate their English and content knowledge.

Practice/Application: Teachers must include a variety of activities that encourage students to practice and apply the content they are learning and practice and apply their developing academic language skills as well. Over several days, all four language skills (reading, writing, listening, and speaking) should receive attention and practice.

Lesson Delivery: A teacher knows that a lesson has been delivered effectively when the content and language objectives have been met, the pacing was appropriate, and the students had a high level of engagement. Classroom management skills play a role in effective lesson delivery.

Review/Assessment: At the end of each lesson, teachers should spend time reviewing key vocabulary and content concepts with the students, who have received considerable input through a new language. Throughout each lesson, teachers need to use frequent comprehension checks and other informal assessments to measure how well students retain information. Teachers must also offer multiple pathways for students to demonstrate their understanding of the content.

By following the SIOP model and the suggested strategies, it is likely that mainstream teachers will be more effective in helping their ELLs attain content standards and develop academic oral language and literacy skills at the same time. (More information and resources on the SIOP model are available at www.cal.org/siop.)

Question

How do you ensure that English language learners develop English language proficiency?

YVONNE S. FREEMAN AND DAVID FREEMAN

According to Krashen (1992), there are two ways of developing a new language: through acquisition or through learning. Acquisition of language occurs subconsciously when we receive messages we understand, what Krashen calls comprehensible input. Acquisition occurs in classrooms when teachers engage students in authentic communicative experiences and teach language through content. We also acquire language through reading. Reading is a rich source better for acquiring academic vocabulary than oral language.

Learning, in contrast, is a conscious process in which we focus on various aspects of the language itself. It is what generally occurs in classrooms when we study grammar, vocabulary, and isolated facts. Learning may help students succeed on tests of isolated bits of information, but learning does not lead to language proficiency.

Acquisition rather than learning results in competent language users. Students acquire language when they receive messages they understand. Teachers, then, must learn how to make the input comprehensible. There are a variety of strategies teachers can use to ensure that they provide comprehensible input (Freeman & Freeman, 2002).

Strategies to Make the Input and Content Comprehensible

If at all possible, teachers should *preview* and *review* the content in the student's first language.

1. Use visuals including graphic organizers, multimedia, and realia (real things). Try always to move from the concrete to the abstract.

2. Use gestures and body language.

3. Speak clearly and pause often.

4. Say the same thing in different ways (paraphrase).

5. Write down key words and ideas. (This slows down the language for English language learners (ELLs).

6. Give students strategies to draw on cognates.

7. Make frequent comprehension checks.

8. Have students explain main concepts to one another working in pairs or small groups. They could do this in their first language.

9. Above all, keep oral presentations or reading assignments short. Cooperative activities are more effective than lectures or assigned readings.

Reading Provides Comprehensible Input

When students understand the language and content that is being taught, they acquire language. They also acquire language when they read. When ELLs read frequently from content texts, they acquire the vocabulary and the structures of academic content subjects. Krashen (2004) claims that reading "is one of the best things a second language acquirer can do to bridge the gap from the beginning level to truly advanced levels of second language proficiency." Teachers of ELLs, then, must provide their students with opportunities to read a large variety of high-interest, comprehensible books to build general vocabulary, and teach them strategies to comprehend content area texts to build academic vocabulary.

When teachers encourage ELLs to read extensively and provide strategies for making both oral and written input comprehensible, their students will acquire high levels of English language proficiency.

Question

When should an English language learner begin to read and write in English?

ERMINDA GARCÍA

We must first shatter the myth that English language learners (ELLs) are not capable of engaging in literacy in English, at least not until they are proficient speakers of the language. Rather than sheltering these students from literacy, we need to immerse them in rich and appropriate literacy experiences (García, 2004). To attain this goal, the language of reading and writing must be meaningful to the learners. Literacy must be based on the knowledge and skills that students bring with them, including linguistic awareness of the alphabet or written symbols from their first language. For students who come from a native language that uses the Roman alphabet, the transfer of knowledge from the first language to English is significant. For students coming from a non-Roman alphabet, the transfer is broader and usually happens at the comprehension strategy level. Regardless of the specificity of the transfer from first to second language, we cannot ignore the power of the knowledge base that children bring to the task of learning English (Hudelson, 1989).

Literacy in English must also be based on the knowledge and skills that students bring with them from their proficiency in oral English. In other words, students can read and write what they can say more easily than they can read and write text they cannot comprehend orally. Then, if we provide appropriate learning supports in a meaningful context and many opportunities and reasons to practice, we can help ELLs become literate in English, their second language. They can, in turn, reap the benefits in accelerated language development that results from reading and writing in that language.

To get ELLs on the path to literacy from the beginning, we need to give them frequent and varied opportunities for reading and writing. A beginning ELL needs to do more than to read controlled pattern sentences and complete sentence starters. Although these types of limited reading and writing activities are helpful, too much reliance on them restricts their written language development. Additionally, it is very hard to expose students to real-life, authentic, meaningful language when we restrict the choice of words in reading or writing material. We need to include the following kinds of reading and writing instruction for beginning level ELLs:

- Daily reading and writing, where students are free to express feelings and opinions.
- Writing in response to literature, where students write about a topic springing from the literature they just read.
- Literacy projects, where students become immersed and invested in first reading, then developing their own writing.

Simply put, to become a reader, you must read; to become a writer, you must read and write. Effective literacy instruction for ELLs begins with a recognition of the assets all students bring with them and with the realization that literacy helps further the development of language proficiency. In this way we can raise not only our own expectations but our students' expectations about what they can accomplish as readers and writers.

✿

LYNNE DUFFY

There is no formula to follow or any magic time to teach reading in English to an English language learner (ELL). A teacher of ELLs must consider the concepts and skills he or she wants to teach with his or her particular students and the types of reading instruction and the strategies he or she will use. Furthermore, the teacher must consider the individual student he or she is teaching. Once we understand these factors, we can decide when we should have an ELL begin to read in English.

Many bilingual teachers will say they do not teach reading in English for several months or even years, yet it is these same bilingual teachers who are in fact teaching English reading almost from day one. A teacher can immerse learners in different kinds of text. The classroom environment, for example, is covered with print. Teachers use written directions to turn in homework, list jobs for the students, label objects, and so on. Often the walls in a bilingual classroom are covered with text written in the native language and English. In an English as a second language (ESL) classroom, the text may be in English with pictures or symbols. Instructional language can be taught using print in the classroom environment as long as it is meaningful and comprehensible to the student.

Reading instruction can be used as a way to develop oral language. Specifically, reading quality literature and nonfiction books to students using comprehensible input will accelerate oral (academic) language skills. It develops vocabulary, promotes fluency, and allows ELLs to hear language in a natural and meaningful context. Building background knowledge and providing comprehensible input, a teacher can use text to help facilitate comprehension skills or knowledge that apply to both (all) languages. Bilingual teachers have a bigger advantage because they can use the native language to help clarify meaning and enhance comprehension. Furthermore, they can help facilitate discussion about literacy and language by pointing out similarities and differences that are specific to each language.

The types of reading instruction and strategies we use with students determine how much English reading a student can handle. We teach word knowledge (phonemic awareness, phonics, and vocabulary), comprehension, and fluency, using guided reading, shared reading, read aloud, and silent reading to individuals, small groups, heterogeneous groups, ability groups, and whole groups. Some of these strategies we can begin in English right away; for others we need to wait.

After we determine what aspects of reading we are trying to teach, we then determine if they are appropriate for the individual student. Let us take an example of a student who is literate in her own language but does not have oral language skills in English. This student understands the concepts of decoding, sentence structure, vocabulary, and different text structures of different genres. She simply needs to learn the specifics of the new language, English. However, this student first needs to develop oral language skills before she is ready to learn how to read in English. She cannot learn sight word vocabulary if she does not understand the words or know how the words fit into a sentence. She cannot learn letter-sound correspondence without first having some experiences with the written symbols and sounds in English, particularly if the native language does not use the Roman alphabet or if a particular sound is not present in her native language.

Other students may not be literate in any language. These students would benefit from being taught how to read in their first language, a language they have oral proficiency in, before they are taught how to read in English. These students are learning many new concepts involved in reading (decoding, text structures, and so on). This task is even more difficult for the student if done in a language that is still being acquired. With policies varying in different states and low-incidence languages found throughout the school system, bilingual instruction is not always possible. Factors teachers need to consider when deciding appropriate instruction are the students' educational history (length of time in school, consistency, and so on), the level of proficiency in their native language, their level of proficiency in English, learning concerns they may have, their age, and their attitudes toward literacy and language. It is only after we consider our students' strengths and needs that we can determine when to teach different concepts and skills of English reading.

MONICA MACCERA FILPPU

The majority of the research on the literacy development of English language learners (ELLs) focuses on students who are sequential bilinguals, that is, they have developed language competence in their native language *before* they are significantly exposed to a second language. In these cases, literacy skills that are acquired in one language transfer to the other language as long as there is continued development of the other language. There has been significant study of which features of language and literacy tend to transfer more readily and which tend to require more explicit instruction.

My struggle as a bilingual educator has been that most of my students do not fit into the sequential bilingualism model. Most of the ELLs I have worked with in Washington, D.C., are simultaneous bilinguals. That is, they are exposed to both languages at home with multigenerational families, by watching television and in the community. In trying to design literacy instruction program for these students (in the context of a two-way immersion program), I was hard-pressed to determine which language was their "native" language. In which language should I introduce literacy? What research could I use to explain their struggles and successes? The most valuable lesson I have learned, therefore, is that for our students, first and second language literacy development are inextricably linked. They are happening at the same time, whether formally or informally and they need to be addressed by the instructional program.

How do we do this at Oyster Bilingual School? We promote a dual language curriculum with simultaneous biliteracy instruction for all students and an emphasis on metacognition and metalinguistic awareness. All students receive literacy instruction in English and the target language (Spanish, in our case). Typically, students are not divided by language dominance for this instruction. In most cases, such a division would be impossible, as most children do not fall neatly into Spanish-dominant or English-dominant classifications. Usually, students have one teacher who is responsible for teaching instruction in Spanish and one who is responsible for literacy instruction in English. Some students have two teachers in the classroom at all times and some students rotate between two classrooms, spending half of their day with each of two teachers. In both situations, however, teacher collaboration is of the utmost importance because it is important that both teachers see themselves as equally responsible for the students' literacy development in both languages. By working closely together, teachers are in a better position to talk with students about the fact that they are learning in two languages and helping them make the connections between what is learned in each language.

We promote a workshop format for literacy instruction in which each child is reading and writing at his or her level and developing the skills he or she most needs for meaningful communication through reading and writing. Along with the types of strategy lessons recommended for such an approach (Taberski, 2000), we include lessons specifically designed to help students understand how their bilingualism affects their literacy development process. For example, I have done mini-lessons, such as *Finding a "just-right" book in my second language* and *What do I do when I don't know the word for what*

I want to say in Spanish/English?, as well as skill-specific lessons that focus on contrastive analysis of Spanish and English. One of my favorites for first grade begins with showing examples of how different students in the class have formed the possessive in Spanish and English and talking about why some students make the mistake of saying "Pedro's casa" instead of "la casa de Pedro". Using reflective practices such as these we are able to develop literacy skills in two languages for all students.

Question

How do you ensure that English language learners can read and write in all content areas?

❦

María Paula Ghiso

Reading and writing are inseparable from learning content—from reading and writing about *real* issues for *real* purposes. This interconnectedness is evident as we witness students' engagement when they are given opportunities to learn about the world and use the processes of reading and writing to delve into topics of interest. How, then, do we include English language learners (ELLs) in this process of inquiry, when at times it appears as if they do not have the language skills to take part in the critical thinking required in content areas?

Provide Rich Content Activities

In an effort to help students achieve, many teachers end up watering down the content to which they expose students or providing students with activities that focus on rote skills. ELLs *can* engage in critical inquiries about content area knowledge. In fact, using reading and writing to learn about the world is interesting work, and often provides the motivation students need to overcome challenges posed by language.

Focus on Academic Language

Although many ELLs may appear to be fluent in English, it takes much longer to acquire academic language than social language. Thus, students may be able to interact in a social setting but may encounter difficulties when dealing with academic texts and tasks. Once we realize that a student may be proficient in social language but still be developing academic language, we can consider how to scaffold the student's experiences and interactions with reading and writing so that he or she may better engage with content area concepts and texts.

Get to Know Texts

Recognizing the difference between academic and social language means that teachers must look closely at content area texts to unpack the implicit language skills needed to access them for particular purposes. A text that at first glance appears easy may in fact pose many challenges to an ELL who is still acquiring academic language. We need to examine the language of the text, identifying potentially difficult vocabulary, sentence structure, genre, rhetorical style, and other features. We need to ask the following questions: What do students need to know to access a particular text? Do they have this background knowledge? What type of language is used in a particular text and in the activities we ask students to engage in? What is challenging about this language for ELLs? Understanding the content area text from a language perspective is the first step toward figuring out how to scaffold a student's interaction with it.

Get to Know Students

A student's background, such as prior educational experiences, level and characteristics of oral and written first and second language acquisition, area of origin, culture, and exposure to particular concepts, influences how he or she interacts with the content area material and the reading and writing processes used to engage with such concepts. Different facets of a lesson might be more or less difficult for different ELLs. For instance, the extent of prior knowledge differs widely, and it is necessary to figure out how to connect students with concepts and experiences that are unfamiliar to them. This can seem overwhelming; however, the English as a second language (ESL) teacher can be a valuable resource for providing information about particular students and suggesting ways of adapting lessons to meet their needs.

Collaborate with Other Teachers

Ensuring that ELLs read and write in all content areas becomes a less daunting task when teachers work together to form nuanced portraits of students, to understand student interactions in different classroom settings, and to align their strategies and expectations of particular students. For this joint work to be most fruitful, it is necessary to break down assumptions about divisions of labor. ELLs are not solely the responsibility of the ESL teacher. Reading and writing are not solely the responsibility of the language arts teacher. However, both the ESL and the language arts teachers can work in conjunction with the content area teachers to ensure that ELLs participate purposefully in the content areas. When the education of ELLs becomes the priority of the school as a whole, we can more successfully foster the engagement and continued growth of students who are often forgotten by the system.

Question

What materials are available for English language learners?

LUCÍA MORALES

When selecting materials for English language learners (ELLs), many factors need to be considered. The most important to keep in mind are the students' ages, their level of language proficiency in English, the amount of schooling they have had in their native language, and the amount of native language support they are receiving in school.

It is critical that the materials selected be age-appropriate and that they support grade-level curriculum. Regardless of the students' English language proficiency, they must have access to materials that focus on concepts being taught at that particular grade level. As an administrator, you may be asking yourself, "How am I supposed to do that when I have students who don't even read a word of English? Wouldn't it be best to give these students materials from a lower grade level, such as kindergarten or first grade?" While this might seem like a logical solution, giving students texts that do not focus on age-appropriate, grade-appropriate concepts could cause students to lose interest in reading (especially if the texts are babyish-looking for their age/grade), as well as cause them to fall farther behind in academics.

What, then, do we do? One possible solution would be to provide students with materials in their native language. The second would be to find materials at a lower readability level that support an age- and grade-appropriate curriculum. A combination of these two types of materials is the most effective for ELLs.

Research shows that the stronger the native language of the child is, the easier it will be for the child to transfer concepts and skills to the second language. Although not all schools are capable of providing native language programs to their students, this does not mean that the school cannot provide access to native language materials to support the child's learning, both in school and at home. There are many great multilingual resources available online for no cost (a list is provided at the end of this question). Some sites have text in as many as 43 different languages. Multilingual books, world news, and content area graphics and word banks are just a few of the materials that can be found on the Internet to support instruction for ELLs. Students provided with these types of resources will have access to academic content in their native language even as they are in the process of acquiring the second language.

When considering what materials to purchase in English for this group of students, one needs to consider which would best lead to high academic achievement. If students are to master grade-level curriculum, then it is obviously best to purchase materials that target those concepts. Fortunately, many publishers have created high-interest books at a variety of readability levels that would be appropriate to use with ELLs. Some publishers have gone so far as to build reading strategies into content area texts and to highlight key terms. (An annotated bibliography of recommended materials, as well as a list of publishers, is available at www.irc-ekits.org.)

But what do these high-interest books look like? What should the teacher or administrator be looking for? The best kinds of books to look for are those that are nonfiction and relate to the themes being studied at the various grade levels in your facility. The books should be highly visual (even for older students)—ones with realistic photography are always great because they can be used at any grade level and tend to appeal to students of any age. When selecting the texts to purchase, it is much better to find four or five books at different readability levels related to the same topic and purchase a few copies of each rather than buying the same book in sufficient copies for every student in the class to have one. By having a variety, teachers will be much better able to differentiate instruction for their students, and students will be more likely to find a book they like and feel comfortable with.

If students are provided with materials to access to the curriculum via the native language and if they are given high-interest materials in English at easier readability levels with graphic and visual support, there is a great chance that they will find academic success. The following is a partial list of multilingual resources:

http://thornwood.peelschools.org/Dual/index.htm
  Online dual language literacy project.

http://thornwood.peelschools.org/Dual/weblinks.htm
  Link to online dual language resources.

http://www.bbc.co.uk/worldservice/index.html
  World news headlines in 43 languages.

http://icdlbooks.org
  International Children's Digital Library: multilingual books online.

www.EnchantedLearning.com
  Great resource for content area graphics and word banks, downloadable
  books in various languages and much more.

http://onlinebooks.library.upenn.edu/archives.html#foreign
  Resources in 34 languages.

http://www.google.com/language_tools?html
  Search any topic in students' primary languages.

http://www.alanwood.net/unicode/#links
  Serves as a guide to use different language fonts/scripts on your
  computer; free access to these downloadable fonts/scripts online.

http://www.textmatters.com/kidstype/multilingual_word_processing.html

http://www.childrensbooksonline.org/library.htm

Question

How can you use technology to support the academic, language, and learning needs of your English language learners?

JOHN HILLIARD

Technology changes so quickly that a list of appropriate software, hardware, or Web resources for use with English language learners (ELLs) would be outdated almost as soon as it was set in print. Even within the somewhat limited category of hardware, there is a dizzying array of items such as personal computers, laptops, tablets, handheld devices, digital cameras, and

LCD projectors that have become an integral part of classroom instruction over the past few years. Furthermore, these items represent only a portion of the technology approved for classroom use. When hardware that enters the classroom illicitly, such as cell phones and gaming units, is added, the result is a mix of technology. The implications of this technology mix for the instruction of ELLs is hard to gauge. Because of the ever-changing technology landscape, administrators might best limit themselves to identifying general guidelines for evaluating the applicability of technology to the instruction of ELLs. These guidelines must be based on the developmental needs of this specific group of learners.

Language Learning and Technology

To make an informed decision about the efficacy of commercially available language software, it is necessary to understand the distinction between *language acquisition* and *language learning.* Young children develop their first language through language acquisition. This developmental process is initiated by natural interaction with the primary caretakers, where the emphasis is on communication and the content of speech. When parents speak to their children, for example, they do not point out grammatical structures or rules that govern the sound system of the language. Older students who *learn* a second language, on the other hand, usually bring a more formal awareness of their first language to bear. For these students, there may or may not be a focus on the grammatical distinctions between the first language and the second. The *language learning* process tends to be less naturalistic and more structured, with the emphasis on the form rather than the content of the message. This approach is readily apparent in the decontextualized types of drills designed for language learners (*Hola, Paco.¿ Que tal?* Who is Paco and why am I saying "hi" to him?). These premeditated phrases are in direct contrast to the original production that is the hallmark of acquisition process.

We can never expect young children to use technology to acquire language, even with the best technology available. There are strong indications that younger learners are not able to distinguish among even the most basic aspects of language through technology. For example, children who are exposed to different versions of target speakers on DVD are unable to develop the necessary auditory discrimination to hear the difference between important phonetic elements of that language (Kuhl, 2004), whereas children who are exposed to the same linguistic input from live speakers easily develop and preserve this discriminatory ability. This has real implications for ELLs who are exposed to English not through interaction with native speakers but primarily through computer-assisted language learning (CALL).

Many of us who have used technology with ELLs have bought into the computer-as-tutor model (Taylor, 1980). This model was based on the intrinsic strengths of the computer, which allow uninterrupted, repetitive drill and practice scenarios with objective feedback. The earlier limitations of CALL software made it much more of a medium for the *learning* of a second language than an environment for *acquisition;* therefore, it was less appropriate for younger learners, who were still acquiring skills in the first language. As CALL software/hardware advances and voice recognition and other interactive technologies become more reliable, it may be possible to incorporate more acquisition types of activities into the software that offer the young second language learner a more natural type of linguistic environment.

The Role of Productivity Software in the Instruction of ELLs

The main challenges to integrating technology into the instruction of ELLs are logistical and economic. The cost of many comprehensive software packages specifically designed for ELLs are beyond the means of many districts with small numbers of these students. For this reason, alternatives need to be considered. The productivity software that is generally found on most PCs or that can be bought at a reasonable cost (such as word-processing, presentation, spreadsheet, and database applications) has a valid role in the ELL classroom. One could even argue that, if properly integrated into content area curriculum, this kind of software can develop language skills without losing the content area focus. The skills developed in using these types of applications are also relevant beyond the educational setting and prepare students for the workplace. An ELL student with the ability to collaboratively create and use a PowerPoint presentation that contrasts his family with the family of a fellow student, in English, is engaged at high levels with both language and content. This engagement is in contrast to the same student sitting alone and passively progressing through a CALL program that exposes him to the vocabulary and grammatical structures used to talk about one's family. Although the CALL software could have a valid use in previewing some of the language associated with this content, by itself it does not allow students to be active users of the language for instructional purposes, and so it should play only a supplementary role.

The World Wide Web

The last important category of technology that has direct relevance to the instruction of ELLs is the World Wide Web. The Web is the single largest repository of information in existence. This resource is multilingual and searchable, open to any user. These characteristics alone make it both a valuable and an intimidating resource for the instruction of ELLs.

Here are some general principles for integrating technology into curriculum for ELLs that follow directly from the points just made:

- ELLs need to be active users of technology to access, evaluate, organize and synthesize, and disseminate information.

- ELLs need to use technology that encourages and assists them in interacting with native speakers in both instructional and social contexts.

- One way to understand the limitations of any commercially available piece of software is to try to identify which language domains (listening, speaking, listening, writing) it is targeting, and whether it relies on language learning or language acquisition activities.

- Computer software should never be used as the primary source for the learning of a second language. This is especially true for younger learners, who do not have access to extrinsic grammatical references in their first language.

Question

How can classroom assessment of English language learners be used in a climate of high-stakes testing?

ELSE HAMAYAN

As high-stakes testing boosts the prevalence of standardized tests in schools throughout North America, the value of classroom assessment increases dramatically. Two aspects of classroom assessment are so valuable that they make this type of assessment an essential component of every classroom for English language learners (ELLs). First, it provides essential information that is sorely lacking from standardized testing to students, their parents, teachers, and administrators. Second, classroom assessment can happen without taking precious learning time away from students because it is integrated with instruction. It follows that for classroom assessment to become accepted in the culture of a school district, it must yield information that is actually useful to different people and it must be fully integrated into the everyday routine of classrooms.

To make classroom assessment useful, results must be obtained and recorded in a way that makes sense to a large number of people: the students themselves, their parents, the teachers, and the administrators. The following guidelines can be helpful (Genesee & Hamayan, 1994):

- Plan assessment by answering the following questions: Who will use the results of assessment, and for what purpose? What will be assessed? When will it be assessed? How will it be assessed? How will the results of assessment be recorded?

- Gather information through a variety of ways and classroom activities, including observation, conferences, student journals, and instruction-based tests.

- Keep good records by keeping track of important information about each student in the form of narrative records and checklists. Narrative records, qualitative in nature, yield information that is particularly meaningful to students and parents, whereas checklists allow information about each student to be quantified. Quantified results of classroom assessment will be particularly appealing to administrators who need to show gain and attainment of standards. Perhaps as a result of the recent need for quantification of classroom assessment, checklists, rating scales, and rubrics that describe different levels of language proficiency are readily available (see O'Malley & Valdez Pierce, 1996, for a comprehensive discussion of effective strategies for assessing and recording information about ELLs).

To integrate classroom assessment into the everyday working of the classroom, teachers must embed assessment in instruction. When this is done successfully, the result appears to the students and to an outside observer as nothing more than just another instructional activity (O'Malley & Valdez Pierce, 1996). Perhaps as a result of the recent push for this type of assessment, many publishers of ESL materials are incorporating assessment activities into the teachers' manuals (see for example, the ESL series *Avenues* from Hampton Brown).

The use of classroom assessment strategies does place greater demands on teachers, and the inclusion of information obtained from these assessments does require advocacy by those teachers and their administrators. But without classroom assessment, it is going to be very difficult for schools to demonstrate what their ELLs are truly able to do.

Letter to an administrator: From a mainstream teacher

——Original Message——

From: Connie Henson [mailto:cbh15@earthlink.com]
To: Jackie Tubman
Subject: My ESL students

Dear Mrs. Tubman,

I need your help and advice about the new ESL students in my class. As you know, we were told that we were responsible for these students, and I am quite happy to have them in my class. I've always been happy to help out, and I've enjoyed having these students from different parts of the world in our school. But I'm feeling quite inadequate as a teacher who, for the first time, has students who are not able to do our 3rd-grade work because of their English.

I have not had much training (hardly any at all) in ESL, so I have no idea what to do with the three students who are at a very beginning level of English. How do I know what they are understanding and what they are not? Then there are the two students who seem to speak English quite well (I hear them chitchatting with English-speaking kids), but they just can't seem to keep up with classroom tasks. I thought that I could use them as peer tutors for the lower level kids, but that's not working out at all. And the big question I have is: I don't speak any of their languages (my high school French is useless), so what do I do about their native language? Do I let them use it in class?

I also have a sense that one of the beginning level students may have some disabilities beyond second language problems. He just doesn't seem to be functioning at the same level as the other students. What do we do about that? When I talked to Ms. Newhart, the special ed teacher, about him, she steered me away from the special ed department and said that it was normal for ESL students to have problems.

I'm wondering if there is any way you could make it possible for me to meet with Miss Lopez, the ESL teacher, on a regular basis. I know she would be a great resource for me. It's practically impossible to find the time within the school day, and I would hate to impose on her after hours.

Please let me know what the possibilities are.

Connie

Survey for Reflection and Action

Use this survey to focus your observations of classes that serve ELLs (mainstream, ESL, bilingual). Use a + when you have observed exemplary practice in this area, a √ when you have observed evidence of this practice, and a − when you found no evidence of this practice. Be sure to jot down evidence of the practice that you observed. Use the data you collect on this survey to focus conversations with teachers and to guide decisions about professional development. Revise the survey to focus your observations on areas of concern (such as particular strategies teachers are targeting in professional development).

Teachers have high expectations for ELLs' academic achievement and English language development	
Observation	**Evidence**
____ Standards-driven classroom instruction	
____ Clear articulation of content and academic language and literacy objectives that are tied to the standards	
____ Lessons are divided into three phases: BEFORE, DURING, AFTER (B-D-A)	
____ BEFORE: Teachers use strategies to activate students' prior knowledge (i.e., past learning, personal experiences, cultural background).	
____ DURING: Teachers use strategies to connect new learning to prior knowledge.	
____ AFTER: Teachers use strategies to extend students' learning beyond the classroom in meaningful ways.	
____ ELLs are integrated into all classroom activities.	

Teachers create an enriching linguistic environment for ELLs/all students	
Observation	**Evidence**
____ Classroom/school is rich in oral and written language, including commercial and teacher-made materials and student work.	
____ Teacher uses sheltered instructional approaches to make complex content area concepts and language comprehensible to ELLs.	
____ A wide range of authentic and appropriate materials is available (in English and/or in the ELLs' L1) and materials are tied to big ideas explored in content area instruction.	
____ The instructional units are multicultural and include contributions and perspectives of the diverse cultural groups represented in the class, school, community, and world.	
____ Students participate in a wide range of teacher-directed and student-directed activity structures, including	
____ whole group	
____ small group	
____ independent	
____ Students use social and academic language orally and in writing for a wide range of purposes (e.g., to ask and answer questions, agree and disagree, seek information and inform, tell stories, give opinions, summarize, synthesize, classify, sequence, compare and contrast, justify and persuade, infer, solve problems, evaluate).	
____ ELLs are actively engaged in all classroom activities.	

Teachers differentiate and scaffold instruction to meet ELLs' needs	
Observation	Evidence
Teacher differentiates instruction to address ELLs' particular strengths and needs in terms of _____ English language proficiency (oral) _____ first language literacy development _____ English literacy development _____ content-area knowledge _____ cultural background _____ learning style **Teacher scaffolds instruction to move from** _____ oral language to written language _____ first language to second language _____ known concepts and skills to new concepts and skills _____ known genres to new genres	

Teachers use alternative classroom-based assessment	
Observation	Evidence
_____ Teacher uses alternative assessment to provide evidence of what ELLs know about the content (regardless of their English language proficiency level). _____ Classroom based assessment of students' performance and development are used to drive instruction.	

Classroom instruction and assessment strengths _____

_____

_____

Action steps _____

_____

_____

References and Additional Resources

Becker, H., & Hamayan, E. (2001). *Teaching ESL K-12: Views from the classroom.* Boston: Heinle & Heinle.

Cary, S. (2000). *Working with second language learners: Answers to teachers' top ten questions.* Portsmouth, NH: Heinemann.

Chamot, A. U., & O'Malley, J. M. (1994). *The CALLA handbook: Implementing the cognitive academic language learning approach.* New York: Addison-Wesley.

Díaz-Rico, L. T. (2004). *Teaching English learners: Strategies and methods.* Boston: Pearson.

Dixon, R. C., Isaacson, S., & Stein, M. (1998). Effective strategies for teaching writing. In E. J. Kameenui & D. W. Carnine (Eds.), *Effective teaching strategies that accommodate diverse learners.* Columbus, OH: Merrill Education.

Echevarria, J., Vogt, M. E., & Short, D. (2004). *Making content comprehensible to English learners: The SIOP model* (2nd ed.). Boston: Pearson/Allyn & Bacon.

Freeman, D. E., & Freeman, Y. S. (2001). *Between worlds: Access to second language acquisition* (2nd ed.). Portsmouth, NH: Heinemann.

Freeman, Y. S., & Freeman, D. E. (2002). *Closing the achievement gap: How to reach limited formal schooling and long-term English learners.* Portsmouth, NH: Heinemann.

García, E. (2002). *Student cultural diversity: Understanding and meeting the challenge* (3rd ed.). Boston: Houghton Mifflin.

García, E. (2004). *Writing instruction for English language learners.* Carmel, CA: Hampton-Brown.

Genesee, F., & Hamayan, E. (1994). Classroom-based assessment. In F. Genesee (Ed.), *Educating second language children: The whole child, the whole curriculum* (pp. 212–239). New York: Cambridge University Press.

Gibbons, P. (1991). *Learning to learn in a second language.* Portsmouth, NH: Heinemann.

Gibbons, P. (2002). *Scaffolding language scaffolding learning: Teaching second language learners in the mainstream classroom.* Portsmouth, NH: Heinemann.

Herrell, A., & Jordan, M. (2003). *Fifty strategies for teaching English language learners* (2nd ed.). Upper Saddle River, NJ: Pearson/Merrill Prentice Hall.

Hudelson, S. (1989). *Write on: Children writing in ESL.* Englewood Cliffs, NJ: Prentice Hall Regents.

Krashen, S. (1992). *Fundamentals of Language Education.* Torrance, CA: Laredo.

Krashen, S. (2000). What does it take to acquire language? *ESL Magazine, 3*(3), 22–23.

Krashen, S. (2004). *The power of reading.* Portsmouth, NH: Heinemann.

Kuhl, P. K. (2004). Early language acquisition: Computational strategies, social influences, and neural commitment in the developing brain. *Nature Reviews Neuroscience, 5,* 831–843.

O'Malley, J. M., & Valdez Pierce, L. (1996). *Authentic assessment for English language learners: Practical approaches for teachers.* New York: Addison-Wesley.

Peregoy, S. F., & Boyle, O. F. (2005). *Reading, writing, and learning in ESL: A resource book for K–12 teachers* (4th ed.). Boston: Pearson.

Richard-Amato, P. A., & Snow , M. A. (1992). *The multicultural classroom: Readings for content-area teachers.* White Plains, NY: Longman.

Taberski, S. (2000). *On solid ground.* Portsmouth, NH: Heinemann.

Taylor, R. (1980). *The computer in the school: Tutor, tool, tutee.* New York: Teachers College Press.

Walter, T. (2004). *Teaching English language learners: The how-to handbook.* New York: Longman.

Chapter 7

Professional Development

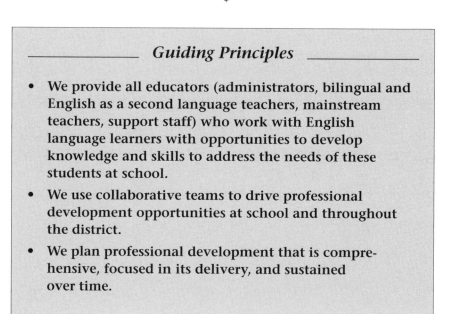

Guiding Principles

- We provide all educators (administrators, bilingual and English as a second language teachers, mainstream teachers, support staff) who work with English language learners with opportunities to develop knowledge and skills to address the needs of these students at school.

- We use collaborative teams to drive professional development opportunities at school and throughout the district.

- We plan professional development that is comprehensive, focused in its delivery, and sustained over time.

Introduction

The education of English language learners (ELLs) is the responsibility of all members of the school community, not only of the English as a second language (ESL) or bilingual education specialists. This means that all members of the school community—administrators, mainstream teachers, ESL teachers, bilingual teachers, and all support staff—must be afforded appropriate professional development opportunities so that they can develop the knowledge and skills they need to serve their ELLs. But what exactly does this mean?

Effective professional development is focused and sustained. Administrators must first identify the professional development needs of their staff—what their staff needs to know and be able to do in order to meet the needs of their ELLs—and then focus professional development activities on these specific needs. Administrators must also sustain educators' attention on the focus of the professional development activities so that educators have the opportunities they need to translate new knowledge and skills into practice. This means that the professional development opportunities that administrators offer concerning the education of ELLs must be aligned with what we know about adult learning and school improvement.

The notion of professional learning communities is key here. We know that school improvement occurs when

- Educators engage in frequent, continuous, and increasingly concrete talk about student learning and teaching practice (using data to inform these conversations).

- Educators frequently observe and provide feedback to each other, developing a shared language to describe their practices.

- Educators plan, design, and evaluate educational programs, materials, and practices together.

Schools and school districts can develop collaborative teams that meet on a regular basis to reflect on their own and each other's practice, share successes, and address the challenges they identify. Through grounded conversations about classroom practices and program development, *all* educators can deepen their understanding of how to effectively address the language and learning needs of their ELLs within the context of their regular practice.

This chapter is organized to facilitate administrators' efforts to address the professional development needs of all of their staff. The chapter begins by identifying what different members of the staff must know and be able to do. The second half of the chapter provides insight into how effective administrators can ensure that all of their staff members develop the knowledge and skills that they need not only to comply with legal mandates but also to appropriately address the needs of their particular students and communities. The chapter concludes with a survey for reflection and action that administrators can use to review the strengths of the professional development opportunities that they make available to their staff, and to identify action steps they may need to take in this area.

Question

What are the legal mandates regarding the professional development of teachers of English language learners?

☙

ADELA WEINSTEIN

Legal mandates regarding the professional development of teachers of English language learners (ELLs) vary from state to state. The first half of this discussion focuses on the specific state requirements for teachers of ELLs in Illinois. The second half looks at the federal requirements under Title III of the No Child Left Behind (NCLB) Act. Administrators are encouraged to consult their state policies, and to look into any changes in federal requirements since the time of this writing.

State Requirements Under State Regulations (23 Il. Adm. Code 228.40(c))

The state of Illinois requires that all certificated and noncertificated (that is, paraprofessional) staff working in bilingual/English as a second language (ESL) programs be annually involved in professional development activities designed to develop or expand their knowledge concerning the education of ELLs. The state regulations specify the areas that must be addressed for new program staff. These areas include basic information on instructional strategies, student identification and assessment procedures, minimum program standards, and program design. The regulations further stipulate that experienced program staff must annually participate in applicable professional development activities at least twice yearly, and identify the areas that must be addressed. These areas include current research in bilingual education, methods of teaching ELLs, language proficiency assessment, cross-cultural communication, relevant culture studies, and issue related to ELL students with disabilities.

Federal Requirements Under Title III of NCLB

The law requires, under Section 3115, that sub-grantee activities use Title III funds to implement professional development activities with the aim of improving the assessment and instruction of ELLs. Such activities are intended to involve a broad spectrum of school personnel. In addition to bilingual/ESL program staff, they should involve general classroom teachers, school administrators, and staff from community-based organizations.

The professional development activities that are to be undertaken must meet certain criteria. They must (1) help increase teachers' knowledge and skills as they relate to effective assessment and instruction of ELLs, (2) be based on scientific research (that is, research that has appeared in a juried publication), and (3) be comprehensive enough to have a meaningful and durable impact on the quality of the instructional program for ELL students. This means that workshops alone, in isolation of a comprehensive plan designed to address the needs of the program staff, would not satisfy the new requirements under this section.

Illinois has interpreted this requirement to mean that school districts must present a long-term professional plan that is designed to address the varied needs of the educators, within given priority groups. First priority is assigned to bilingual/ESL teachers who are in need of training to meet the state's definition of "highly qualified staff." Second priority is assigned to those general program teachers with ELL students in their classrooms or who will be receiving students who are transitioning from the bilingual/ESL program. Other priorities are assigned to professional development activities that involve school administrators, particularly those with responsibility for the supervision of these programs, as well as school counselors, support staff, and other ancillary personnel.

Question

What kinds of knowledge and skills does an administrator need in order to implement an effective program for English language learners?

BARBARA MARLER

An administrator needs to understand the basic processes of second language acquisition and acculturation so that he or she can support teachers in their work with English language learners (ELLs). To serve as an exemplary manager in this area, however, simple knowledge of the two processes is not sufficient. An effective administrator must know how to apply this knowledge to help and support staff in creating and managing optimal school environments for learning. Such information should be used as a guide in decision making in such areas as: planning for staff development for all educators (not just bilingual/ESL staff), allocating resources (staff, materials, and classroom space), crafting program design and supportive infrastructure (scheduling, language allocation, instructional priorities, collaboration opportunities), implementing policies and practices that will facilitate smooth student transitions (program entry, subject area transitions, and program exit), and designing parent involvement activities that will appeal to language-minority parents.

Additionally, an administrator needs to know the research in the area of effective instructional/assessment strategies for English language learners and the efficient use of standards-based data in order to serve as an instructional leader. Such knowledge allows the administrator to coach or direct teachers into creating and sustaining classroom environments that result in maximum academic achievement and linguistic progress for ELLs in the building or the program. This information also helps the administrator to accurately interpret student performance data in a meaningful way that has an impact on instruction and to communicate the data to a variety of stakeholders. Also, the administrator who is knowledgeable in these areas is a more effective and credible role model for staff as he or she demonstrates in his or her daily professional life what matters most in the education of ELLs.

Finally, an administrator needs to know the federal and state law as it applies to English language learners. Many administrators are well versed in the legal requirements and legislation and court decisions pertaining to special education students. The law in relation to ELLs is less prescriptive and less prolific than the law in relation to special education. However, it does set minimum standards for education for ELLs and ensures the protection of the civil rights of language-minority students, and is therefore essential for an administrator to know.

Question

What kinds of knowledge and skills do mainstream teachers, English as a second language teachers, bilingual teachers, and support staff need to implement an effective program for English language learners?

🍵

JoAnn (Jodi) Crandall
with Holly Stein and John Nelson

We begin by looking at the knowledge and skills needed by all teachers; then we address each of the specific categories of teachers, indicating what knowledge and skills they are likely to have, as well as those for which they are likely to need special professional development. Finally, we discuss some special considerations for school personnel (guidance counselors, school secretaries, other support staff). We also provide a list of suggestions for professional development activities to promote better understanding and skills for promoting effective instruction for English language learners (ELLs).

As indicated in Crandall (2000, p. 285) "There is substantial agreement within the educational community regarding the knowledge, skills, and attitudes (dispositions) that all teachers need to be able to effectively teach today's diverse students." One way of identifying these knowledge, skills, and attitudes is to look at the requirements for all teachers in states such as Florida or California, where there are large numbers of ELLs. Florida requires the following as topics for pre-service teacher education or professional development for those who are already teaching:

- Knowledge of first and second language acquisition and literacy development.
- Knowledge of differences in cross-cultural communication and educational experiences and expectations concerning the appropriate roles of teachers, learners, and parents in school, as well as strategies for linking instruction with language and literacy activities in the home and community.

- Strategies for adapting materials and instruction to accommodate differences in language and literacy development (methodology for teaching ELLs both academic content and English).
- Appropriate assessment strategies.

Similar areas were identified by California (where more than one-third of all ELLs reside), resulting in the restructuring of teacher licensing to include the Cross-cultural, Language, and Academic Development (CLAD) and Bilingual CLAD (BCLAD) options, which encourage all teachers to include a focus on language development, culture, and integrated language and content instruction in their teacher preparation.

Mainstream Teachers

There is a growing gap in the background, educational experiences, and expectations between teachers and the students in their classrooms. While national and state accreditation of teacher education programs may emphasize the importance of diversity and the need to "differentiate instruction" (which often translates as a need to provide for special education students), the majority of teachers have had little preparation for teaching students whose languages, cultures, and educational experiences differ substantially from their own. Thus, most mainstream teachers will need professional development on:

- Knowledge of how ELLs acquire and develop their first and second languages.
- Knowledge of how ELLs develop first and second language literacy.
- Knowledge of cross-cultural differences in communication.
- Skills in adapting instruction to accommodate students of differing levels of English proficiency (sometimes referred to as sheltered instruction, or SDAIE; see Echevarria & Graves, 1998).
- Skills in providing instruction that is appropriate for different learning styles (oral/aural, visual, kinesthetic; a preference for working alone or in groups).
- Skills in conferencing with parents who may not speak English (such as finding and working with an interpreter) and who may have different expectations about the appropriate roles and responsibilities of parents and teachers in the education of their children.
- Skills in assessing learning (often referred to as "accommodations") that provide ELLs with an opportunity to demonstrate their under-

standing in a variety of ways, without relying on oral or written English that is above the level of the proficiency of ELLs.

- Knowledge of the types of English as a second language (ESL) or bilingual programs and services offered to students and skills in working collaboratively with these teachers in coplanning or coteaching lessons.

ESL Teachers

Novice ESL teachers usually have at least an undergraduate degree in TESOL (Teachers of English to Speakers of Other Languages) or, more typically, a graduate degree, in which they will have developed at least the following;

- Knowledge of the structure of English (pronunciation, grammar, vocabulary, and so on) and skills in teaching that English structure to ELLs.

- Skills in helping ELLs to develop oral (listening and speaking) and written (reading and writing) proficiency in English.

- Knowledge of first and second language acquisition and how to teach English, through English, to ELLs with different English proficiency levels (it is not necessary to speak a student's language to teach that student English).

- Knowledge of cross-cultural communication and differences in learning styles and some skills in creating lessons for learners with diverse learning styles.

- Knowledge of the basic laws and regulations governing the education of ELLs.

They will usually have had experience learning and using another language, and they may have lived abroad or in diverse communities where they became interested in ESL. Thus, they will be prepared to have learners from different language and cultural backgrounds in their classes and to accommodate different levels of English proficiency in their instruction. Like all novice teachers, however, they will need:

- Knowledge of the policies and procedures related to ELLs in the school and district, including intake and placement procedures, the types of programs and services offered, regulations governing standardized assessments (exemptions and accommodations), and reports required.

- Knowledge of specific responsibilities, including whom to report to (principal, district supervisor, other).

- Knowledge of state or district curriculum and standards related to instruction for ELLs.

- Knowledge of the content taught in mainstream classes (through curriculum guides for the mainstream content areas or review of instructional materials) and skills for integrating academic concepts, texts, tasks, and tests into the ESL classroom.

- Skills to work collaboratively with mainstream teachers in coplanning, coteaching, or previewing/reviewing content in ESL instruction that effectively integrates academic content into the language focus.

- Knowledge of resources available to ELLs and their families and skills in accessing these resources, including working with district staff, guidance counselors, and district staff.

- Skills in managing classes with a seemingly continual intake and outflow of students (resulting from the mobility of immigrant students and the differences in the rate of development of English language proficiency).

- Skills in working with students who have experienced severe shock or trauma as victims of revolution or war.

- If teaching in more than one school, knowledge of responsibilities and skill in functioning without the support of a school or even a regular classroom.

- If teaching in an elementary school, knowledge of scheduling and skill in negotiating time for "pulling out" ELLs for ESL instruction.

- If teaching in a middle or high school with ELLs who have limited prior schooling or literacy, including students from countries in which a Creole variety of English is spoken, skills in teaching initial literacy in English (Crandall, 2003; Crandall & Greenblatt, 1999; Hamayan, 1994).

Veteran ESL teachers will have most of the same knowledge and skills as novice ESL teachers, with the following exceptions: They may be teaching with methods and techniques that do not adequately focus on the academic concepts and language and literacy needs of their students, since a focus on integrating language and content instruction is relatively new in ESL teacher preparation. They may also be unaware of or resistant to standards developed for teaching ESL and will need focused attention to curriculum or lesson planning that reflects those standards.

Like all experienced teachers, they may also be suffering from burnout, which can be especially severe for teachers who have seen a constantly shifting population of learners from different parts of the world, with different backgrounds and needs. Ways to provide needed professional development and refreshment include pairing these experienced teachers with novice ESL teachers, which can result in a mutually rewarding experience for both, and forming a relationship with a nearby university's TESOL teacher education program, which can bring teacher education faculty, teacher candidates, and graduate students in applied linguistics and TESOL as resources to the school (see Crandall, 2000). These teachers would also benefit from being able to attend a local or national TESOL conference.

Bilingual Teachers

Novice bilingual teachers who have a degree or endorsement in bilingual education have the knowledge and skills to teach content areas through the students' primary language (usually Spanish). Being bilingual and bicultural themselves, they also share a great deal with the experiences of their students and are able to provide emotional and educational support to students, who can continue to learn through their primary language while they are also learning English.

Novice bilingual teachers will have much the same knowledge and skills as ESL teachers but with the additional ability to teach through a student's primary language. They should also have preparation in teaching ESL, but may have limited experience in doing so. They will need:

- Knowledge of the policies and procedures related to bilingual learners in the school and district, including intake and placement procedures, the types of programs and services offered, regulations governing standardized assessments (exemptions and accommodations), and reports required.

- Knowledge of state or district curriculum and standards related to instruction for bilingual students.

- Skills in working collaboratively with ESL and mainstream teachers, especially in transitioning students from bilingual classes to ESL, sheltered, or mainstream classes.

- Knowledge of bilingual resources available in the community and skill in helping families, the school, and the district to access these resources, including help for guidance counselors, nurses, and other school staff who work with bilingual students.

- Skill in helping serve as a cultural interpreter for other school personnel.

- Skill in managing classes of students with diverse backgrounds, including differences in proficiency in the home language and English.

- Skills in working with students who have experienced severe shock or trauma as victims of revolution or war.

Like experienced ESL teachers, experienced bilingual teachers will need opportunities to learn new approaches and techniques for teaching bilingual learners and ways to align their instruction with new standards and assessments. They may also be experiencing teacher "burnout" and need a chance to work with a less experienced, but enthusiastic bilingual teacher in a mentoring relationship from which both will benefit. They will also benefit from being able to attend local or national NABE (National Association for Bilingual Education) or other professional conferences, participate in teaching in-service programs focused on bilingual/bicultural students, or other approaches to broaden their perspectives or provide an opportunity to share the wealth of their experiences with other teachers and school personnel.

Support Staff

Effective schooling for ELLs requires understanding and assistance from all school personnel; however, most will have had little education or experience in dealing with students from a wide range of linguistic and cultural backgrounds. We discuss briefly some of the knowledge and skills needed by key personnel in the school. Experienced ESL, bilingual teachers in the school or district personnel who work with ELLs, and university faculty who teach in ESL or bilingual teacher preparation programs can all provide training and assistance to these personnel. If there is a large population of students from the same linguistic and cultural background, it may also be helpful to have a series of schoolwide in-service programs focused on the language, cultural practices, educational experiences, and other important features of that community. A series of these programs will help all school personnel become more familiar and comfortable with the diversity of students in the school. Some schools have also provided classes in basic language instruction ("Spanish for Educators").

Guidance Counselors

Although guidance counselors have the knowledge and skills to interact with students and their families and to provide academic and other counseling, they are likely to have had almost no preparation for dealing with culturally and linguistically diverse students and families. They will need the following to help them tailor what they do for ELLs and their families:

- Understanding of basic differences in communication patterns (degrees of formality or informality, directness or indirectness, and so on) and the ability to present information in simple but noncondescending English.

- Knowledge of different educational systems and beliefs about appropriate roles and responsibilities of teachers and parents in schooling and skill in helping reluctant parents to participate in school events.

- Ability to work with an interpreter when needed.

- Knowledge of basic differences in beliefs and practices concerning mental and physical health and skills in interacting with culturally diverse students and families when discussing these topics.

- Knowledge of the ESL or bilingual programs offered in the school and skills in working with ESL and bilingual teachers in designing appropriate courses and schedules for ELLs.

- Knowledge of the educational systems and policies in the home countries of the ELLs or their parents and skill in helping both students and families to make the transition to American schools and colleges (Crandall & Greenblatt, 1999).

- For middle and high school, skill in helping ELLs to negotiate the complex path to college preparation, application, and financial aid, which may be especially difficult for students who are the first in their families to attend or even consider attending college (Crandall & Greenblatt, 1999).

Secretaries

Secretaries are often the first to meet the families of ELLs, who may come to their neighborhood school to begin enrolling their children. These secretaries may have had no prior experience or training to help them in their role as the first point of contact for ELLs. They will need:

- Knowledge of the steps required for registration and placement of new ELLs.

- Knowledge of available resources for translation or interpretation, including a roster of language capabilities of all school personnel and students who can be called upon, especially for providing emergency translation or interpretation.

- Skill in greeting new parents and students and helping them feel welcome across language barriers.
- Skill in working with ESL or bilingual teachers.

Nurses

Nurses need to have a clear plan for how they will deal with emergency situations for all students, including ELLs. They will need:

- Knowledge of how to locate interpreters and translators for emergencies.
- Knowledge of whom to contact for translation of common forms or where translated forms are available.
- Knowledge of differences in medical practices and skill in explaining new medical practices to ELLs and their parents.

Instructional Aides

Instructional aides are often a very diverse group. They may have high or limited levels of educational achievement; they may be members of the ELL's community or not. Depending on their background, they may be assigned different roles and will have different needs. It is important that administrators regularly assess the effectiveness of the aide, especially if that aide has a principal role in instruction of ELLs. At a minimum, instructional aides will need:

- Training in how to work to support ELLs in mainstream and ESL/bilingual classrooms.
- Basic knowledge of the cultural backgrounds of students and effective ways of interacting with them.
- Training in instructional strategies for teaching/tutoring ELLs that complement those used by the classroom teacher.

Custodians, Bus Drivers, Cafeteria Workers

All of these personnel will need:

- Cultural awareness and sensitivity training to help them understand differences in student behavior.

- Basic instruction in modifying their language to make it understandable to ELLs (restating in simple language, demonstrating, using gestures, enlisting the aid of someone who speaks the student's language).

Some Professional Development Approaches for All Teachers

To help all teachers to develop greater understanding of and skills in meeting the needs of ELLs, the following professional development approaches may be useful:

- Peer observation, with mainstream and ESL or bilingual teachers observing each others' classes. This is particularly helpful if the teachers share some students and if the focus is on the students rather than the teachers.

- Collaborative curriculum development or lesson planning by ESL/bilingual and mainstream teachers. This is an excellent summer inservice program where teachers work closely together and learn from each other.

- Team teaching. Opportunities for ESL/bilingual and mainstream teachers to coteach, especially in the upper grades, can provide opportunities for teachers to learn instructional strategies from each other.

- Teacher inquiry or research groups. Small groups of teachers can be encouraged to engage in an extended program that focuses on better understanding the instructional needs of ELLs.

- Participation in a professional development school or similar internship site with a university that has a TESOL or bilingual teacher education program. This will increase the number of ESL or bilingual teachers in the school, provide opportunities for mainstream teachers to have an ESL/bilingual intern for part of the internship, and may lead to a longer-term collaboration focused on the needs of ELLs in the school.

- Courses cotaught by language and mainstream teachers or university teacher educators on topics such as how to teach and assess linguistically and culturally diverse students. It is important to develop collaborations among mainstream and language teachers to encourage sharing of knowledge, experiences, and concerns.

- Parent classes (especially in ESL) or after-school or weekend sessions for parents of ELLs and the ELLs focused on academic skills such as literacy or math, or community resources. Parents of ELLs may be reluctant to come to school or to participate in parent-teacher conferences or associations, but a program that focuses on their interests and needs can bring them to school and help make them feel more comfortable.

- Professional development programs focused on the culture and educational backgrounds of immigrant students in the school or district. These programs may include shorter programs, with visits to community centers or students' homes, or a longer program that focuses on the language, educational system, teacher and student roles and responsibilities, and parental expectations of the school. A good model for the latter is a semester-long program that brings students, members of the community, and teachers together in the learning process. Students can talk about their experiences, community members can explain cultural and educational traditions, and teachers participating in the program can tutor and learn from ELLs who need additional attention (see Crandall, 2003).

Question

What levels of language proficiency in the language of instruction does a bilingual teacher need to have in order to teach effectively in a bilingual program?

DAVID ROGERS

Since acquiring English is a primary goal (or one of the primary goals) of the program for English language learners (ELLs), it is imperative that the instructor have a command of the English language, as well as an intimate understanding of language acquisition, its steps, and the instructional strategies to facilitate acquisition. The teacher also needs to be able to modulate his or her language to make it more comprehensible and to build on the student's personal experience and scaffold the academic concepts, including that of language.

If the ELL is fortunate to be supported by content instruction in the home language, the teacher delivering that instruction must possess native-like fluency and an academic level of proficiency in the language of instruction. This is often overlooked as a primary concern in developing an effective program for the ELLs at school. Finding qualified instructors who can deliver quality instruction in the home language of ELLs can be a great challenge. Many teachers are fluent in the native language of their ELLs but do not possess the knowledge, vocabulary, or experience to deliver effective instruction in that language. And many times the teacher lacks the requisite native fluency to ensure proper modeling and further development of the language.

Above all, the instructor who has the requisite native fluency and academic language level must have a clear understanding of the educational model (bilingual or ESL) selected by the school and must to be able to vary the use of the student's two languages in a way that fits into the long-term language plan for that student.

New Mexico offers the *La Prueba* examination for Spanish fluency which all teachers must pass in order to complete and receive their bilingual endorsement. This endorsement permits them to deliver instruction in the language of their endorsement. The fifteen subtests of this comprehensive examination include fluency, grammar/conventions of the language, regional dialects, academic levels of language, and so on. It is not uncommon for a teacher to retake this test in order to successfully complete at least three of the four components of the test. Referred to as a "progressive" test, once the test is successfully completed, the site administrator can be confident that the teacher possesses a good foundation for instructing in the language. Instructor Proficiency Examinations, which identify an instructor with native proficiency skill in a student's home language, are currently being developed in New Mexico in Navajo, as well as Keres, one of the primary languages of the Pueblo People.

Question

How can administrators sustain and extend teachers' professional development regarding English language learners?

❦

KELLY ESTRADA AND RENEA HAMILTON

In order to achieve the goals of an effective program for English language learners (ELLs), English as a second language (ESL) teachers, bilingual, and mainstream teachers must work together to develop comprehensive English language fluency, the types of academic English associated with specific content areas, and mastery of the content itself, whether it is in the native language or English.

Start with the End in Mind

Effective professional development is outcomes-based, where outcomes are tangible and result in significant improvements in student learning and achievement. We suggest setting attainable goals and designing a program of professional development that will provide teachers and other school personnel with the tools they need to meet these targets. It is equally important to solicit and support the participation of school administrators, who typically have a stake in closing achievement gaps between ELL and mainstream students. We have found that these administrators can provide the best grassroots leadership for schoolwide professional development efforts targeted to students such as ELLs.

Build Capacity

Since the numbers of ELLs are growing, sustaining and extending ELL professional development throughout the school and district setting is an opportunity for capacity building. Professional development for teachers of ELLs should target effective learning strategies. Such strategies should result in improved achievement for all students, but they are especially effective for

ELLs. Further, to be effective, professional development must be of the quality and duration to affect changes in classroom practice, changes that result in improvements in student learning. School administrators should therefore approach professional development as a long-term commitment. We recommend that schools develop an ongoing, sustained program of ELL professional development that incorporates core components of the school improvement plan. Using this approach, teachers will have the opportunity to translate professional development more effectively into classroom practice.

Develop Shared Goals

Take advantage of the expertise represented in district teaching staff. For example, many districts employ full- or part-time ESL teachers who have specialized knowledge in the teaching of English to speakers of other languages. ESL teachers are excellent resources for content teachers and can provide high-quality support for lesson planning, instructional adaptation, and ELL student assessment. Also, we find that teachers work together best as special teams—small groups of teachers that engage in sustained professional development experiences with colleagues and expert others (university consultants, professional development providers). Various criteria can be used to form these teams—grade level, content area, high ELL classroom population, high desire for professional development experience, low ELL student performance in a content area, and so on. Once teams are assembled, they work closely with the professional development provider to develop a program that will complement and enhance existing or planned districtwide or schoolwide professional development activities. The ELL professional development program should do the following:

1. Address the highest priority needs with respect to improving ELL student outcomes.

2. Ensure that the focus of the ELL professional development program is an extension of the professional development focus for the entire school.

3. Target those "best practice" methods and strategies that will have the most impact on ELLs, both in their specialized classroom setting and in the mainstream and the wider school setting.

Focus on Practice

High-quality teacher professional development offers a variety of educational opportunities to learn, practice, and hone the skills necessary to improve ELL student learning. Thus, teachers need to participate in such professional development experiences as:

- Face-to-face sessions
- Classroom observation and feedback with respect to the focus of professional development
- Analysis of student outcomes (such as student work from lessons in which new strategies were implemented)
- Analysis of formative and summative student data (aligning instruction with classroom goals and objectives as well as with academic standards)
- Tracking of student progress over time in relation to instructional strategies implemented
- Participating in peer coaching and mentoring relationships

Teachers need ample time to modify, discuss, reflect upon, and analyze the results of changes in their practice. Various initiatives compete for the limited professional development time that is allocated for teacher learning. Therefore, it is critical that administrators provide ample time for teams of teachers to engage in all aspects of the professional development experience. This time should be set aside throughout the year or if possible over multiple years to allow for wider dissemination across the school or district and to promote in-depth exposure and broad coverage.

Question

How do you ensure that teachers and staff have the professional development they need to implement an effective program for English language learners?

KIMBERLY THOMASSON

As the leader of a learning community with a population of English language learners (ELLs), one of my main concerns is that teachers have the knowledge to implement effective programs for ELLs. To ensure that teachers and staff have the professional development they need to implement such a program, there are four identified steps: needs assessment, timely and valuable professional development, evaluation, and reflection.

Once a clear vision is established, the next step is to find out what teachers and staff know and what they want to know. Conducting a needs assessment will give valuable information that can be used to make a plan for professional development. By conducting a simple survey with questions about the kinds of training teachers have participated in and by asking what they want to know more about, staff needs can be quickly assessed. For training to be meaningful and valuable to teachers and staff, there should be a need and a desire for the information. After identifying the information that is needed by teachers and staff, administrators should arrange for high-quality professional development that will help teachers improve instruction for ELLs.

Time is always a challenge when it comes to professional development; therefore, short, structured, meaningful, and frequent staff development activities are most successful. Facilitators must create opportunities for teachers to internalize professional development so that information learned becomes a part of daily classroom practice. It is not just about sitting and receiving information. Information and new strategies learned in the course of professional development need to be implemented in the classroom. Teachers should have time to practice new skills and talk about how they have worked. For instance, professional development could be scheduled for two hours one afternoon a week for several weeks. Once a new strategy is presented, teachers are encouraged to practice it in their classrooms. During the following session the administrator and teachers talk about the implementation, address any concerns, and share successes. At the next session a new technique, so on. This approach allows time for implementation in the classroom and continual support for teachers as they learn and try new approaches to teaching.

Once new practices for ELLs start being implemented in the classroom, it is time to evaluate whether or not those practices are having an impact on student achievement. Teachers are an integral part of this process. Their observations of student achievement, both academic and affective, give valuable information on student progress. The evaluation may include statewide test results but other kinds of data gathered at the classroom level are likely to yield more meaningful information. Administrators should be cautious and remember that any changes worth making take time to become evident. After all, the goal is long-term student achievement.

Involving teachers in the entire professional development process is key to an effective ELL program, and it creates a vested interest among teachers in the success of ELLs in the school. Through this process, teachers become

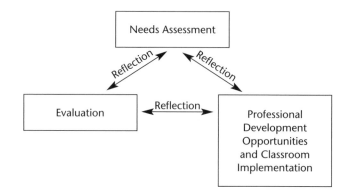

Figure 7–1. Fundamental processes in an effective professional development system.

empowered. Empowerment is the way to ensure that teachers and staff have the professional development they need to implement effective programs for ELLs. The product is a self-sustaining system that is reflective, and a cycle for continuous improvement is created. This system is represented in Figure 7–1.

María Torres-Guzman

Assessment data can be used in various areas of decision making, including the assessment of professional development needs. When I started collecting data on dual language programs in New York City, the school district and I decided to assess teacher needs in the areas of dual language education. We gave the teachers of all dual language schools a survey we had jointly constructed to ask them the following questions:

- Who are your students?
- What does your program look like?
- What instructional and evaluation issues are you facing?
- What is your educational and experiential background? How do you develop professionally, and in what areas?

Analysis of teachers' answers to these questions provided a grounded basis for decisions about program and professional development.

We looked at individual schools and at a subset of schools, and completed a comparative analysis of two types of schools. The subset consisted of literature-based dual language programs (that is, programs that are aligned with the research on effective dual language programs) that were stable. Stability was defined as being in existence for three or more years. Each of the three types of analysis gave us different information for decision making.

The data on individual schools gave administrators information about how the teachers in their schools characterized the students they worked with, whether they were on the same page with respect to the basic elements of the program they were implementing, what issues came up for them in instruction and in assessment, and how teachers saw their own development. The data from the subset of similar schools and the data from two different types of schools gave us information about the needs of dual language programs at different levels of development. Our analysis provided answers to important questions like the following:

- Are the teachers' views of the students in the dual language program accurate when compared with the results that the school district provides? What would I (the administrator) have to communicate to the staff to get them to shift their understandings?

- If the way that the teachers described the dual language program in their school did not meet the literature-based criteria for dual language programs, what was obstructing the implementation of the dual language program? What else would be needed?

- Is a dual language program the best program option, given the staff and language distribution that was possible within the context of the school?

- Would it be more appropriate to acknowledge that the program implemented at the school was actually a second language/heritage language enrichment program rather than a dual language program?

- What instructional issues did the teachers raise, and how can I ensure staff development in the area of expertise they need?

- How might we transform the way staff development is done so that it becomes more teacher initiated?

Our analysis of teachers' answers to these kinds of questions led to the identification of three levels of staff development that are necessary at the district level.

Schools that were in the beginning stages of a dual language program needed staff development on what a dual language program is and how to build one. Schools that were beyond the beginning stages needed to focus on instructional and assessment issues. Where the program was well developed instructionally, teacher-led, teacher-initiated types of professional development, such as teacher study groups and teacher inquiry projects, were important areas for staff development.

When administrators use data on how their dual language programs are interpreted and implemented at the local school level, they can develop professional development activities that target the specific needs of teachers. Such a data-driven approach can ensure that schools that say they have dual language programs actually implement dual language programs that are aligned with research in the field.

Question

What types of professional development for teachers of English language learners have you found to be effective for your staff?

❧

KELLY ESTRADA AND RENEA HAMILTON

The recommendations we make to administrators planning effective professional development programs are the result of our experiences implementing a model that incorporates each of the following four components. To synthesize the growing body of research on effective professional development (cf. NCTAF, 1996; Darling-Hammond & McLaughlin, 1995), teachers need (1) classroom-based opportunities to practice, assess, observe, and reflect on the new knowledge and skills they are learning; (2) engagement with a network of peers and experts that allows for discussion and knowledge sharing; (3) sustained, intensive experiences that include activities, such as modeling, coaching, analysis, and problem-solving, and (4) a solid foundation in research and methodologies that is derived from and addressed to teachers, their practice, and their students.

The model we have developed is the result of our experiences providing professional development about the education of English language learners (ELLs) to teachers and administrators in nine districts that are served by the

Delaware County Intermediate Unit (DCIU) in Pennsylvania. Our focus is on improving the academic achievement of ELLs in accordance with state standards for academic subjects (that is, reading, mathematics, science, and social studies). Although this focus targets a categorically defined "special needs" population, we strongly recommend that school leadership emphasize that professional development about ELLs is an integral part of school improvement efforts. Thus, we explicitly communicate to those districts with which we work that the model is applicable to any small- or large-scale initiatives targeted to improving achievement for *all students*.

The model requires a minimum of ten weeks of participation, although the timeline for implementation can be tailored to the individual school calendar for teacher professional development. There are five professional development sessions, each of which is followed by a week of observation and teacher feedback. The overall goal of the experience is to facilitate the implementation of research-based sheltered instruction strategies by targeting the strategies to teachers' academic goals for ELLs. These materials (Short & Echevarria, 1999) address the specific needs of teachers working with ELL students at the elementary levels.

A critical design feature is the provision of an ongoing and sustained professional learning experience that engages teachers in a community, both within their own school and across districts that participate in the project. In our model, small teams of content teachers, peer coaches, professional development providers, and university consultants constitute a learning community. Learning community members participate in professional development sessions, discussions, reflections, analysis, critical inquiry, and application to classroom practice through problem solving with one another over an extended period of time, both face-to-face and online. Peer coaches, who are generally English as a second language (ESL) teachers experienced with sheltered instruction methods, facilitate classroom teachers' participation in the professional learning experience by assisting them in the formulation of instructional goals, conducting classroom observations of new methods of instruction, providing teachers with feedback on implementation, and analyzing ELL lesson outcomes in relation to the instructional goal. The peer coaches also assist teachers by coplanning and instructional modeling.

Classroom observations and feedback are provided via an observational rubric that targets specific strategies presented and modeled for content teachers over the course of the professional development experience. In conjunction with each session, teachers develop instructional goals from what they have learned. Classroom observations focus on the degree to which these goals were achieved. In addition to providing observational feedback, peer coaches assist teachers in reviewing and analyzing ELL work samples collected from lessons in which sheltered instruction methods were implemented. The framework of analysis for student work samples are the individual teacher's instructional goals developed with reference to the ongoing professional development experience.

Our experiences to date in implementing this model in one school district in southeastern Pennsylvania have been positive. The strengths of the model were related to our teacher-centered approach. As most professional development workshops tend to be short-term experiences, ours benefited from being both ongoing and sustained and from having a focused curriculum. The teachers we worked with were released early one day per week for professional development. This dispensation allowed us the opportunity to provide immediate feedback and follow-up sessions after every classroom observation. Feedback sessions focused on the goals classroom teachers developed in relation to the ELL professional development session in which they participated. The teachers, who participated in grade-level teams, had increased opportunities for interaction with peer coaches and with one another.

Given that this was an elective experience rather than one that was mandated by the school administration, we found that teacher participation varied. To support teacher participation, we recommend that the school administration encourage and support participation and that teacher-based incentives be offered. Further, teacher schedules must allow for adequate time for participation in the entire cycle of the professional development experience. Finally, although many efforts were made to foster and maintain a high level of teacher engagement, we encountered various forms of resistance to ELLs and their needs. The resistance occurred most often in relation to our expectations that teachers would make changes in classroom practice to meet the needs of ELLs. Thus, it is imperative that a "whole school" approach be taken to integrating ELL professional development with school-wide improvement efforts.

☙

LYNNE DUFFY

A pebble dropped into a lake causes a ripple effect. As the waves form and move away from the original entry site, they get bigger and bigger, spreading to distant shores. The same effect is seen over and over again with teaching: by introducing one teacher at a time to new practices, modeling those practices, and providing observational feedback, we can see the circles of information and best practice expanding throughout the school and school district. Sometimes we need individual teachers or a grade-level team to start a practice, work through the training, implement the strategy or practice, and fine-tune it to fit the needs of the particular grade levels, team, school, or student population. It is the willing pioneer who then can become the mentor to others. These teachers can be bilingual or English as a second language (ESL) teachers, or they can be mainstream teachers.

For the experienced teacher, it is usually fairly easy to go to a conference, listen to the description of a new idea or strategy, and go back to the classroom and implement it. A change in practice is more difficult when a more complex strategy is introduced, or a new area of teaching is addressed, or when the new practice requires a shift in teaching philosophy. For many teachers today, it may be the way we teach or think about English language learners (ELLs). Changes such as these are a process, not an event. Staff development, therefore, should also be a process, not just an institute day.

The most successful experiences I have had with teachers have come from working through a process. Typically it starts at a workshop. Often I ask the teachers, as an exiting activity, to list what they have learned and what they would like to learn more about. I also ask them to identify a time I could come to their classroom to continue the discussion. I then meet individually with the teacher, and I am better able to get a sense of what the teachers know about a specific strategy or topic and what they need to know. Typically we talk about the students' strengths and needs in the classroom. We figure out a time frame and plan a series of lessons. I then come to the classroom and usually implement the first few lessons. We team-teach the next lesson or two, and then the teacher takes over. Sometimes the teacher is able to implement the lessons from the start. Those teachers often ask me simply to observe and provide feedback on their teaching. At other times the process takes longer. During the first few classes I model the strategy. After each lesson, I sit down with the teacher and explain how I plan and execute the lesson. It is after they see the process done that they are ready to start planning and executing the lessons themselves.

Differentiation with teachers is as necessary as it is with students in the classroom. Modeling strategies after instruction is the most powerful and meaningful way to get teachers to understand and use them. This requires time: time to discuss, plan, observe, execute, debrief, and adapt; time to introduce the strategy, time to plan, time to watch or observe the strategy in action in one's own classroom. The more thorough we are, the more confident we become about sharing our experiences with others and spreading the knowledge.

Question

How should an administrator evaluate teachers of English language learners?

JACK FIELDS

Few tasks required of a teacher supervisor are more intimidating then having to evaluate a teacher who is teaching children in a language other than English when the evaluator is a monolingual English speaker. Too often the evaluator opts to limit his or her observations to classes of English as a second language (ESL), which is unfair both to the teacher and to the children being served. Limiting observations to ESL lessons does not provide a full spectrum of observations in the process of retention or dismissal. As a bilingual program director working with many such principals and supervisors, I have identified a number of preparations and strategies that can be done to help administrators provide more effective and relevant observations when first language instruction is being observed.

Preparation

Smaller districts with fewer resources usually depend on the building administrator to make evaluative decisions regarding staff. Even in large school districts where an ESL or bilingual director is employed by the district, evaluations leading to continuing employment or dismissal are usually the responsibility of the building administrator. This often makes administrators uncomfortable and threatens teachers, who feel they are being evaluated by someone who may not understand bilingual/English language learner (ELL) instruction. The risk of continuing the employment of an ineffective teacher because of discomfort with the language of instruction only endangers the teaching of more children for years to come.

The following *program questions* need to be answered before observing the teacher.

1. What is the philosophy and program design that are being implemented in your district?

2. What are the entry and exit criteria for children being served?

3. How is the appropriate language of instruction determined, and who determines it? (In my first job as a teacher, I simply switched to Spanish whenever a supervisor entered the room, and they rarely stayed long. They almost never asked what I was doing.) In many rooms, the appropriate language of instruction may be different for different students in different subjects.

4. What academic performance does the English-only teacher expect from students transitioned into their rooms?

The following *classroom questions* need to be asked of the teacher when possible before the observation.

1. The Observation: What are the objectives of the lesson? How does the lesson fit into a series of lessons or objectives that are being taught? What activities will be used? How will the teacher evaluate the outcome of the instruction? If the language of instruction is a language that you do not know, having this information in advance will help you better understand what is going on in the room during the observation.

2. The Students: What assessment has been made of the students to establish the need for the instruction? What prior experience have the children had in preparation for the class? What special needs, if any, exist in the class? Obtain a seating chart so that in the follow-up conference you can refer to specific children in context with activities or behavior observed.

3. The Teacher: What professional preparation or teaching experience has the teacher had before entering the classroom? This background information may be helpful in developing later recommendations and providing support that the teacher needs.

Observation

The evaluator should arrive prior to the observation time to be able to observe how the class is initiated. Nothing is more frustrating for the teacher than the feeling that the evaluator missed something important at the beginning of the lesson that affected the observation later during the class.

Good instruction is normally good instruction, regardless of the language. We want to see classrooms where children are interactively involved in the lesson. The evaluator should observe children and their reactions to the lesson or the presentation. The evaluator should also remember to make notes regarding specific situations using the seating chart and time for conferencing later.

Behavior

Does the children's behavior reflect that they know the class rules and follow them? Does the teacher have to constantly remind them of rules (not yet established or new for the visitor)? Do the children appear to be safe and comfortable in their interaction in the classroom? Or are they afraid to participate?

Instruction

Look for the qualities you see in any good classroom. Who does most of the talking? Are children asked to explain or clarify? Be aware of the length of children's responses. Short answers usually are an indication that lower level questions are being asked. Do many or all children have the opportunity to participate? After an assignment is given, are the children able to do it? Move around the room when children are doing seatwork and ask children what they are doing. Observe the support the teacher offers children when they are doing seatwork.

Conference

Have the conference as soon after the observation as possible. This will allow the teacher to respond more meaningfully when you ask about the class. Ask teachers to evaluate their own lesson by sharing what worked well, what they would change, and so forth. The best teachers learn to evaluate their own and their students' work. Remember that "bilingual teachers" are often hired for their language skills and may have little background in research and instruction of English language learners. Much of the responsibility of the evaluator will fall in the area of determining what kind of a learner the teacher is and making decisions about growth potential of the candidate and whether or not the candidate shows sufficient promise in his or her professional development for continuing employment. It is critical that the evaluator communicate a willingness to support the candidate in professional growth, using the evaluation process as a tool.

Begin the conference by having the teacher review the lesson plan (preparation) and the lesson implementation. Ask the teacher to share his or her own observation of the lesson or class. It is very important for teachers to develop the skill and willingness to self-evaluate. Using your notes and seating chart, ask the teacher to explain events or activities that were of concern to you or that you did not understand. If you are unsure of whether or not the appropriate language was being used in a particular lesson, ask the teacher to explain why the language was used or what other issues interfered with the teacher's doing what ideally should have been done. If you lack confidence in the teacher's answers, contact someone with expertise in the field so that your facility and students will develop appropriate instructional designs.

Question

What are recommended resources for the professional development of teachers who work with English language learners?

NANCY CLOUD

One of the challenges administrators face in providing professional development to teachers and other personnel is locating resources for the great variety of staff development that is possible. Staff development can take many forms, including

- Specialized graduate course work
- Attendance at conferences, learning institutes, or workshops
- On-site, sustained staff development provided by district experts or external consultants
- Networking among schools or programs
- Mentoring or peer coaching in classrooms
- School-based collegial circles or study groups
- Hands-on working sessions among colleagues designed to improve assessment or curriculum

Staff development initiatives work best when they are focused on particular school improvement goals and in a format that would best respond to the personnel's level of expertise, role, and student population served. Teachers and other personnel need to feel that they are receiving valuable information that is advancing their practice. Quality staff development needs to be reality-based, practical, and delivered from trusted sources. Administrators also need to provide incentives for participation in professional development, such as financial support (paying the cost of conference registration or course work), release time, or professional recognition (letters for their personnel file, acknowledgements in district newsletters).

Where can busy administrators go to locate useful resources for their local staff development purposes? The following listing is designed to assist with this process.

Graduate Course Work and National Board Certification.

Graduate programs and course work can be used to substantially advance the knowledge or skills of assessment and instructional personnel; sometimes resulting in new teaching endorsements or licenses. Often course work can be offered on-site through continuing education at a reduced cost. As an additional incentive, cost-sharing arrangements can be implemented in which participants pay a portion of the cost and the school or district pays a portion. Teachers of English to Speakers of Other Languages (TESOL, www.tesol .org) maintains a directory of teacher education programs with course work specific to working with English language learners (ELLs). Beyond delivering course work, college faculty working in these programs might also serve as partners for district- or school-based initiatives.

Another option for expert teachers is to seek national board certification. The National Board for Professional Teaching Standards (NBPTS, www.nbpts .org) has developed standards in English as a new language (ENL) for this purpose. Administrators can support teachers by providing access to support groups while teachers prepare their portfolios, release time to complete the requirements, or financial rewards upon completion.

Professional Associations

A variety of associations provide professional development resources, most notably, the National Association for Bilingual Education (NABE, www.nabe .org) and TESOL (www.tesol.org). The corresponding state affiliates of these two international associations offer parallel in-state professional development opportunities. In addition to conferences and institutes, professional associations provide Web-based discussion forums, online courses, and a variety of published professional development resources. Associations also exhibit professional development and classroom resources at conferences that can support local professional development initiatives, and they publish periodicals focused on best practices in teaching and assessment. Some journals are now offering continuing education units for reading and responding to topic-focused issues. All of these mechanisms can be used as specialized sources of professional development.

Other associations with specialized resources to tap include the following:

- The International Reading Association (IRA, www.ira.org)
- The National Council of Teachers of English (NCTE, www.ncte.org)
- The National Association for the Education of Young Children (NAEYC, www.naeyc.org)
- The Council for Exceptional Children (CEC, www.cec.sped.org), which offers a bi-annual Symposium on the Education of Culturally and Linguistically Diverse Exceptional Students)

State Departments of Education and Funded Centers

State education departments receive funding specifically earmarked for professional development. In addition to statewide institutes and workshops, state-funded personnel may be available to conduct in-house trainings. Grant and foundation-funded centers also provide professional development resources. For example, the National Clearinghouse for English Language Acquisition (NCELA, www.ncela.gwu.edu) of the Office of English Language Acquisition, Language Enhancement and Academic Achievement for Limited English Proficient Students (OELA, U.S. Department of Education); the Center for Applied Linguistics/CAL (www.cal.org); and the Center for Research on Education, Diversity and Excellence (CREDE, http://crede.uscs.edu) are a few of the funded centers to offer online support, published materials, and professional development resources (videos, CD-ROMs) or special training events.

School/Program Visits and Demonstration Teaching

Sometimes the best way to offer professional development is to visit a school or program in your region known to be effective. In this manner teachers and administrators can witness firsthand the type of assessment, curriculum, and instruction that makes a difference in the achievement of ELLs, and can ask questions that help them better implement school-improvement initiatives. Similarly, demonstration teaching sessions conducted in live classrooms can often clarify for teachers how to implement research-based teaching approaches better than merely reading about them. Video-recorded teaching demonstrations also serve this purpose.

Publishers of Professional Development Materials

Professional reading is a main contributor to professional development whether done in a collegial circle, in conjunction with credit-bearing course work, or independently. It would be impossible to mention all the publishers of this type of material but, in addition to the professional associations and funded centers already mentioned, some representative publishers specializing in this type of material include Heinemann (www.heinemann.com), Hampton-Brown (www.hampton-brown.com), and Pearson Education (www .pearsoned.com/us-school/index.htm). Publishers also offer professional development to schools and districts through consultants and representatives, particularly as it relates to their curriculum materials. Some offer online courses around their professional books or video-taped series designed to advance teaching skills in classrooms.

Letter to an administrator:
From a member of the school leadership team

Dear Mrs. Henderson,

As the school year draws to a close, I would like to share with you my thoughts about our building's staff development plan. Because of my role on our school improvement team, many colleagues share their ideas and concerns with me. As you know, staff members and parents are upset about the budget constraints that we are facing for the coming year. I think that this can be an opportunity for us to rethink what is done in staff development.

Our school has offered each teacher the benefit of attending a professional conference or workshop. It's nice to hear new ideas and to find out what other schools are doing. However, I always come away a little disappointed. Each time I harbor the naïve hope that this workshop will offer the *key* to becoming a good teacher. No presenter has ever accomplished that. I come away with some new ideas or activities, but big changes seem difficult to implement. Often I don't seem to have the appropriate materials, the necessary time, or the right students to enact the suggested ideas. Sometimes I implement some of the new instructional strategies, but they don't seem to work out well, so I go back to doing things the "old way."

This budget cutback could be the opportunity for us to change our staff development into a more facility-based approach. I believe that we have a lot of expertise and talent within our staff. We could share the strategies that work with our students, our curriculum, and our textbooks. To implement continuous improvement we need the time for collaboration and planning. Our staff is very dedicated. I believe that if we agreed on a focus for building-wide improvement we could gather the research and instructional activities to address that issue. We don't need to travel to the city or hire an "expert." We have the talent and expertise within our staff or within our district to work toward improving this area.

For example, with the growing bilingual population in our school, one of the critical issues for us to address in staff development is the effective instruction of second language learners. Certainly, we need to provide guidance for our bilingual and ESL teachers. They seem to have less experience than most of the staff members at our school. So they need additional support in classroom management and effective instructional techniques. They may also need some specific guidance in fostering the development of language and literacy for students whose native language is not English. However, those insights would be helpful for our *whole* staff. The strategies that are valuable for our bilingual and ESL classes would help all staff work with students as they are mainstreamed from ELL classes. In addition, most teachers have children in our classes who speak English in school but another language at home. So this need for staff development includes all teachers.

As we work with you to plan for next year, it is important for the school improvement team, the budget committee and the staff as a whole to develop a shared vision. Our data should lead us to select one or two areas for instructional improvement that all teachers will work to address. This will lead to a focus for school-based professional development. This alignment with our comprehensive plan will provide an opportunity for our staff to work collaboratively to meet learning goals and maximize the effectiveness of our staff development funds.

I thank you for the opportunity to share my thoughts. I look forward to working with you to make our school a great place to learn for both students and staff!

Sincerely,

Lore Levin

Survey for Reflection and Action

This survey reflects the guiding principles for effective professional development that were articulated in the introduction to the chapter. Survey the professional development opportunities that are available for the staff at your school/school district. Use a + when your school/school district is exemplary in this area, a √ when your school/school district is working on this aspect of your professional development opportunities, and a − when there is no evidence of this guiding principle in place in your school/school district. Use a ? when you don't know. Use the results of your survey of the professional development offered in your school/school district to determine what, if any, actions you should take to improve your professional development plan.

All educators who work with ELLs have the knowledge and skills that they need to address the needs of ELLs at our school.

____ Mainstream teachers

____ Bilingual teachers

____ ESL teachers

____ Administrators

____ Resource teachers (e.g., special education, reading specialists)

____ Support staff (e.g., counselors, secretaries)

____ Community liaisons

School-based collaborative teams drive the professional development opportunities at our school/school district.

____ Educators at our school/in our district engage in frequent, continuous, and increasingly concrete talk about student learning and teaching practice.

____ Educators have developed a shared language to describe their practices.

____ Educators use data on actual student learning (e.g., formative assessments) to guide professional development.

____ Educators use data on actual teaching practice (e.g., videotapes and/or observations of teaching) to guide professional development.

____ Educators have ongoing opportunities to observe each other's practice.

____ Educators have opportunities to provide feedback to each other in a supportive, non-threatening environment.

____ Educators plan lessons, programs, materials, and practices together.

____ Educators review and evaluate lessons, programs, materials, and practices together.

Our professional development is comprehensively planned, focused in its delivery, and sustained over time.

_____ Educators in our school/school district regularly assess professional development strengths and needs based on new developments in the field, reflective conversations about practice, evidence of student performance, and observation of teaching practice.

_____ Educators have a comprehensive professional development plan with realistic and attainable goals to address professional development needs.

_____ Professional development focuses attention on specific strategies that target specific goals and that are to be implemented in practice.

_____ Educators have opportunities to implement new strategies in their practice.

_____ Educators observe the implementation of new strategies (self and/or peer observation).

_____ Educators reflect on the implementation of new strategies, using classroom-based data on student learning and/or teaching practice to inform the reflective conversation.

_____ Educators continuously identify professional development needs, and the cycle begins again.

Strengths of our professional development regarding English language learners _____

_____

Action steps _____

_____

References and Additional Resources

Center for Applied Linguistics. A complete set of digests and Q & As for teachers and other school personnel can be found at www.cal.org.

Center for Applied Linguistics. (2000). *Enhancing English language learning in elementary classrooms.* Washington, DC: Center for Applied Linguistics and Delta Systems Co.

Center for Multilingual, Multicultural Research, University of Southern California, Rossier School of Education. Available at http://www-rcf.usc.edu/~cmmr/BEResources .html. Provides links to the major centers, networks, and Web sites; full-text articles, and PD resources.

Crandall, J.A. (2000). The role of the university in preparing teachers for a linguistically diverse society. In J. W. Rosenthal (Ed.), *Handbook of undergraduate second language education* (pp. 279–299). Mahwah, NJ: Erlbaum.

Crandall, J. A. (2003). They DO speak English: World Englishes in U.S. schools. *ERIC/ CLL News Bulletin,* Summer/Fall.

Crandall, J. A., & Greenblatt, L. (1999). Teaching beyond the middle: Meeting the needs of underschooled and high-achieving immigrant students. In M. R. Basterra (Ed.), *Excellence and equity in education for language minority students: Critical issues and promising practices* (pp. 43–80). Washington, DC: Mid-Atlantic Equity Center, American University.

Cuevas, G.J. (1994). Mathematics learning in English as a second language. *Journal for Research in Mathematics Education, 15,* 134–144.

Darling-Hammond, L., & McLaughlin, M. W. (1995). Policies that support professional development in an era of reform. *Phi Delta Kappan, 76,* 597–604.

Echevarria, J., & Graves, A. (1998). *Sheltered content instruction: Teaching English-language learners with diverse abilities.* Boston: Allyn & Bacon.

Hamayan, E. (1994). Language development of low-literacy students. In F. Genesee (Ed.), *Educating second language children: The whole child, the whole curriculum, the whole community* (pp. 278–300). Cambridge, UK: Cambridge University Press.

Jamison, J. (1999). *Enriching content classes for secondary ESOL students: Complete inservice training materials for middle and high school content.* Washington, DC: Center for Applied Linguistics and Delta Systems Co.

Killion, J. (2002). *Assessing impact: Evaluating staff development.* Oxford, OH: National Staff Development Council.

Mills, G. E. (2003). *Action research: A guide for the teacher researcher* (2nd ed.). Upper Saddle River, NJ: Pearson Education.

Office of Bilingual Education and Minority Language Affairs. (1995). *Model strategies in bilingual education: Professional development.* Washington, DC: U.S. Department of Education. Available at http://www.edu.gov/pubs/ModStrat/index.html.

Olsen, L., Crandall, J. A., Jaramillo, A., & Peyton, J. K. (2000). Diverse teaching strategies for diverse learners: Immigrant children. In R. W. Cole (Ed.), *More strategies for educating everybody's children.* Alexandria, VA: American Society for Curriculum and Development.

National Commission on Teaching and America's Future. (1996). *What matters most: Teaching for America's future.* New York: Columbia University, Teachers College.

National Staff Development Council (2001). *Standards for staff development.* Oxford, OH: Author.

Rosenthal, J. W. (1996). Teaching science to language minority students. Clevedon, UK: Multilingual Matters.

Short, D., & Echevarria, J. (1999). *The sheltered observation protocol: A tool for teacher-researcher collaboration and professional development* (Educational Practice Report No. 3). Santa Cruz, CA, and Washington, DC: Center for Research on Education, Diversity & Excellence.

Sparks, D., & Hirsh, S. (1997). *A new vision for staff development.* Alexandria, VA: Association for Supervision and Curriculum Development.

Chapter 8

When Challenges Arise

> ### *Guiding Principles*
>
> - We assess the special needs of our English language learners as challenges arise.
> - We assess the special needs of our school regarding English language learners as challenges arise.
> - We provide the most appropriate services available to address the student and school needs that we identify.
> - We collect, analyze, and use valid and reliable data on the special needs of English language learners to drive our decision making when a challenging situation arises.

Introduction

English language learners (ELLs), like any other group of students, come from varied backgrounds and have extremely different skills and abilities. ELLs come from different language backgrounds, with different levels of proficiency in their native language and with different literacy skills. They come with different levels of English language proficiency, and they come with different types of schooling. Some of them arrive having experienced significant trauma in their lives. They come from different socioeconomic backgrounds, and they bring with them varied cultural norms and values. They arrive at our schools at different times of the year, at different ages, and with different expectations and dreams.

Despite the fact that diversity creates a richer environment for everyone, diversity can also bring challenges. Thus, ELLs who seem to have higher levels of difficulty than would be expected in school, those who have specific learning disabilities, those who arrive at school past first or second grade not having had the expected level of education, and those who arrive in the middle of the year do pose challenges for their teachers and schools. ELLs who speak less commonly taught languages (Mixtec, Pashto) may also pose challenges because schools may not have ready access to bilingual resources in these languages.

This chapter is organized around the questions that administrators are asking about how to address these kinds of challenges as they arise. The responses in this chapter are from experts who have experienced challenges like these in their schools, and they offer insight into ways that schools can meet the needs of all of their ELLs while they enrich and strengthen the diverse environment at school for all of their students. The chapter concludes with a survey for reflection and action that administrators can use to determine how prepared they are to address the challenges that arise for their English language learners and for their school overall.

Question

What do you do when English language learners seem to take a particularly long time to acquire English? How do you even know what that is due to?

Nancy Cloud

In answering this question, it is important to remember that there is tremendous variation in the rate of language acquisition among children and youth. The statistics often cited indicate are that it should take up to two years to develop everyday language for social interactions and five to seven years to develop academic English sufficient to compete with monolingual agemates. However, these figures are averages compiled from a wide range of individual learning times. I have worked with students who took off like rockets and others who plodded along but continued to progress. Learning itself is often uneven, with periods of limited development followed by rapid growth spurts. Obviously, our programs, teaching expertise, teaching methods, and curriculum all interact to influence student progress.

With all of this in mind, I like to take a step-by-step approach to analyzing the situation when it seems that students are taking a long time to acquire English:

First: *Look at the Student's Opportunity to Learn.* To improve the learning situation, we have to understand (1) any significant disruptions in schooling, (2) the types of programs and services that have been provided and the quality, comprehensiveness, and continuity of those services, (3) the expertise of the individuals working with the student, (4) the teaching approaches that have been used with the student and their effectiveness, (5) the responsiveness and known effectiveness of the curriculum for English language learners (ELLs), and (6) the level of involvement of the family and the supports that are available outside of school to extend school learning. Teachers should work on improving these elements first to improve students' growth in English.

Second: *Look for Any Constricting Influences.* Because the status of the primary language has a great effect on the development of the second language, we need to look closely at the first language. Is the student's first language well developed? Is the family clear on using their most proficient language with their child at home, rather than using an underdeveloped language that would constrict both the quantity and quality of language used in the home? If English is used at home, have we documented the characteristics of the child's speech community? Do we know what variety of English is spoken and any limitations (such as limited vocabulary) that may exist in the parents' proficiency that could explain patterns that we see in the child? When bilingualism is the goal, both languages must be well supported, rather than one favored at the expense of the other. We especially want to avoid the situation Jim Cummins calls the "square wheel deal" (picture a bicycle with two flat tires) in which neither language has been adequately developed to support learning.

What about motivation? Is the child motivated to learn English, and does the child feel accepted by and comfortable with English speakers? How is the affective climate in which the child is learning English? Is the child drawn in to communication with English speakers or rejected by them? Does the child feel encouraged and supported or negatively judged and overly corrected?

What about important learning differences? Have the child's experiential background knowledge and culturally determined learning characteristics really been taken into account in instruction or only given lip service? How is the room arranged? How are students grouped?

What learning styles are favored? Are the participant structures (ways students are asked to participate) culturally compatible? Has the child been given sufficient learning opportunities and feedback for his or her unique needs? All of these things are known to influence language development, and to the extent that we strengthen these, we contribute to more successful English acquisition.

Third: Look for Learning Difficulties in the Child. Only after we have assurance that all of the requisite learning conditions are fully met—the programs, learning conditions, curriculum and instruction—should we suspect learning difficulties on the part of the child. At that point we will seek to understand the possible disabilities that may be in our way (sensory, neurological, cognitive, social/emotional) so that we can account for them in the approaches and materials we choose to better support the learner.

❧

ESTER DE JONG

English language learners (ELLs) face the challenge of simultaneously acquiring content matter and English, in addition to adapting to a new culture. Since their native English-speaking peers continue to progress cognitively and linguistically, ELLs are trying to catch up with a moving target. As a result, it may take a long time for ELLs to catch up with their peers and to be able to demonstrate their learning at age-appropriate levels on standardized achievement or reading tests. It is well known that a wide range of social and individual factors influence the rate of second language (L2) development. Furthermore, the quality of services offered to ELLs and the resources available to ELLs and their teachers play a crucial role. Together, these factors can either accelerate L2 development or significantly slow down the process of mastering English for academic purposes.

If a second language learner takes longer to acquire academic language proficiency, it does not therefore imply that the child has a learning or language disability. More information must be gathered to see if a student has a disability and should receive special education services. Determining whether the lack of progress is due to a disability or to normal second language development is challenging, particularly if the school or district does not have access to bilingual services. Standardized tests used for determining disabilities are generally inappropriate for ELLs because of issues of validity, norming groups, and language and cultural bias. As a result of inappropriate identification, many ELLs are overrepresented in special education services. More recently there has also been a trend toward failing to appropriately identify disabilities, leading to underrepresentation.

When setting expectations for L2 development, schools must carefully consider how the learning context may have affected a particular student's trajectory in English. Specifically, teachers and administrators need to take into account whether the following factors that define effective instructional practices have existed or are currently in existence:

1. High quality of services offered to ELLs. A curriculum should be implemented that reflects ELLs' linguistic and cultural experiences and that has high expectations for ELLs.
    - The curriculum should valuing L1 as a resource and use the students' native language for instruction.
    - The curriculum should use appropriate sheltered English teaching techniques.

2. The use of ongoing assessments that document individual students' annual growth in language and content development.
    - Authentic assessments that assess the curriculum being taught should be used.
    - Scaffolding assessments for students' L2 proficiency as well as L1 skills should be undertaken.

We also need to take into account the influence of background variables on individual student's language and literacy development and content learning, including (but not limited to):

- L1 schooling experiences and L1 literacy background
- Sociopolitical context of the minority group in the United States and the immigration history
- Individual factors, such as age, personality, attitudes, and motivation

Given current trends in accountability, administrators play a key role in mediating the tension between standardized expectations of growth for ELLs and the actual growth that can be expected, given the learning context. On the one hand, they must ensure that all the elements of quality instruction are in place for ELLs and provide teachers with the necessary resources and professional development. On the other hand, they must advocate for ELLs by understanding the limitations of standardized tests for ELLs and by being able to appropriately interpret achievement data within the context of their school.

Question

How can we distinguish between a language difficulty and a learning disability?

CRISTINA SANCHEZ-LOPEZ

Administrators can create school environments that make it easier for school staff to find out what could be causing academic difficulties for English language learners (ELLs). Three factors can greatly affect the school-based pre-referral team's efficacy. First, an ELL's difficulty cannot be considered a disability when it is observed only in the child's second language (English). It is important that the pre-referral group have access to information in the child's primary or home language(s), no matter the age or grade level of the child. It is critical, then, that the school administrator create an environment in which children's languages and cultures are treated as resources at all times rather than as problems or barriers. Schools can successfully invite the children's languages and cultures into the school even in multilingual settings (see, e.g., Walker, Edwards, & Blacksell, 1996).

The second factor that helps pre-referral teams sort out this issue is when school administrators schedule ongoing professional development programs that address second language acquisition, sheltered instruction, literacy and language instruction across the curriculum, and other topics related to ELLs. All school staff, both general education and special education teachers, administrators, speech and language pathologists, school psychologists, social workers, counselors, and other staff, must have a working knowledge of these topics in order to accurately interpret the student's difficulty and be able to offer appropriate interventions.

The third factor that could influence the decision of whether to place an ELL child in special education classes or not has to do with the extent to which appropriate literacy instruction has been provided for the ELL population. As ELLs become more proficient in English, they are able to "word call" but have limited reading comprehension. Teachers misinterpret word calling as actual reading, which leads to difficulties across all content areas and sometimes to the incorrect diagnosis of reading disability. If administrators shared with their teachers the recommendations of the International

Reading Association (2001) to "provide initial literacy instruction in the children's primary language whenever feasible and make certain that ELLs develop some measure of oral language proficiency before introducing formal reading instruction in English," more ELLs would get the literacy instruction they needed, no matter what their grade level. However, teachers beyond first grade would have to learn about reading theories and methodologies. ELLs benefit when their oral language and literacy is supported across the content areas and throughout their school experience.

There are many recommendations that influence how well a school does in diagnosing ELLs' learning disabilities and avoiding overrepresentation of ELLs in special education, but I have focused on three areas in which school administrators could have a great impact. Principals can create an environment at their schools that invites the students' languages and cultures into each classroom. The students' languages are viewed as resources, thereby ensuring that all school staff will have access to primary language data at any time and will be able to determine whether the difficulties that evince when the children use English are also present when they use their other languages. If so, this observation might point to a more intrinsic cause of the problem. Principals can also seek out professional development opportunities for their entire staff related to second language learning theory. This would help team members better interpret the possible causes for an ELL student's difficulty. Finally, all staff should learn about how important primary language literacy is as a predictor of second language literacy development, as well as learn about how to support language and literacy across the content areas and throughout the grade levels as a means of avoiding unnecessary reading difficulties and hence providing ELLs access to the academic content and concepts.

Question

How can we best serve English language learners who do have special needs, such as a disability?

☙

NANCY CLOUD

The best way we can serve English language learners (ELLs) who have special learning needs is to place them in classrooms with qualified teachers who can simultaneously address their cultural, linguistic, and disability characteristics. An "add-on" service approach, whereby ELLs are placed in unmodified special education settings (with special education teachers who have not been prepared to serve second language learners) and then receive some unmodified English as a second language (ESL) or bilingual support services (by ESL or bilingual teachers who have not been prepared to serve students with disabilities), does not make a quality program, despite everyone's best intentions.

What is needed are special educators (or inclusion teams of special and general educators) who can deliver well-integrated services because they have the specialized professional preparation required to fully meet *all* of the students' learning needs—as a second language learner, as a culturally diverse learner, and as a special needs learner. Such teachers would have knowledge and skills from the fields of special education, second language education, and bilingual/multicultural education.

These teachers would select teaching methods and materials that are known to be effective with students with disabilities and at the same time known to be effective with second language learners. Such methods might include (1) cooperative learning, (2) visual learning approaches (use of graphic organizers, maps, webs, graphics), (3) multisensory and whole body teaching approaches (arts-based learning approaches using music, drama, and visual arts; total physical response), (4) experience-based learning approaches (such as language experience approach; discovery learning), (5) process-based teaching approaches (readers/writers workshop; traits-based writing approaches), and (6) technology-based learning approaches (assistive technology, interactive CD-ROMs). Curriculum materials would also be selected to match the child's learning needs, culturally and experientially determined background knowledge, and language characteristics. Multicultural materials would be plentiful.

Teachers would have clear goals for learners in terms of language development, literacy development, and academic learning, and they would know how to create culturally responsive learning environments, as well as how to scaffold instruction to bypass identified disabilities and to support learning through a second language.

To serve ELLs with special needs we would carefully link in-school efforts with the student's other primary learning environment, the home. We would provide the best guidance to parents with respect to their language use with their child, namely, to consistently use their most proficient language with their child using communication that is developmentally appropriate for the child.

In cases where the language of instruction at school is different from the home language, we would link our efforts at the *learning objective level,* rather than ask parents to use a language in which they have limited proficiency, which would restrict both the quantity and quality of the language used. This would mean that if at school we are working in English on labeling objects or describing actions or taking notes while listening, these objectives would be worked on at home in the native language. In other words, we would link our efforts at the goal or objective level and let the language of instruction vary. In this way, the child would be assisted to build and transfer desired skills across the two primary learning environments.

Finally, all service providers working with the student (speech and language clinician, counselor, occupational therapist) need to be on the same page regarding the culturally responsive learning conditions and teaching approaches to be used. They must be given the time needed to carefully coordinate their efforts so that together they fully address the child's cultural, linguistic, and learning needs. These are the major guidelines to follow in providing quality services to ELLs with special learning needs (Cloud, 2002, 2005; Hearne, 2000; Winzer & Mazurek, 1998).

Question

How should we deal with overage English language learners who come to school with a low level of literacy in their first language?

☙

YVONNE S. FREEMAN AND DAVID FREEMAN

Older English language learners (ELLs) present a challenge for teachers. Some arrive with adequate formal schooling, but many others have limited formal or interrupted schooling. Felipe is a typical overage ELL. He attended a rural school in Mexico for two years. When he came to the United States, he was placed in second grade. His education has been frequently interrupted by return trips to Mexico and by absences when the family moved to other parts of the country with the crops. Felipe will enter middle school next year. He cannot read or write in Spanish. His English literacy is below grade level, and he is behind his classmates in math, science, and social studies. There are many overage ELLs like Felipe in U.S. schools (Freeman & Freeman, 2002).

Teachers frequently ask, "How can I help my older ELLs read and write in English when they cannot read or write well in their first language? What strategies and texts should I be using with overage ELLs?" We have found that successful teachers follow certain practices. In addition to teaching language through content and organizing curriculum around themes, these teachers do the following:

1. They draw on and validate their students' strengths.
2. They engage students in hands-on activities, working in cooperative groups.
3. They use materials that are culturally relevant.
4. They use the preview, view, and review strategy.

1. Teachers can draw on and validate students' strengths by recognizing their life experiences and using their first language. When teachers draw on their students' life experiences and recognize common cultural values, struggling students respond positively. Teachers can also use strategies with students to help them recognize cognates, which often include important academic vocabulary.

2. Many studies have shown the benefits of cooperative learning for language minority students. When academic assignments include projects during which students work together, overage ELLs become more involved and experience more success. Teachers can differentiate their instruction by having limited formal schooling students participate by illustrating concepts, labeling, and writing short contributions.

3. Teachers can read aloud or have available in the classroom books that include events, settings, and characters that are familiar to the students. Students want to read and are willing to work hard to read culturally relevant texts because they reflect the here and now of their lives (Freeman, Freeman, & Freeman, 2003).

4. Preview, view, and review is an excellent strategy for working with limited formal schooling students. If the teacher, a bilingual peer or cross age tutor, a bilingual aide, or a parent can simply tell the English learners in their native language what the upcoming lesson is about, the students are provided with a preview. During the view the teacher conducts the lesson using strategies to make the input comprehensible. With the help of the preview, the students can follow the English better and acquire both English and academic content. Finally, it is good to have a short time of review during which students can work in same-language pairs or groups to clarify and summarize the lessons and then report back in English.

Teachers who are successful with working with overage students use the above strategies to help their students move towards academic success (Freeman & Freeman, 1998).

Question

How can we best serve migrant English language learner populations?

NADEEN RUIZ

In 2002 the U.S. Department of Education commissioned a report on the educational context of migrant students, *The Same High Standards for Migrant Students: Holding Title I Schools Accountable.* The three-volume report highlighted a number of contextual features of schools with high numbers of migrant students such as poorer schools, differences in curriculum between districts "sharing" migrant students that added to the serious problem of academic discontinuity, and inability to estimate the percentage of migrant students who actually participated in statewide and district accountability systems or to disaggregate their scores. These school-site features, along with migrant families' mobility, low income levels, and lack of English proficiency, led the National Commission on Migrant Education to note, "Some educators view both currently and formerly migratory children as having greater needs than other disadvantaged populations" (p. 31). In turn, the U.S. National Migrant Office has documented the academic outcomes of these ineffective educational contexts over the past decade and a half, showing a persistent and dramatic achievement gap between migrant and nonmigrant students.

Despite this sobering picture of migrant students' educational needs at the national level, we have found through our own work in the *Migrant Optimal Learning Environment (OLE) Project* (Migrant/OLE Project, 2004) that these patterns of underachievement can be reversed. Our research shows that when educators offer *optimal learning environments* to migrant students, that is, evidence-based literacy instruction and practices, migrant students traverse the achievement gap and actually outperform nonmigrant students matched for language background in areas such as emergent literacy skills, standardized writing scores, and overall academic achievement. The optimal conditions for instruction of migrant students used by the Migrant/OLE Project are shown in Figure 8–1 (Ruiz, García & Figueroa, 1996).

How can administrators put in place what is needed to replicate the success of schools and programs like those in the Migrant/OLE Project?

1. Working with your local migrant director or coordinator, disaggregate the achievement data for migrant students in each school, at each grade level, and closely examine the instructional programs offered to migrant students.

   Brad Doyle, Migrant Education Director for a Northern California region, conducts what he calls "reading audits." Brad literally sits down with administrators in each of the schools in his region and closely examines the literacy program offered to migrant students. The audit focuses on identifying the primary literacy program and supplemental programs, the profiles of students receiving native language reading support, assessments that are curriculum-based evidence of reading performance, and expected and actual reading levels for each migrant student in grades K–3. In a study conducted by the Migrant/OLE Project we discovered what we believe is an outcome of this region's reading audits and emphasis on evidence-based literacy instruction: the migrant students in this

1. Student Choice
Students exercise choice in their learning when possible: writing topics, books, research projects, and thematic cycles.

2. Student-Centered
Lessons begin with students' personal experiences, background knowledge, and interests.

3. Whole Texts for Explicit Teaching of Skills and Strategies
Lessons begin with whole, communicatively functional texts (e.g., books, poems, newspaper articles) to maximize the construction of understanding; then move to the analysis of components of reading and writing processes, such as strategies, text organizations, or smaller units of language forms (e.g., phonics, spelling, punctuation).

4. Active Participation
Students actively engage in lessons with frequent and long turns at producing both oral and written language.

5. Meaning First, Followed by Form
Students construct meaning from (reading) or through (writing) text first, then move to a focus on correct forms of language such as spelling and grammar.

6. Authentic Purpose
The end-products of lessons have a real-life function that often extends beyond the classroom; real audiences, real purposes.

7. Approximations
Students are encouraged to take risks and successively approximate language and literacy skills (following a developmental course).

8. Immersion in Language and Print
The classroom is saturated with different print forms and functions, and with opportunities to understand and use language for a wide range of purposes. All teachers act on their charge to teach language across the curriculum.

9. Demonstrations
Teachers demonstrate their own reading and writing, and share their ongoing efforts with students. "More expert" students also serve as models for their peers.

10. Response
Students receive timely responses to their oral and written texts that go beyond letter grades to personalized and thoughtful acknowledgments of their ideas, experiences, and efforts.

11. Community of Learners
Students, parents, and teachers form a community of readers, writers, and learners who explore a range of questions relevant to them. Students have the opportunity to discover and develop their academic identities.

12. High Expectations
Teachers, parents, and the students themselves expect that students will become proficient and independent speakers, readers, and writers. Teachers make sure that scaffolds are in place to help students meet these expectations.

Figure 8–1. Optimal Conditions for Language and Literacy Learning: *The Migrant/OLE Project*

particular region outperformed the students in any other region in California in numbers reaching the 50th percentile in reading achievement scores (Figueroa, 2004).

2. Offer an evidence-based literacy instruction to migrant students.

    Unfortunately, in a recent meta-analysis of 38 studies from the National Reading Panel, only one included English language learners (ELLs) (Ehri, Nunes, Stahl, & Willows, 2001), and consequently it cannot be considered scientifically or evidence-based because of the lack of fit between the children in the studies and ELLs such as migrant students (International Reading Association, 2002; Ruiz & Figueroa, 2004). There is, however, a robust body of literature on best literacy practices with ELLs as cited throughout this volume and reflected in Figure 8–1. That information should be used by schools to create optimal learning environments for migrant students wherein, despite the often harsh realities of the migrant life circumstances, migrant students can academically thrive.

Question

How can we best serve "newcomers," students who come with interrupted formal schooling and from educational backgrounds that are very different from those in the United States?

Barbara Marler

Newcomers can be well served through a newcomers' program that takes into account the unique needs that such English language learners (ELLs) bring to our schools. Many of these students have interrupted formal schooling, putting them at risk of failing in their academic subjects if adequate support services are not provided. Still others have had limited opportunities to fully develop literacy in their native language. Additionally, the need to become fully cognizant, competent, and savvy in the new, non-native culture can be a daunting task, especially when fluency in the target language is limited and when little support is available in the students' native language. A portion of the existing bilingual/English as a second language (ESL) program should be devoted to the needs of the newcomer.

This programming can take the form of a Newcomers' Center (usually in the same vein as a "school within a school") or a series of courses that new arrivals are expected to participate in during the first few months of enrollment. Newcomer Centers are usually set aside from the rest of the school, but successful models have also been established where the newcomers are integrated with their English-speaking peers or other ELLs who have been in U.S. schools for a few years. Regardless of the separateness of the Newcomer Center, such programming options are to be considered short-term, intensive interventions, designed to give such students an added advantage as quickly as possible. Once students reach a certain level of English proficiency and become skilled in the culture of school, they can be gradually transitioned into the existing bilingual/ESL classes or the mainstream.

Newcomer programming includes the following components:

- Instruction in the native language (whenever possible) in academic areas and literacy. At this entry point in the newcomers' life, the native language is going to be the most efficient route to literacy and to content area knowledge attainment.

- Survival English and initial English literacy instruction. This must be given by a highly skilled ESL teacher who knows how to integrate language with content instruction and how to connect oral language development with beginning literacy. Intensive survival English (for six to twelve weeks) prepares students for the demands of U.S. schools and allows instruction to move more rapidly from social language to academic language.

- Understanding American culture and U.S. schools. Newcomers must be introduced to the way things work in their community and the larger society, such as public services and public transportation, as well as in their school, such as lockers and cafeteria rules. When students are prepared to deal with the cultural chasms they are likely to encounter they are better able to focus comfortably on academic and linguistic pursuits.

For older students, career/vocational/post-secondary schooling awareness and planning is important. This helps to contextualize learning for new arrivals and guide them as they begin to make choices that influence their future.

Newcomers' programming cannot remedy lost years of formal schooling, but it can help students reach a level where content area instruction in regular bilingual/ESL classrooms becomes more meaningful and can be provided closer to the age-appropriate grade level.

Question

How can we best serve older English language learners who are returning to school after having dropped out, or who have arrived in the United States after age 18?

☙

JOE REEVES LOCKE

Older English language learners (ELLs) in pursuit of a high school diploma find themselves dealing with not only the intricacies of an academic learning experience in a non-native language but also with the day-to-day grind of life in an alien environment. They may be faced with seemingly overwhelming issues at home or at work, and now they have taken on the pursuit of a high school diploma! An adult high school format provides the needed venue for the older ELL in pursuit of an academic learning experience. Like all ELLs, but even more so for adults, they need encouragement, support, and flexibility.

Encouragement should begin with the initial contact of the learner with the program. Assure the learner of his or her ability to be successful in an academic endeavor. Make it simple to get started in the learning experience. Keep registration and assessment to a minimum, and if possible have them occur at the same location as the learning experience. Apprise the learner of the number of credits, required classes, and electives needed to graduate. Detail for the learner not only the daily class schedule but also the possible amount of time it will take to reach the ultimate goal of a high school diploma.

Support for the older ELL, as for all older learners, is intrinsic in the adult high school venue. When the adult high school is able to offer ELL classes, then that support is enhanced for the older ELL. Adult learners often are more focused, more motivated, and more likely to be supportive of each other in the classroom. Adult learners are in the adult high school because of a self-perceived need to obtain their high school diploma. The climate of an adult high school enables teachers, ELL as well as mainstream, to provide individualized attention at particular points of need.

Flexibility in attendance, scheduling, and statute of limitations greatly aids older ELLs in their academic learning experience. Older ELLs have so many calls on their time that an illness in the family, a change in transportation arrangements, or a change in a work schedule may mean missing days of class, or may even necessitate a hiatus in attendance. Make it possible, if needed, for students to easily arrange for make-up sessions with teachers for time missed. Simplify the process of schedule changes, so that students will not dread the procedure and will not hesitate to do it. Reduce the amount of paper work connected with reentry into the program. Give credits the longest possible life, so that reentry will be a continuation and not another new beginning. The encouragement, support, and flexibility in the academic learning experience for the older ELL does not mean a reduction in the quality of the instruction. The older ELL, just as the under 18 ELL, should be held to district, state, and national standards. Older ELLs are in the class because they are taking the time and making the effort to be there, and they want quality learning that will make a meaningful difference in their lives.

Question

What happens when there are only a few English language learners in a school district?

SUE WAGNER

Immigrant families from different cultural and language backgrounds sometimes arrive in school districts that have so few English language learners (ELLs) that there is no specific program for them. Regardless of age, ELLs arrive with varying amounts of school knowledge and literacy experiences and will need to be placed at the grade levels of their age group peers. Administrators and teachers designing the program for the ELL students need to assess the background knowledge of the children and build a program for them that addresses three academic needs: (1) how they will learn grade-level concepts, (2) how they will learn (or continue to learn) to read and write, and (3) how they will develop academic English language proficiency.

Assessing Knowledge, Language, and Literacy

When new ELLs arrive, a first step is to conduct an educational background interview. For ELLs in primary grades, use an interpreter to have a "getting to know you" conversation with the parents. Ask background questions about their region and the schools that their children have attended. Talk directly with older learners (through the interpreter) about their previous school experiences. Whenever possible, conduct an informal literacy screening for children who have attended school. Using a children's book in the child's language, ask the new ELL student to read a paragraph. Ask him or her to retell information. Ask the new ELL to complete a writing sample in his or her native language (such as writing a paragraph or two about the family). Through the interpreter, ask the student to tell you about what he or she wrote. Was the student able to retell what he or she read? Look at the writing. Does it appear than the student has been in school regularly? After the ELL is comfortable in the school, conduct an English language proficiency test. Most states recommend a specific test for ELLs. However, the measures described here may be more useful in developing an instructional plan.

Assessing Grade-level Academic Concepts

If the new ELLs have a history of irregular school attendance, low literacy skills in their first language, or have missed major concepts in school, providing native language instruction is the most effective way to help them catch up to the academic knowledge of their English-speaking peers. For ELLs who come to school with age-appropriate knowledge and literacy skills, initial native language support will help them learn academic concepts with their grade-level peers. Their literacy and cognitive knowledge will serve as a strong foundation that will help them learn.

Teachers can find creative ways to provide native language support even when resources are limited. Perhaps there are language-minority community members who would work for a few hours a week as tutors. Older children from the language group who are more proficient in English can be trained as cross-age tutors. Parents can be taught to support their children's learning at home. For example, plan a weekly "Apple Letter" process. Through an interpreter, explain to the parents that their children will be bringing short, special letters home every week about how to help their children. Explain that since the teacher doesn't know their language, the short letter will be in English and will have a special graphic apple around the paragraph. The apple letter tells the parents about what their child is learning that week so that they support their children's learning. The family interpreter will need to read these letters to the parents.

Learning Academic English

Regardless of how few ELLs a district has, the students will need specific English as a second language (ESL) instruction to develop academic language. Avoid traditional ESL approaches that teach the children social language that they are likely to learn on their own. Employ a sheltered, content-based ESL instructional approach, and be sure to coordinate the lessons with the content that they are currently studying in the English-speaking classroom.

Literacy Development

Research suggests that initial literacy instruction be provided in the child's native language whenever possible. However, for districts that do not have the resources to provide formal literacy instruction in the native language, the National Research Council recommends postponing formal reading instruction until an adequate level of proficiency in spoken English has been achieved (Snow, Burns, & Griffin, 1998). Therefore, it is important that, in addition to daily ESL instruction, ELLs have a chance to build their oral English proficiency through meaning-based literacy experiences. The literacy learning activities should be connected to the content instruction they receive in their classrooms and the vocabulary that they are learning in ESL (Miramontes, Nadeau, & Commins, 1997).

Question

How can we best serve English language learners when we have many different languages represented in each class and throughout the school?

BARBARA MARLER

One important issue that administrators need to be concerned about is different patterns of grouping English language learners (ELLs) for instruction. Administrators should be cognizant of the many ways of grouping students, be aware of each grouping pattern's advantages and disadvantages, be able to communicate this information to teachers, and be willing to provide teachers with the support they need to carry out a variety of student grouping patterns. Teachers may group students according to grade level, language proficiency level, interests, or tasks. Teacher should make student-grouping decisions based on instructional goals and reflective of the strengths and needs of the students they are teaching.

Administrators can provide teachers with support simply by changing the way in which they approach scheduling of classes in their building. Most building administrators typically begin to plan their building's schedule by first plotting the days and times of the "specials classes" (typically physical education, music, art, library time, and computer instruction). The practice is understandable: many of the "specials" teachers are itinerant, so the way buildings share their services should be well planned. Additionally, most of the "specials" teachers provide instruction to every student in the building, and therefore their schedules do influence the daily schedule of every other teacher. After the "specials" classes are scheduled, administrators typically go to the general education teachers to incorporate reading, math, science, and social studies into the building schedule plan. Generally, teachers of ELLs are invited to create their teaching schedules (which include student-grouping patterns) after the entire building schedule is set. When there are many languages groups represented in each class or throughout the school, this becomes a daunting task. The resulting schedule is not geared to the needs of the ELLs but rather is a reflection of instruction offered when the students are available. If administrators consider the academic and linguistic instructional needs of the ELLs served in the building before establishing the building schedule for the "specials" classes and the general education classes, many more student-grouping patterns can be supported. Administrators should meet with the teachers of ELLs prior to establishing the building schedule to become fully aware of the grouping patterns the teachers intend to pursue during the following school year to meet the academic and linguistic instructional needs of their students.

In a pull-out program, administrators can also provide support to different student grouping patterns by clustering ELLs into targeted general education homerooms. Many administrators believe that assigning students randomly to homerooms is a good idea: student diversity and student needs are distributed equitably throughout the school. Actually, assigning ELL students randomly into general education homerooms compromises their instructional program. In an elementary school with five or six grade levels, the teacher of ELLs is expected to communicate and collaborate with upward of ten to fifteen teachers. In a middle school with teams, the teacher of ELLs is expected to communicate and collaborate with more than two teams. Both situations are impossible to manage, and the resulting lack of communication and collaboration seriously compromises the effectiveness and efficiency of the educational program for ELLs. Instead, the administrator should implement a practice of clustering ELLs students at a given grade level into a targeted homeroom or into a targeted team. With clustering, resources (both instructional and professional development) can be easily shared with the students and staff involved, and the teachers can more easily find time to communicate and collaborate. Additionally, ELLs may be grouped, either in and out of the clustered general education homeroom or in and out of the team, according to the instructional goals and the student's strengths and needs.

Even though there may be many different languages or language groups in each class or throughout the school, such a situation does not preclude the need for native language instruction and support. Administrators should attempt to recruit and hire bilingual and ESL teachers that have fluency in the largest language groups. For example, in a facility with twelve Gujarati speakers, six Polish speakers, four Japanese speakers, and three Russian speakers, a bilingual or ESL teacher with fluency in both English and Gujarati can provide ESL instruction to all twenty-five ELLs and native language instruction and support to the twelve Gujarati speakers.

For the students who do not have native language representation among the building staff, the school should take full advantage of the fact that there are many cultures and languages represented in the student body. All students in the building, be they ELLs or not, will benefit from a linguistically and culturally rich environment. School staff must communicate to parents the value of the native language and culture and actively encourage parents to continue to use the native language at home with their children. All school staff should endeavor to make sure that parents have access to instructional or content materials in their native language, whether on the Internet or in materials that the school provides in their learning center or library. In addition, schools should work in partnership with other community agencies, such as the community library and other local schools. Administrators who work with their community library will be certain that the library is cognizant of the native language concerns and needs of the community. An active relationship with the local high school may lead the administrator to discover that many sophomores have service learning requirements. Such graduation requirements can be linked to foreign language study for many students who wish to practice their foreign language skills but cannot afford an AFS experience or a summer living in a foreign country. These students can be engaged to provide cross-age tutoring or hired to assist teachers during summer school programs. Schools should foster relationships with all residents of the community, not just the parents of the students they are currently serving. Fostering such relationships expands the pool of volunteers as well as the pool of individuals willing to translate, interpret, and provide native language support to students.

Letter to an administrator: From a bilingual program teacher

Dear Dr. Rosen:

I'd like to propose a project for our school and I hope that you can support me with it. An ancient Haitian proverb tells us, "We see from where we stand." You have many educational concerns in sight as you strive to ensure the academic success of students in multiple classrooms, while my feet have been firmly planted inside a third grade classroom for eight years. Academic achievement for all my students has been my primary concern and passion. When I received my first group of Spanish-speaking children seven years ago, I was both challenged and excited. We've come a long way to knowing how best to educate these children. But from where I stand, it is clear that there is something more we can do to enable all our English language learners (ELLs) to achieve a higher level of success in our school. As you know, last year we received a few students from Laos, Somalia, Serbia, and Russia. I have four of them in my class this year.

From where I stand, I see that we desperately need a schoolwide language policy, language development goals, and a carefully developed program model that can address the needs of these new students in the same way that we serve our Spanish-speaking students. I believe that the policy, goals, and model will provide a firm foundation for our classroom practice for all ELLs, not just the Spanish-speaking students for whom we have readily available resources. I would like to suggest not only that we form a committee to look into establishing a well-articulated language policy, goals, and program model for these new ELLs but that we also take this opportunity to assess what we've been doing with our Hispanic students, as well. We have not had anything in writing for our Spanish-speaking students, so this would be beneficial for all our students.

The students from these new language backgrounds are having a tremendous impact on classroom teachers like me as well as our ESL teachers in a way that is different from the Spanish-speaking students. We all need to put our heads together to figure out the best way to deal with this new challenge (and opportunity for growth).

I see from where I stand. As a teacher who has paid special attention to English language learners, I see the need for this firm foundation of a well-articulated language policy, collective goals, and program model. Standing firmly on this foundation, I envision a program shared, valued, and further developed through professional development involving the entire school community.

I hope that you can support me in getting a group of staff together so that we can get closer to our wish to help our ELLs as best as we can. Hoping that my proposal will enhance what you see from where you stand, I look forward to hearing from you.

Sincerely,
Bonnie Rivers

Survey for Reflection and Action

Use this survey to review how your school addresses challenges regarding the education of English language learners. Use a + when your school has clear policies, programs, practices, and assessments to address challenges that arise and these are understood and supported by everyone, a √ when there is evidence of practical efforts to address this challenge proactively but no clear policy, and a − when your school has no policies, programs, practices, or plans in place to address this challenge. Use a ? when you don't know. Use the results of this survey to guide decisions about your policies, program and professional development, and classroom practices.

We appropriately assess the students', school's, or district's needs to determine the nature of the challenge

_____ Personnel who are responsible for assessing the challenge have an understanding of second language acquisition AND the area for which they are assessing (e.g., for a learning disability, or having many languages represented in each classroom).

_____ In the case of an individual challenge, outside contextual influences have been explored (e.g., home factors, prior schooling, first language) before a special education referral is initiated.

_____ In the case of an individual challenge, students' opportunities to learn have been explored.

_____ In the case of a school/district level challenge (e.g., limited resources in a given language), resources within the entire community have been tapped.

We provide appropriate services to address the needs

_____ Services provided to address the challenge (e.g., the learning disability, the academic needs of overage ELLs) are based on appropriate assessment of the challenge.

_____ Services to address the challenge are provided by highly qualified personnel.

_____ Services to address the challenge are implemented with the necessary resources (e.g., materials, time).

We use valid and reliable data to drive decision making

_____ Educators collect valid and reliable data on students' performance and development over time.

_____ Educators use that data to drive decision making (e.g., to inform instruction, program and professional development, and policy).

Strengths _____

_____

_____

Action steps _____

_____

_____

References and Additional Resources

Artiles, A. J., & Ortiz, A. A. (2002). *English language learners with special education needs: Identification, assessment and instruction.* McHenry, IL: Delta Systems.

Baca, L. (2004). *The bilingual special education interface* (4th ed.). Saddle River, NJ: Pearson/Prentice Hall.

Cloud, N. (2002). Culturally and linguistically responsive instructional planning. In A. J. Artiles & A. A. Ortiz (Eds.), *English language learners with special education needs: Identification, assessment, and instruction* (pp. 107–132). Washington, DC: ERIC Clearinghouse on Languages and Linguistics, Center for Applied Linguistics.

Cloud, N. (2005). Including students who are culturally and linguistically diverse. In D. Schwartz, *Including children with special needs: A handbook for educators and parents.* Westport, CT: Greenwood Publishing Group.

Ehri, L. C., Nunes, S., Stahl, S., & Willows, D. (2001). Systematic phonics instruction helps students learn to read: Evidence from the National Reading Panel's meta-analysis. *Review of Educational Research, 71,* 393–448.

Figueroa, R. A. (2004). *Migrant students' achievement in language arts in California: A historical and contemporary analysis.* Manuscript submitted for publication. California State University Sacramento: The Migrant/OLE Project.

Freeman, Y., Freeman, A., & Freeman, D. (2003). *Home Run* books: Connecting students to culturally relevant texts. *NABE News, 26*(3), 5–8, 11–12.

Freeman, Y., & Freeman, D. (2002). *Closing the achievement gap: How to reach limited formal schooling and long-term English learners.* Portsmouth, NH: Heinemann.

Freeman, Y. S., & Freeman, D. E. (1998). *ESL/EFL teaching: Principles for success.* Portsmouth, NH: Heinemann.

Genesee, F., Paradis, J., & Crago, M. B. (2004). *Dual language development & disorders: A handbook on bilingualism and second language learning.* Baltimore, MD: Paul H. Brookes.

Hearne, J. D. (2000). *Teaching second language learners with disabilities: Strategies for effective practice.* Oceanside, CA: Academic Communication Associates.

Igoa, C. (1995). *The inner world of the immigrant child.* Mahwah, NJ: Erlbaum.

International Reading Association. (2001). *Second language literacy instruction: A position statement of the International Reading Association.* Newark, DE: Author.

International Reading Association. (2002). *What is evidence-based reading instruction?* Position statement. Newark, DE: Author.

Migrant/OLE Project. (2004). Available at http://edweb.csus.edu/Projects/ole.

Miramontes, O., Nadeau, A., & Commins, N. (1997). *Restructuring schools for linguistic diversity.* New York: Teachers' College Press.

Mora, J. K. (2001). Effective instructional practices and assessment for literacy and biliteracy development. In S. R. Hurley & J. V. Tinajero (Eds.), *Literacy assessment of second language learners.* Boston: Allyn & Bacon.

O'Malley, M., & Valdez-Pierce, L. (1996). *Authentic assessment for English language learners: Practical approaches for teachers.* Reading, MA: Addison-Wesley.

Piper, T. (2001). *And then there were two: Children and second-language learning.* Toronto, ON: Pippin.

Ruiz, N. T. & Figueroa, R. A. (2004). *"Scientifically-based reading research": The definitional dilemma for California Migrant education students.* Manuscript submitted for publication. California State University, Sacramento: The Migrant/OLE Project.

Ruiz, N. T., García, E., & Figueroa, R. A. (1996). *The OLE Curriculum Guide: Creating optimal learning environments for bilingual students in general and special education.* Sacramento, CA: State Department of Education Publications Bureau.

Snow, C. Griffin P., Burns, M. S. (Eds.). (1998). *Preventing reading difficulties in young children.* Washington, DC: National Academy Press.

Walker, S., Edwards, V., & Blacksell, R. (1996). Designing bilingual books for children. *Visible Language, 30*(3), 268–283.

Winzer, M. A., & Mazurek, K. (1998). *Special education in multicultural contexts.* Upper Saddle River, NJ: Merrill

Chapter 9

Advocacy

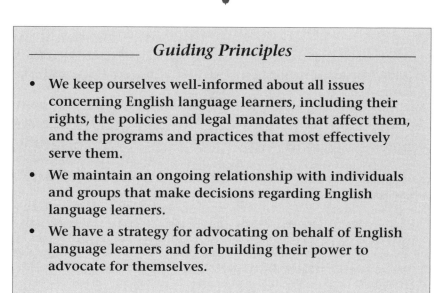

_____ *Guiding Principles* _____

- We keep ourselves well-informed about all issues concerning English language learners, including their rights, the policies and legal mandates that affect them, and the programs and practices that most effectively serve them.
- We maintain an ongoing relationship with individuals and groups that make decisions regarding English language learners.
- We have a strategy for advocating on behalf of English language learners and for building their power to advocate for themselves.

Introduction

Public education, schooling provided by the government and paid for by taxes as well as other sources, is a right that we have come to take for granted in the United States. However, English language learners (ELLs) do not represent and are generally not well represented by the brokers of power in public education. As long as ELLs do not constitute the powerful majority in this society, they remain, in most states, an afterthought in educational policy and planning. To make things worse, many people see ELLs as a burden to society, and they perceive diversity as a challenge to schools rather than a source of richness. Thus, as long as ELLs remain an afterthought, and as long as there are people who see these students in a negative light, we need to advocate. This advocacy must be all-inclusive: We need to advocate on behalf of the program for ELLs and we need to advocate on behalf of ELLs, their parents, and their teachers.

Advocacy on behalf of the program for ELLs must be comprehensive. Instruction and assessment are the two primary foci for most districts, but other aspects, such as extracurricular activities and physical building issues, are also candidates. Advocacy must also happen in every phase of the development of the program. When a school is starting a new program for ELLs, it must begin by advocating for the program. As the program is developing, administrators need to advocate for changes in that program. Even for well-established programs, there is a constant need to make sure that the effectiveness of that program is advertised and understood by everyone involved in the school community. Advocacy must reach the widest range of individuals involved in the school community. The range can include parents, local business owners and community members, and state and federal legislators.

With respect to advocating on behalf of ELLs, two issues emerge. First, it is essential that we advocate for all ELLs equitably, remembering that the same treatment for everyone does not constitute equal treatment. Second, and perhaps most important in all discussions of advocacy, we must keep in mind that advocacy on behalf of people must have as a primary goal the empowerment of those people to become activists and advocates themselves. We advocate on behalf of ELLs, their parents, and their teachers so that they may in the future advocate on behalf of themselves.

This chapter is organized to answer questions that administrators ask about advocacy for ELLs. The answers that experts provide offer insight into strategies that administrators can use to advocate and stimulate action in their schools and communities. Effective advocacy is critical in light of the confusion, conflict, and controversy surrounding the education of ELLs that we hear in the popular media today. The chapter concludes with a survey for reflection and action that administrators can use to consider their approaches to advocacy, and to identify action steps they can take to improve this important aspect of educating ELLs.

Question

What are some key elements in advocating for educational programs for English language learners?

Stephen Krashen

Language educators have serious public relations problems. This is because the views of professionals are often very different from personal theories held by the public, and the "commonsense" views of the public have won all the recent battles. Despite consistent evidence supporting bilingual education, voters in three states voted to dismantle it. Despite substantial evidence showing the limits of phonics and the power of real reading, intensive systematic phonics is strongly supported by state departments of education and the federal government.

In addition, there is the familiar problem of dealing with the media. In general, reporters, often overworked and facing deadlines, cannot study educational issues in depth, and get their information from other newspapers, press releases, and conservative think tanks (Stafancic & Delgado, 1996). Although it is possible to inform the public and even change public opinion, this will never happen if we don't try. Here are some steps we might take.

Step One: Get Informed

Many educators feel that they are too busy to read professional literature, or don't know where to find it. But we can inform ourselves quickly and easily, thanks to some high-quality Web sites and reader-friendly books (a list of Websites is provided at the end of the chapter).

Step Two: Share with Allies

If our colleagues are not aware of what we and others are doing, there is no hope. All too often professionals find out about significant events only after they have appeared in the press, and have been misrepresented.

In sharing information, we discover groups that either already hold similar views or are open to hearing our point of view. This results in a rapid diffusion of ideas. Similar battles are being fought in different areas of education, and the arguments and data that help in one area can help in another.

Sharing ideas these days is easy, requiring only forwarding items to others electronically.

Step Three: Express Your Own Point of View, From Your Own Experience and Expertise

To paraphrase Susan Ohanian, the public needs to hear from those who have been in the classroom, not from those who have never in their lives been shut up in a room with a large group of seventh graders for a full day. I suggest you write (or talk) about any issue in which you, as a professional, have knowledge that the public does not have and needs to have.

Publish your opinions anywhere you can. At least tell us, your colleagues, by posting on listservs. Others will learn from your ideas and might be able to use them. There are of course other possibilities: letters to the editor, op-eds, blogs, articles in professional journals, general-interest magazines, newsletters, and so forth.

Each person has to discover what is comfortable for him- or herself. I like to write journal papers and letters to the editor, and I stick to these formats. For some reason, I find it hard to write op-eds or general-interest articles. (Thomas Feyer, letters editor for the *New York Times*, has provided some good advice on writing letters to the editor; Feyer, 2004.)

Right now, the public is hearing only from amateurs with little or no experience in educational practice or research. The public needs to hear from the real experts.

The acceptance of new ideas depends on a variety of factors: One factor is obvious—how much people know about the new idea. Rogers (1983) notes that we see no acceptance of new ideas until potential "adapters" have a minimum amount of information. But once a certain threshold is reached, increases in information result in substantial increases in acceptance of the new idea (p. 235). We are, in my view, far below the minimum. Getting information to the public, and eventually to opinion leaders, is a task we must all take part in.

๛

SHARON M. O'MALLEY

The process of advocacy for English language learner (ELL) education programs is multifaceted and is most effective when it is driven by an intense passion for ELLs. One must interface with diverse constituencies, including parents, local communities, district personnel (central office, principals, and teachers), school boards, and state and federal governments.

First, at the local level, parents must have a voice in decision making. There must be ongoing parent-teacher partnerships to ensure that children are succeeding in school. Program administrators must advocate at the district level for support for all parents (through, for example, parent workshops, classes, and family support linkages) that ensure that all parents have equitable opportunities to participate in school and to make decisions that shape school programs. There is a need to link students and families with community and cross-city resources to create comprehensive coordinated support networks. A parent advisory council can help to review program policies and get input from parents.

Second, the community must have a voice in decision making. A program administrator should be visible and serve on boards of local community-based agencies that serve the families of ELLs. Take the time to educate community members of the needs of ELLs. Make sure that the public understands the program and its effectiveness. Families and other community members need access to achievement indicators in concise, user-friendly formats and in a language they know and understand. As the community learns about the services that the school provides, the administrator can make them aware of how they can help support the cause. For example, community members can collaborate with the school by offering small grants for specific projects, or they might volunteer to help teachers in the classroom or after school.

Third, at the district level, educate the superintendent, central office, and the school-based administrative staff. Identify a key bilingual person who can represent the population through serving on the school board. Often the composition of school boards is not representative of the entire population it serves. A voice is needed to push the agenda. Another way of being in the forefront of district policy is to have an ELL representative be part of every district committee. This person can remind committee members who may not have ELLs on their mind of their specific needs and how the decisions being taken by that committee might affect ELLs. It is imperative that the ELL population is considered while decisions are being made, not afterward, and that there is an equity framework to guide educational decisions. Have ongoing professional development on ELL issues to all staff. Clearly describe different program models and the benefits of additive versus subtractive bilingualism. Provide presentations of whole-school, classroom, and individual school data, including disaggregated data that present the strengths and special needs of a historically underserved student population.

Fourth, at the state level, legislators and state boards of education should be made aware of ELL issues to enact policy change. Engage staff and students in letter-writing campaigns to educate legislators about policy issues that affect ELLs. Invite politicians to your district as they are usually disconnected from the real problems facing schools. Talk one on one with politicians who may be sympathetic to your cause. Mobilize stakeholders and have the views of parents, community members, teachers, and students known by testifying at public hearings. In addition, it is important to work with other ELL program administrators and form a network for sharing, working on common issues, advocacy, and enacting policy changes. Be a voice through task forces or volunteer for state-level committees at the Department of Education.

Fifth, enter in an ongoing dialogue with media. Spend the time to make the local media aware of issues and highlight successes (Ryan, 1991). Public attitudes are often negative with regard to bilingual education but can be influenced positively by the media.

Finally, advocacy is involvement in professional organizations. Organizations such as the National Association for Bilingual Education (NABE) and Teachers of Speakers of Other Languages (TESOL) advocate for the rights of ELL students. You can make a difference through the local, state, and national affiliations.

In summary, to be effective program administrators, we must gain the trust and respect of everyone we serve. Our advocacy will inevitably have an impact if we involve all stakeholders in the political and educational process. Together we can further the educational interests of ELLs.

Kelly Estrada

As a former English language learner (ELL) program supervisor, I have used the following elements to promote an advocacy-based approach to program design and implementation (U.S. Department of Education, 2005). These elements resulted in a significant degree of ELL program success, despite the fact that we were functioning in a chronically underperforming school environment.

Increase Visibility

In districts where ELLs are not the majority, they tend to become invisible to school staff that are focused on improving mainstream student achievement. By merit of the fact that ELLs and their parents most often do not speak English well enough to be vocal, their silence often results in a lack of attention to their educational needs. One way to increase ELL visibility is to attract parents and community members to come to school. That can be accomplished by making sure that school communications, especially student handbooks and school meetings (schoolwide and parent conferences) are available in the students' native languages. Free and low-cost translation assistance is available through hospitals, churches, local community agencies, and even parents with greater fluency in English.

Become Knowledgeable

What are the legal requirements for educating ELLs? What constitutes a compliant ELL program? What are the educational rights of ELLs and their parents? With greater access to reliable information via the Internet, it is relatively easy to become knowledgeable regarding compliance and effectiveness of programs. The Office of English Language Acquisition (OELA) in Washington, D.C., provides many useful resources on its Website, as well as links to other important sources of information (additional resources are listed at the end of this chapter). Taking advantage of these and other widely accessible resources will empower school administrators to act as advocates for ELL students. For even greater effect, share knowledge with other stakeholders in the school and district, such as parents, teachers, and central office administration.

Establish and Maintain Appropriate Program Funding

When I first began working as an ELL programs consultant for a district in southeastern Pennsylvania, there was no ELL program budget. The first order of business was therefore to establish one. As per state and federal requirements, this budget was funded from the core instructional budget for the district.[1] Once the ELL program was part of the district budget, we were legitimized; this funding gave us a seat at the table in terms of district function. It was astonishing to me at the time to witness how others within the school administrative hierarchy sat up and paid attention to our ELL program needs once we were funded and so legitimized. Beyond core instructional funds, there is a wide range of federal discretionary and external institution funds that can support ELL programs. Tap the expertise within the district in applying for such funds. Form a team of grant writers who can become yet another advocacy network that could potentially enhance the quality of your program.

Use Data to Advocate for ELL Students

The data I maintained during my tenure as program supervisor included measures of English language proficiency, academic achievement (standardized test results, grades), attendance, and length of time in the program. I suggest conducting careful analysis of ELL data as compared with that of their native English-speaking peers. By using these results to formulate clear and concise presentations to district stakeholders, I was able to ensure proper identification of ELLs, the provision of ELL services to those students who needed it, and appropriate placement for instruction. In addition, we were able to increase the duration and quality of English language learning and to promote adaptations of content instruction to increase academic achievement for ELLs in mainstream classroom settings. We also used the data to ad-

---

1. Title III funds, funds allocated on a per pupil basis to support ELL program implementation, are supplementary funds and cannot supplant core instructional funds for ELL students.

vocate for ELL program budget increases. These funds resulted in our ability to add ELL instructional staff and to purchase core ESL instructional materials. With respect to advocacy, it is clear that cold, hard facts often translate into action where none was taken before.

Question

How can I use information about the program for English language learners to advocate for further development?

Else Hamayan

Having information about your English language learner (ELL) program is essential for advocacy purposes. Gathering that information should be part of the routine functioning of every school that has an ELL population. This way, you have access to the information you need when you need it. You cannot go back in the spring when budgetary decisions are being taken by the school board and assess the level of proficiency that students started the academic year with. That information has to be there from the very beginning of the year.

The following is a partial list of the information that could be useful to advocate on behalf of the program for ELLs.

- Scores on tests: Make sure that you can show development and growth over time. If possible, interpret the scores or performance levels on the basis of whatever standards are being used for ELLs.

- Scores obtained from qualitative data such as checklists, rating scales, and rubrics. Again, explain what different levels of scores mean in terms of performance on a given subject matter.

- For programs where ELLs exit the services provided once they reach a certain level of proficiency: Provide a description, either numeric or qualitative, of how well students who are functioning in the mainstream with little or no specialized support are doing.

- Student work samples: Select students' best work that clearly represents parts of the curriculum.

- Gather success stories from individual students, either those who are still in the program or those who have graduated.
- Save testimonials from parents of ELL students.
- Save testimonials from employers of ELL students.

When it comes time to present this information, an administrator must be sure it is done in a way that appeals to the particular audience it is being presented to. Finally, it is easiest for people to relate to someone who is like them. If you are appealing to your superintendent, get another superintendent to talk to him or her. If you are talking to parents, get another parent to do the presentation, or talk to them yourself as a parent rather than as a researcher or administrator.

Question

Regarding English language learners, whom do we advocate with, and about what?

MARÍA JOSEFINA (JOSIE) YANGUAS

With all the different stakeholder groups, one of the most important elements of advocacy begins with putting forth positive and accurate information about programs for English language learners (ELLs) in your school and district. All too often there are negative perceptions regarding programs for ELLs that can be countered with a school visit or a school report. Therefore, whenever there is an opportunity to showcase ELL students in a school, not only should notices be sent to the parents, school officials, and school board members, they should also go to other groups in the community, including the media and local elected officials. Any follow-up reports about such events or additional documents that describe the academic progress and other accomplishments of ELL students should also be sent to these different stakeholder groups. Such reports need not be long and elaborate but rather brief and to the point.

Table 9–1 lists the various stakeholders and the most crucial information administrtators need to obtain about them, as well as the information stakeholders might be most interested in.

Table 9-1. Regarding ELLs, who do we advocate with and what about?

What Level?	Who?	What Would Be Useful to Find Out?	What Do We Advocate About?
State elected officials	Governor	Who are gubernatorial staff members that help shape state education policy and budgets?	• Adequate funding for ELL/bilingual education. • Lobby in favor of/against specific legislative and budgetary proposals that affect ELLs.
	State representatives and state senators	Who are the key leaders at the House and Senate level knowledgeable about education? Who are educators and parents who reside in the districts of these officials who can speak/serve as advocate for ELL/bilingual education? Do these elected officials have constituency-based education committees that help shape local educational policy? Who are elected officials who are well-meaning but have little knowledge/information about ELLs?	• Have elected officials sponsor specific legislation that would be favorable for ELLs; e.g., if there is no provision in state law for ELL/bilingual education, find an elected official willing to sponsor such legislation. • Lobby in favor of/against specific legislative and budgetary proposals that affect ELLs. Consider volunteering for (or even forming) such committees to assist with the formulation of possible ELL/bilingual education legislation.
Federal elected officials	U.S. Senators and U.S. Representatives	Make the distinction as to whether a policy is a federal or state mandate; e.g., Title III monies are federal monies that support ELLs, yet at the same time the majority of funds that support ELL education come from state/local monies.	• Keep federal officials apprised of how the state is supporting the needs of ELLs.
State Board of Education or State Dept. of Education		• Is the state superintendent an elected position? An appointed position? • Is there a designated individual/department at the state level that supports ELL education?	• Statewide policy decisions related to ELLs, particularly critical within the context of NCLB and its high-stakes accountability and assessments expected for ELLs. • Supplemental funding for ELL education.
Local school board		How many members understand and/or are supportive of ELL policies?	• Encourage parents knowledgeable in ELL programs to get elected to the school board.

(continued)

235

Table 9-1. (Continued)

What Level!?	Who?	What Would Be Useful to Find Out?	What Do We Advocate About?
Parent groups and parents	PTAs, school-based committees with parent members (e.g., NCLB and/or bilingual parental advisory committees, local school councils), other formal or informal parent group at a school.		• Encourage parents to participate in some kind of formal/informal group at school that will help parents better understand (and ultimately advocate for) ELL. • Encourage parents knowledgeable about ELL programs to testify at school board meetings for any new policy initiatives for ELL students.
Media	Print, TV		• Invite the media to visit the school, and send reports to the media that highlight ELL students and their accomplishments.
Local community/business groups/ local chambers of commerce/community-based organizations (CBOs)			• Could be a source of income to help support small projects related to ELLs. • Can talk and testify to other stakeholders (such as school board members and elected officials) on behalf of ELL students and any possible program needs.
Education associations and national advocacy groups	Some examples include MALDEF, Aspira, NABE, TESOL, and state associations of these national groups.		• Can advocate for different ELL/bilingual education policies through member newsletters and events. • Can talk and testify to other stakeholders (such as school board members and elected officials) on behalf of ELL students and any possible program needs.
School District level	District superintendent and other central office administrators; teacher unions; teacher leaders within a school, departmental chairs; teacher assistants, other school support staff.		• Can advocate for different ELL/bilingual education policies through membership newsletters and events. • Can talk and testify to other stakeholders (such as school board members and elected officials) on behalf of ELL students and any possible program needs.

Question

What are some resources to help us advocate on behalf of English language learners?

NANCY CLOUD

Language-minority students and parents may not advocate for themselves, for many reasons. First, they may lack the proficiency in English to engage in this sophisticated verbal interplay, or for cultural reasons they may shy away from speaking up. Second, they may not fully understand the expectations of democratic institutions and may instead believe that the institution will respond to their needs without prompting. Third, they may have other reasons for nonparticipation, such as fear of reprisal based on their residency status or ethnicity, or negative past experiences. For all these reasons, administrators and teachers need to advocate on behalf of this student group to ensure that they get the best education possible.

What does it take to advocate for this group? First, we must be familiar with the relevant laws and legislation to make certain children and parents get all of the services and protections to which they are entitled. To get this information, we can start at the U.S. Department of Education, Office for Civil Rights, which has issued guidelines for program development and evaluation (*Programs for English Language Learners: Resource Materials for Planning and Self- Assessments,* updated through March 28, 2000, available at http://www.ed.gov/about/offices/list/ocr/ell/index.html). Another helpful contact is the National Clearinghouse for English Language Acquisition and Language Instruction Educational Programs, which has published a fact sheet entitled "What Legal Obligations Do Schools Have to English Language Learners?" (available at http://www.ncela.gwu.edu/expert/faq/23legal.htm). Finally, we can contact the Council of Chief State School Officers, which has published the "Summary of recommendations and policy implications for improving the assessment and monitoring of students with limited English proficiency," as well as other policy-oriented documents directed toward the appropriate education of ELLs (available at http://www.ccsso.org).

Second, we need to understand best practices for ELLs. For this, we can turn to our professional associations to learn of the position statements they have issued with respect to the assessment and education of language-minority students. We can also join with them in their advocacy efforts on behalf of ELLs. There is a great degree of consistency among the recommendations they make, which should give us the ammunition we need to defend the policies and practices we wish to implement on behalf of ELLs. Associations that have issued policy statements of interest include Teachers of English to Speakers of Other Languages (TESOL), the National Association for Bilingual Education (NABE), the International Reading Association (IRA), the National Council of Teachers of English (NCTE), the National Association for the Education of Young Children (NAEYC), the National Education Association (NEA), the American Educational Research Association (AERA) , the National Council on Measurement in Education (NCME), and the American Psychological Association (APA). Collectively, they support the use of the native language in instruction and assessment, the active development of bilingualism/multilingualism in our multicultural society, respect for and responsiveness to children's primary languages and cultures at school, and the active involvement of language-minority parents.

Finally, to advocate effectively, we need to understand the goals and requirements of the major program models designed to serve ELLs so that we can select appropriate models and implement them well. A great source for this purpose is Fred Genesee's *Program Alternatives for Linguistically Diverse Students* (Center for Research on Education, Diversity & Excellence, University of California, Santa Cruz, 1999, available at http://www.cal.org/crede/pubs, along with many other helpful publications).

Being well-informed should form the foundation of our advocacy efforts at all levels of the educational system—state, district, and school. All issue policies and establish practices that need to work for ELLs. Obviously, it works best if our advocacy happens early on, as policies are being formulated and practices are being determined. Whether it is high-stakes testing or curriculum decisions, advocacy is needed to make sure that the needs of ELLs are fully considered. Administrators are in an ideal position to advocate on behalf of ELLs, and it is in their best interest to do so, as their success hinges on doing the right thing for the populations they serve.

Question

How can we move from advocacy for English language learners to activism by English language learners and their families?

❦

NANCY SANTIAGO-NEGRÓN

Advocate: *one that pleads the cause of another; specifically: one that pleads the cause of another before a tribunal or judicial court*

Activism: *a doctrine or practice that emphasizes direct vigorous action especially in support of or opposition to one side of a controversial issue*

—Merriam-Webster Dictionary

So many of us that work in education like to think of ourselves as advocates for the children we teach, for the families in our schools, or for the community our schools serve. But how many of us think of ourselves as activists? I believe that to truly change the world of the children we serve, we cannot continue to simply advocate or speak for the community. Instead, we need to help the community speak for itself.

As an advocate, your pleas may still go unanswered, your requests for support unmet, and your sole voice ignored. But if you wish to create change for your students, you must move a community to speak together. To be a true agent of change you must create situations that allow the community to speak together loudly and allow the community to be understood regardless of the language spoken.

The summer that the state took over control of the School District of Philadelphia taught me many things, but the most important lesson was how to create real change. Philadelphia was in the beginning phase of the most unprecedented experiment in public education in many generations. The very face of public education was about to change forever in Philadelphia, yet when I looked around my community during this very tense period I noticed something very worrisome—silence. The public education system was about to undertake the most drastic change in its history, yet the community had very little to say on the matter. I, along with some fellow advocates, started to voice our concerns over the impending changes. We called meetings, wrote letters, and made telephone call after telephone call to school district and state officials requesting help, to no avail. After several months of advocating, I realized that we had to regroup and try another strategy quickly.

I then tried to "preach from the pulpit," spewing out information on what was happening to all who would listen. I tried to get the community and parents to write letters and make telephone calls, hoping that this would draw more attention to the issue. What I did not realize then was that listening and engaging are two very different things. Parents and community residents politely listened to me and my colleagues, but nothing of what we said made a difference in their behaviors because they were not invested in us. Actually, when I review these events more objectively today, I realize that I was not invested in them either—at least not yet. I was invested in the "cause," in the issue of equal access to quality education. I was invested in the issue that I thought automatically translated to being invested in children, but I was wrong. I needed to become invested in the day-to-day lives of my students and the community, both inside and outside of the school walls. Once parents felt me reach out to them in a sincere way, in a way that said "we are partners," not "I am that expert here to help you," they felt comfortable. Once I invested my time and energy to build a relationship that felt safe for both of us, parents started to invest their time and energy in me and our school district.

The building of these relationships started with a simple question. Instead of running in and out of schools "raising awareness" about the impending takeover, I decided to ask questions. Our road toward real change started with one question: Do you know what is happening to our schools? It seems like such a simple question at first, but it opened floodgates of ideas, opinions, and insights into what makes a community work. The question almost never received the answer that I thought that I would hear— the way that I thought it should be. I received one answer when I visited a church, another answer when the question was asked in a community-based organization and yet another answer altogether when I met with parents at the park for a community event. What I realized is that the answer was more complex than I had originally thought, but the solution seemed closer with each person I talked to that summer.

The question began a dialogue, a true exchange with parents, students, community leaders, and residents. This dialogue took me out of the safety of a central office building and into community-based organizations, community and civic meetings, churches, grocery stores, and parents' homes. This new conversation helped me understand the importance of opening my schools' doors to the community. I learned to open the doors of our schools to basketball games, first-time homebuyer workshops, and community aerobics classes. I let the community into my home, and they welcomed me into theirs. This exchange eventually took us to marching in the streets and speaking up at board meetings. The shared communication led to "actions" that guaranteed that our parents, not outside advocates, would be listened to. Parents and community residents were the activists that caused actions (and reactions) that later made all of the difference in their children's schools and educational process.

If I try to organize the steps we took on our road to change together, it would probably look like this short list:

Leave Your Building: Take a walk or drive in your school's community and conduct a survey. See what resources exist. Make a list of those resources, including names and contact numbers. Drop in at the community grocery store. Visit community landmarks.

Reach Out to Your Neighbors: Find out what services the community-based organizations in the area provide. See if they have something they can offer to your students and families. If they conduct workshops, offer them your space to provide one of those workshops. Many of these organizations are trying to reach the same families that you serve. Keep a contact list handy and available to your staff at all times.

Support Your School's Community: Buy your breakfast, lunch, snacks, and lottery tickets in that neighborhood grocery store. Listen to the conversations while you are there. Pick up the local newspapers while you are there. Get into the habit of talking regularly to the store owners and ask them questions about the community. Leave information about your school and school events at the stores. Make sure that community residents always have a way to contact you should they need you.

Bring People, Other Than Students, Into Your Schools: Offer the community different workshops in your schools via your community partners and municipal agencies (how to purchase a home; tax prep; CPR/first aid, and so forth). Sit in on those workshops as a participant and not just the coordinator. Have these workshops take place during hours that allow working parents to attend. Open student performances and special events to community leaders, business owners, and volunteers. Build relationships with adults outside of your school staff and parents.

Create a Climate of Trust and Reciprocity: Ask questions and allow folks to be as honest as possible. Gather information from all sources—parents, students, and school volunteers. Have a feedback loop that allows people to give you information in an anonymous way (such as a suggestion box or email address), and then act on those suggestions if appropriate. Organize community forums on education with a partner (and make sure that you always have someone there who can translate if necessary). The creation of the forum agenda should not be up to the school staff. Have a community-based partner take on this responsibility; you just help them get the word out.

Share: Share information, share space, share time, share history, and share celebrations. Share information in the languages that all parents can understand. Share your concerns and causes with them. Chances are they will share the same concerns with you.

Our time frame was relatively short, and things didn't take place in the most organized or sequential of timelines, but they happened. One at a time, great new partnerships started to form and take hold of parent groups, of community meetings and eventually of the issue of the state takeover. When it was time to fight for change, parents, community residents, business owners, leaders, and elected officials were ready. They were armed with information and whole community support. The state and district entities now realized that they could not move on this very prickly issue until they listened and reacted to the concerns being raised by the local community.

Question

What is bilingualism worth, and how much should I be willing to invest in it?

Eugene García

Too often, bilingual persons in the United States are perceived as monolingual. Latinos in the United States are considered to be Spanish speakers who are intent on retaining their language and culture while refusing to incorporate English and the values of the greater "American" culture. Crawford (2002) indicates that Latinos in the United States are gaining English language competencies faster than they are growing. Suro (2003) in a recent Pew Hispanic Center study indicates that 20 percent of Hispanics are Spanish dominant, 38 percent report being able to communicate in Spanish and English, and, 42 percent are dominant in English. Therefore, 80 percent are English speakers.

Yet, as Gavrilos (2003) reports in her examination of journalistic reports regarding Latinos and their language, a consistent construction of an "imagined community" of Latinos in the United States generates a profile that Hispanics are mostly immigrants and speak Spanish. It is Anzaldua (1987) who first observed with regard to Latinos that language serves as an important category of identity and is symbolic to non-Latinos of national, ethnic race and class. Using this notion, Gavrilos (2003) studied news coverage surrounding a language controversy in 1980 in Miami after the passage of an anti-bilingual ordinance. That ordinance was eliminated in 1993 in Miami when Spanish was becoming a business necessity. The study pointed out that in 1980, the *Miami Herald* had created an "imagined community" of Latinos in Miami that spoke Spanish and spurned English, while at the same time building on an "imagined community" that considered English an absolute ingredient of being American. This juxtaposed community representation created extensive controversy within and between various Latino and non-Latino groups. In 1993, the "imagined community" representing "American-ness" in Miami had shifted to include Spanish and dual language abilities in Spanish and English.

This study suggests that national identities, positive and negative, do not exist as fixed, easily identifiable attributes or cultural traits. Negatives can be changed to positives and positives to negatives. Currently, Latinos and their perceived embrace of Spanish as opposed to dual language competence is clearly a negative. This seems to be a result of our public media defining "American" only in contrast to foreigners—the label still sticking to Latinos, although less than 60 percent are foreign born. The media may only be reflecting the presence of such a process operating at various levels of U.S. culture; nevertheless, the media seem to steadily portray Latinos not as dual language competent.

It may be time to move in the direction of changing this perception in the mind of the public and in the media. As the research has pointed out, developing dual language competencies is doable, and it is good for the individual, good for business, and good for society. (It is important to speak the language of those whom you serve, whether you are a fireman, policeman, doctor, nurse, lawyer, or president—doing so is good for the service provider and the individual who is provided important services.)

Ultimately, ample U.S. and international research indicates that there are no specific linguistic, cognitive, or cultural costs to becoming dual language competent (bilingual), particularly during the early years of a child's or student's life. Quite the opposite: there may even be some cognitive and social benefits or advantages. A dual language competent child can distinguish subtleties in achieving communicative success with others and adapt the languages she or he uses, including switching between languages when necessary. A child competent in two languages can also understand the subtleties of cultural rules of making meaning that accompany the use of certain languages. This social advantage, again, maximizes the potential success of the communication. Last, at a cognitive level, a dual language competent child more fully comes to understand the abstract features of language and communication.

❦

Rebecca Freeman and Else Hamayan

The fact that we are asked what bilingualism is worth and how much we should invest in it is an indication that we are far from being a society that values proficiency in two (or more) languages. Yet in this day and age we should be very concerned that despite the fact that many students in U.S. schools speak a language other than English at home, few of these students graduate from high school with proficiency in that language. Since the early 1900s, immigrants have experienced strong pressure to assimilate to monolingualism in English. Even among the Spanish-speaking population today, we see clear evidence of an ongoing language shift toward English, despite the large numbers of immigrants that revitalize this language throughout the country. For the majority of immigrants, today as in the past, the native language is generally lost after three generations (Peyton, Ranard, & McGinnis, 2001).

The cost to the individual of losing a native language is serious and significant. When children refuse to speak the language of their home, family, and community because English has more prestige, they can become alienated from these critical connections that help them understand who they are relative to others in the world. When children believe they must reject their home language and culture in order to participate and achieve in a monolingual, English-speaking world, they deny an important part of their sociocultural identity. They also limit opportunities that could be readily available to them if they were to maintain and develop their home language.

Contrary to popular belief, maintaining and developing the native language by no means hinders an English language learner's ability to acquire English. Add to that the evidence that shows tremendous benefits to bilingualism, both individual and societal. A wide range of research shows educational, cognitive, sociocultural, and economic benefits of bilingualism for the individual. Bilinguals tend to perform better than monolinguals on cognitive tasks that call for divergent thinking, pattern recognition, and problem solving, and they tend to demonstrate sophisticated levels of metalinguistic awareness. People who can use more than one language can generally communicate across language and cultural boundaries more effectively, and they generally have a wider range of professional opportunities available to them in the global economy (Cloud, Genesee, & Hamayan, 2000).

The evidence about English language learners (ELLs) in particular and Latinos in general demonstrates that these student populations score disproportionately low on standardized tests and drop out of school at disproportionately high rates (Genesee et al., 2005). At the same time, the evidence on well-implemented dual language programs (such as two-way immersion and one-way developmental bilingual programs) shows that these programs enable ELLs to close the achievement gap with their English-speaking peers in five to seven years (Lindholm-Leary, 2000; Thomas and Collier, 2002). These data suggest that when schools have the linguistic resources available to implement dual language programs that lead to additive bilingualism and biliteracy, they are well worth the investment.

Promoting bilingualism is not only good for the individual, their families, and the local community, it is good for the nation overall. According to the National Foreign Language Center,

> the United States has critical needs for genuine communicative competency in a range of languages, a level of competency that can rarely be attained by native English speakers in a classroom setting. The ethnic communities constitute a valuable and unique resource in producing true multilingual ability in English and languages that are essential to the national interest (NFLC, 1995, p.1).

Peyton et al. (2001) argue that a national policy that viewed these languages as resources to be preserved and developed rather than as obstacles to be overcome could contribute significantly and in a relatively short time to America's expertise in foreign languages.

Bilingualism is the expectation and the norm in most other countries in the world today. Many countries have language policies that promote the teaching of additional languages beginning in elementary school. Although there is no such language policy or expectation overall in the United States today, schools can challenge the assimilation process on the local level by investing in bilingualism. In our opinion, the benefits clearly outweigh the costs.

Letter to an administrator: From a parent

Dear Mrs. Jacharek:

I am writing to you about something that has been bothering me for a while. I am sorry to be contacting you formally (with copies and so on; as you know, Mr. Wilson, one of your board members, is a neighbor of mine and I thought it wouldn't hurt for the board to know that I am bugging you about this issue), but I have not been able to leave messages for you very easily, at this busy time of year.

My frustration reached its limit this evening as I struggled in Spanish class. The company that I work for is expanding its business in Central America and I couldn't turn down an opportunity when they asked me if I would take over that program. As you know, I am of Mexican descent, and my boss thought it was best to have someone who was at least a little familiar with Spanish. So, I sit in a Spanish class two nights a week very frustrated at not being able to become fluent in Spanish quickly and easily. What makes it most frustrating is that I came to this country at the age of nine speaking Spanish! At that time, about twenty years ago, not only did my school not care if I and the other Mexican children lost our language but they did everything in their power to keep us from speaking it! My parents were so anxious to "fit in" that they didn't even seem to mind that I couldn't talk to my grandmother anymore… and after only one year of being in the United States!

Now I find myself really regretting that I didn't make more of an effort to put our son Jay in a school where Spanish is taught. So, I would like to speak to you about starting a Spanish program at Skinner School. I would be happy to help any way that I can. I spoke to my Spanish instructor, and she told me that there are, in fact, some schools in Missouri where they teach Spanish in elementary schools. I know there are other parents who are interested in having their children become fluent in Spanish. Interestingly, they are Anglo parents for the most part! (I personally can't understand why every parent in this community would not be demanding that their children be taught Spanish or Chinese.) Our country is in a huge island, but we cannot continue to pretend that we do not share a border and a whole continent with people who speak Spanish.

Mrs. Jacharek, I just don't want Jay to lose this precious gift that we can give him. My teachers and principals gave me a good education, but shame on them for allowing me to lose one of the most valuable assets that I brought to school. For that, I will not forgive them. Let us not do the same thing to our children.

I can come to see you any afternoon next week. Please let me know what would be convenient for you. You can reach me most easily at work at 314–555–1212.

Sam Alvarez (Jay Alvarez's father, in Miss Johnson's KG class)

cc. Ray Wilson
Dr. Ellen Morgan

Survey for Reflection and Action

This survey is based on the guiding principles about advocacy that were articulated in the introduction to the chapter. Read the following statements about your school's advocacy efforts on behalf of your ELLs. Indicate the extent to which each of the following applies to your school: DK = don't know; 1 = strongly disagree; 2 = disagree; 3 = agree; 4 = strongly agree. Use the results of your survey to identify your advocacy strengths and needs to determine what, if any, actions you should take to improve these efforts.

Everyone at our school is well informed about legal mandates and the rights of English language learners:

- Everyone at our school understands the program for ELLs to be able to advocate on its behalf.   DK 1 2 3 4

- There is a system in place through which new information is gathered and disseminated efficiently.   DK 1 2 3 4

Members of our staff/school leadership team have an ongoing relationship with the following constituents:

- Parents and community members   DK 1 2 3 4

- District level administrators   DK 1 2 3 4

- State legislators   DK 1 2 3 4

- Federal legislators   DK 1 2 3 4

- Mass media (newspaper, radio, etc.)   DK 1 2 3 4

- Other advocacy groups (organizations, resource centers)   DK 1 2 3 4

Our staff/leadership team has strategies for advocacy:

- We have an advocacy plan in place.   DK 1 2 3 4

- We implement the advocacy plan.   DK 1 2 3 4

- We gauge the effectiveness of our advocacy strategies and revise our plan as necessary.   DK 1 2 3 4

- ELLs and their parents become advocates on their own behalf.   DK 1 2 3 4

Program Development Strengths _____

_____

_____

Action Steps _____

_____

_____

References and Additional Resources

Anzaldua, G. (1987). *Cultural and language aspects of ethnic and gender identity.* Boston: Sage.

Center for Applied Linguistics/CAL. Web site: http://www.cal.org.

Cloud, N., Genesee, F., & Hamayan, E. (2000). *Dual language instruction: A handbook for enriched education.* Boston: Heinle & Heinle.

Coalition of Essential Schools. Web site: http://www.essentialschools.org.

Crawford, J. (2002). Comment: Bilingualism and schooling in the United States. *International Journal of the Sociology of Language, 155/156,* 93–99.

Education News. Web site: http://educationnews.org.

Feyer, T. (2004). The Letters Editor and the reader: Our compact, Updated. New York Times, May 23, 2004. [Online] Available at http://www.nytimes.com/2004/05/23/opinion/23READ.html?ex=1098781586&ei=1&en=167fb22576f65f52. [Accessed Oct. 17, 2004]

Freeman, R. (2004). *Building on community bilingualism.* Philadelphia: Caslon.

Gavrilos, A. (2003). *Latino perceptions in the US news media.* Unpublished doctoral dissertation, University of Miami. FL.

Genesee, F., Lindholm-Leary, K., Saunders, W., & Christian, D. (2005). English language learners in U.S. schools: An overview of research findings. *Journal of Education for Students Placed at Risk, 10*(4), 363–385.

Lindholm-Leary, K. (2000). *Dual language education.* Clevedon, UK: Multilingual Matters.

National Foreign Language Center. (1995). *Heritage languages in the national interest.* Washington, DC: Author.

National Clearinghouse for English Language Acquisition (NCELA). Website: http://www.ncela.gwu.edu.

Peyton, J., Ranard, D., & McGinnis, S. (2001). *Heritage languages in America: Preserving a national resource.* McHenry, IL: Delta Systems Co.

Rethinking Schools. Website: http://www.rethinkingschools.org.

Rogers, E. 1983. *Diffusion of innovations* (3rd ed.). New York: Free Press.

Ryan, C. (1991). *Prime time activism: Media strategies for grassroots organizing.* Boston: South End Press.

Samway, K. D. & McKeon, D. (1999). *Myths and realities. Best practices for language minority students.* Portsmouth, NH: Heinemann.

Stefancic, J., & Delgado, R. (1996). *No mercy: How conservative think tanks and foundations changed America's social agenda.* Philadelphia: Temple University Press.

Suro, R. (2003). *Pew Hispanic fact sheet.* Washington, DC: Pew Hispanic Center.

Teaching for Change http://www.teachingforchange.org

Thomas, W., & Collier, V. (2002). *A national study of school effectiveness for language minority students' long term academic achievement.* Santa Cruz: Center for Research, Education, Diversity, and Excellence, University of Clifornia, Santa Cruz. http://www.crede.ucsc.edu/research/llaa.1.1.html.

U.S. Department of Education, Office for Civil Rights. (2005). *Developing Programs for English Language Learners.* [Online] http://www.ed.gov/about/offices/list/ocr/ell/programeval.html.

U.S. Department of Education, Office of English Language Acquisition (OELA). (2005). [Online] http://www.ed.gov/about/offices/list/oela/index.html?src=oc.

Additional Internet Sources

Bilingual education: http://ourworld.compuserve.com/homepages/JWCRAWFORD/

General news on education: http://susanohanian.org.

Language acquisition and literacy: http://www.TRELEASE-ON-READING.COM http://www.sdkrashen.com.

Testing and standards: http://susanohanian.org, http://www.alfiekohn.com.

Glossary

Words in italics within a definition are defined in another entry in this glossary.

Academic language proficiency   The type of language proficiency required to participate and achieve in content area instruction (contrast with *conversational fluency*). There are different varieties of academic English associated with different content areas (such as the language of science, of social studies, of math). According to research, it may take at least five to seven years and up to eleven years for ELLs to acquire the academic English proficiency they need for academic success in U.S. schools. Cummins used the term cognitive academic language proficiency or CALP in his earlier work to refer to this idea.

Additive bilingualism   The process by which an individual adds proficiency in a new language (such as English) without losing proficiency in the first language (contrast with *subtractive bilingualism*).

Bilingual education   A well-planned educational program that uses two languages for instructional purposes. All bilingual programs in the United States aim for high levels of proficiency in English and academic achievement in English as important goals (some bilingual programs have additional goals). A program that is taught exclusively through English but that provides some translation to the native language is not a bilingual program. There are several different types of bilingual education programs (see *transitional bilingual education, dual language education, developmental bilingual education, two-way immersion, immersion*).

Conversational fluency   The type of English that is acquired through everyday social interaction. It generally takes English language learners approximately one to two years to acquire conversational fluency. Contrast this with *academic language proficiency*. Cummins used the term basic interpersonal communication skills or BICS to refer to this concept in his earlier work.

Developmental bilingual education program (DBE)   A type of *bilingual education* that targets *English language learners* and/or *heritage language speakers* and aims for high levels of proficiency in English and in the students' home language and strong academic development. Students generally participate in these programs for at least five to six years, receiving content area instruction in English and in their home language. Developmental bilingual programs are also sometimes referred to as one-way developmental bilingual programs, maintenance bilingual programs, or late-exit bilingual programs. This guide considers one-way developmental bilingual programs to be a type of *dual language education* because they share the goals of *additive bilingualism* with other types of dual language programs.

Dual language   A model of bilingual education that aims for (1) bilingualism, (2) biliteracy, (3) strong academic development, and (4) positive cultural understanding and intercultural communication skills. Students generally participate in dual language programs for at least five to six years. They receive content-area instruction in two languages; at least 50 percent and up to 90 percent of that content area instruction is through the minority language (language other than English in the United States). Under the broad definition of dual language programs used in this guide, we find three types: *one-way developmental bilingual education, two-way immersion,* and *second/foreign language immersion* that differ in terms of their target populations.

English as a second language (ESL)   Developmentally appropriate English language instruction tailored for English language learners' level of English proficiency; also known as English language development (ELD). While English language learners receive ESL/ELD instruction, they also receive content instruction from other sources (for example, in a bilingual program, in mainstream classes). There are different types of ESL classes, including *pull-out, push-in,* or *self-contained. Sheltered instruction programs* are another type of English-only program associated with the term ESL.

English language learner (ELL)   A student who is in the process of learning English as a second/additional language. While these students should all be designated as ELLs by schools, educators may find ELLs who are designated as fully English proficient (FEP) by local exit criteria. However, because many districts use inappropriate exit criteria, we find many ELLs who have developed *conversational fluency* in English but who are still acquiring *academic language proficiency* in English.

Fully English proficient (FEP)   An official designation for a former English language learner who has met all exit criteria of an ESL or bilingual program and is considered ready for participation in the all-English academic mainstream. However, because many districts use inappropriate exit criteria, we find many ELLs who have developed *conversational fluency* in English but who are still acquiring *academic language proficiency* in English.

Heritage language program   A language program for *heritage language speakers* that aims to broaden the linguistic repertoire of these students. Heritage language programs may be offered by community-based institutions (such as Chinese programs at Saturday schools or Korean programs at church) or by public schools (such as a world language for these students). The most common heritage language programs offered in public schools are *Spanish for Spanish speakers* or *Spanish for Native Speakers* (SNS) programs. We also find programs that promote Native American languages or other less commonly taught languages.

Heritage language speaker   A student who speaks a language other than English (their heritage language) at home. Heritage language speakers, as a collective, have a wide range of expertise in their heritage language. Some heritage language speakers may be able to speak, understand, read, and write for a wide range of purposes, while others may only be able to understand their heritage language when they are spoken to by a family or community member about a familiar topic.

Immersion program A type of *dual language program* that exclusively targets *language majority* students (such as English speakers in the United States). These programs provide content area instruction through English and another language (for example, French, Spanish, Chinese) and aim for bilingualism, biliteracy, academic achievement in two languages, and positive cultural understanding and intercultural relations. They are sometimes referred to as second or foreign language immersion programs. NOTE: Sometimes the term immersion is used to describe all-English programs for *language minority students;* however, when schools do not structure the learning environment of English language learners (by, for example, using *sheltered instructional* strategies), this experience is better understood as submersion, or sink-or-swim. Contrast this with *sheltered English programs* or s*pecially designed academic instruction in English/SDAIE programs,*that is, English-only programs that are specially designed to meet the language and learning needs of ELLs.

Language majority student A student who speaks the dominant societal language. In the United States, this refers to a standard English speaker.

Language minority student A student who speaks a language other than the dominant societal language. In the United States, this refers to a speaker of any language or variety of language other than standard English (for example, black vernacular English or Ebonics, Spanish).

Limited English proficient (LEP) An official designation for students who are designated as in need of instruction in English. This term has been criticized because it defines the student in terms of a deficit, namely, limited English proficiency. The term *English language learner* is increasingly used.

Newcomers Students who have just arrived into the United States, typically with limited formal instruction. Most newcomers, as a result of their interrupted or limited schooling, have no or low levels of literacy in their native language.

Newcomer programs Specially designed programs for *newcomers* (recent arrivals to the United States who have no or low English proficiency and often have limited literacy in their native language). The goal is to accelerate their acquisition of language and academic skills and to orient them to the United States and to U.S. schools. Some follow a *bilingual* approach and others focus on *sheltered English.*

Pull-out A teaching arrangement whereby a specialist teacher (such as ESL or bilingual) takes small groups of students out of the mainstream classroom for short periods of time to give them specialized support (such as ESL or native language instruction).

Push-in A teaching arrangement whereby a specialist teacher (such as ESL or bilingual) comes into the mainstream classroom to give specialized support to a small number of students, or to help the mainstream teacher who has those students in her or his classroom.

Sheltered instruction   Offers English language learners grade-level core content courses taught in English using instructional strategies that make the content concepts accessible while students are acquiring English as a second language. These programs are sometimes referred to as sheltered English *immersion* or *specially designed academic instruction in English (SDAIE)*. The term sheltered instruction may also be used to describe pedagogy rather than a program design. Sheltered instruction practices and individual sheltered instruction courses can be and often are implemented in conjunction with other program alternatives.

Sheltered Instruction Observation Protocol (SIOP) model   A proven, research-based approach for *sheltered instruction* that helps English language learners develop oral language proficiency while building academic English literacy skills and content area knowledge. The SIOP Institute, trademark, and copyright are owned by LessonLab/Pearson Education.

Spanish for Spanish/Native Speakers (SNS)   A *heritage language program* for students who speak Spanish as a home or *heritage language*. These programs aim to broaden the linguistic repertoire of Spanish speakers, and they often focus on ensuring that Spanish speakers learn to read and write in Spanish (while not stigmatizing the vernacular variety of Spanish that the students speaks at home and in the community).

Specially designed academic instruction in English (SDAIE)   Another term for *sheltered instruction*.

Subtractive bilingualism   A process by which a second language is learned, but at the expense of the first one. As a person becomes more proficient in the new language, proficiency in the first language diminishes, or worse, the person loses that first language altogether (contrast with *additive bilingualism*).

Transitional bilingual education (TBE)   A model of *bilingual education* that provides content area instruction to English language learners (ELLs) in their native language while they learn English (to varying extents for varying lengths of time). As the ELLs acquire English, they move to all-English mainstream classes, typically after one to three years (also known as early-exit bilingual programs).

Two-way immersion (TWI)   A type of *dual language education* that targets balanced numbers of English language learners and English speakers and aims for (1) bilingualism, (2) biliteracy, (3) academic achievement in two languages, and (4) positive cultural understanding and intercultural communication. TWI programs provide content area instruction through two languages to students in integrated classes, and they typically last for five to seven years. There is considerable variation across TWI programs in terms of how they allocate languages for instructional purposes. NOTE: The term *dual language* is sometimes used as a synonym for two-way immersion programs. This guide takes a broad view of dual language education, by which we mean any bilingual program that promotes bilingualism and biliteracy (that is, *additive bilingualism*), academic achievement in two languages, and positive cross-cultural understanding for its target populations. Under this broad view, a two-way immersion program is one type of dual language program.

Index